AUDITING CANADIAN DEMOCRACY

Published in association with the Centre for Canadian Studies at Mount Allison University

Advisory Group

William Cross, Director (Carleton University)
R. Kenneth Carty (University of British Columbia)
Elisabeth Gidengil (McGill University)
Richard Sigurdson (University of Manitoba)
Frank Strain (Mount Allison University)
Michael Tucker (Mount Allison University)

Titles

John Courtney, *Elections*
William Cross, *Political Parties*
Elisabeth Gidengil, André Blais, Neil Nevitte, and Richard Nadeau, *Citizens*
Jennifer Smith, *Federalism*
Lisa Young and Joanna Everitt, *Advocacy Groups*
David Docherty, *Legislatures*
Darin Barney, *Communication Technology*
Graham White, *Cabinets and First Ministers*
Ian Greene, *The Courts*
William Cross, ed., *Auditing Canadian Democracy*

AUDITING CANADIAN DEMOCRACY

Edited by William Cross

UBCPress

20 19 18 17 16 15 14 13 12 11 10   5 4 3 2 1

Printed in Canada on FSC-certified ancient-forest-free paper
(100% post-consumer recycled) that is processed chlorine- and acid-free.

Library and Archives Canada Cataloguing in Publication

Auditing Canadian democracy / edited by William Cross.

(Canadian democratic audit; 10)
Includes bibliographical references and index.
ISBN 978-0-7748-1101-9 (set). – ISBN 978-0-7748-1919-0 (bound);
ISBN 978-0-7748-1920-6 (pbk.)

1. Democracy – Canada. 2. Canada – Politics and government – 1993-2006. 3. Canada – Politics and government – 2006-. I. Cross, William P. (William Paul), 1962- II. Series: Canadian democratic audit; 10

JL75.A93 2010   320.971'09051   C2010-905321-4

e-book ISBNs: 978-0-7748-1921-3 (pdf); 978-0-7748-1922-0 (epub)

Canadä

UBC Press gratefully acknowledges the financial support for our publishing program of the Government of Canada (through the Canada Book Fund), the Canada Council for the Arts, and the British Columbia Arts Council.

The editor thanks the Harold Crabtree Foundation for its support of the Canadian Democratic Audit project.

UBC Press
The University of British Columbia
2029 West Mall
Vancouver, BC V6T 1Z2
www.ubcpress.ca

This volume is dedicated to Vera, and to the children and grandchildren of all the "auditors," in hopes that the Canada they inherit will be a prosperous and vigorously democratic one.

Contents

Figures and Tables

Acknowledgments

Ten years ago, a group of political scientists gathered at Mount Allison University in Sackville, New Brunswick, to begin work on an audit of Canadian democracy. Those brave academics who accepted the call to take part in the first comprehensive assessment of Canadian democracy probably didn't realize they were embarking on an enterprise that would last a decade. Nonetheless, I think I speak for all of them in saying this has been a special project offering great rewards, both professionally and personally. Through the course of spending many hours together, we have learned a great deal from one another, and strong bonds of friendship have been formed. We have been helped along the way by scores of colleagues from across the country and internationally, who have offered encouragement and advice. Through this project, I have experienced the generosity and talents of so many members of the Canadian political science community and am grateful to them all.

The Audit would not have been possible without the significant support of the Harold Crabtree Foundation in Ottawa, which provided funding for the endeavour. The Centre for Canadian Studies at Mount Allison University provided the time and space for much of the early work on this project. At that institution, Peter Ennals, A. Wayne Mackay, Michael Fox, and Joanne Goodrich were all keen supporters, and given the early skepticism of others, the Audit would never have gotten off the ground without them.

At Carleton University, which has been my academic home for the past five years, the generosity of Dr. Ruth Bell in funding the Honorable Dick and Ruth Bell Chair for the Study of Canadian Parliamentary Democracy has allowed me the time to bring this project to conclusion.

This is the tenth volume in the Audit series, and we have been incredibly fortunate to partner with UBC Press in the publishing enterprise. Emily Andrew was one of the very first persons I talked with about the possibility of a Canadian Democratic Audit. From that first conversation over a cold drink on a hot summer day in Quebec City, Emily has been a full partner. Peter Milroy and all of his staff at the press have been terrific to work with and have brought much added value to the series. All authors should be so fortunate as to work with such a professional and agreeable group.

My biggest debt is to my partner, Emma. Since our days together in graduate school, she has been a constant source of support and encouragement. I can't imagine life without her.

William Cross

AUDITING CANADIAN DEMOCRACY

CONSTRUCTING THE CANADIAN DEMOCRATIC AUDIT

1

William Cross

Several years ago, a team of political scientists agreed to participate in a democratic audit of Canada. Over the course of the intervening years, the Audit project has resulted in the publication of nine monographs, all investigating the state of individual public institutions and discrete areas of democratic life. This collection brings together the findings of these assessments and in doing so provides a single, more comprehensive, view of the status of Canada's democratic practice in the first decade of the twenty-first century.

Each of the essays in this book uses the Audit benchmarks of participation, inclusiveness, and responsiveness to evaluate a particular aspect of Canadian democracy. In doing so, each chapter both synthesizes and updates the findings of the monographs in the Audit series. Collectively, the chapters provide both a critique of current democratic practices and a potential road map for future democratic reforms.

The Democratic Audit project was principally inspired by several factors, including the apparent popular discontent with the state of Canada's democratic institutions and practices, the generation of democratic assessments in other Western states, a desire to produce a framework to facilitate a cohesive and comprehensive assessment of Canadian democracy, and an opportunity to identify and explore potential democratic reforms. The discussion that follows outlines the motivation for the project and the considerations involved in constructing a democratic audit.

At the beginning of the twenty-first century, many indicators suggested that Canadians were uneasy with their set of democratic arrangements. Recent years had seen the publication of reports from two wide-ranging investigations of democratic practice, both of which found evidence of a serious malaise. The Citizens' Forum on Canada's Future (commonly known as the Spicer Commission) conducted scores of public meetings and other types of consultations, in which Canadians were invited to comment on the state of public decision making in their country. As expressed in the following passage from its final report, the Spicer Commission found considerable dissatisfaction with the state of our democracy:

> One of the strongest messages the forum received from participants was that they have lost their faith in both the political process and their political leaders. They do not feel that their governments, especially at the federal level, reflect the will of the people, and they do not feel that citizens have the means at the moment to correct this. (Citizens' Forum 1991, 135)

Similar findings were reported by the Royal Commission on Electoral Reform and Party Financing. This commission found evidence that "many Canadians are critical of their existing political institutions. Many are concerned that these institutions are not sufficiently responsive to their views and interests" (Royal Commission 1991, 229).

These findings were supported by public opinion data showing that large numbers of Canadians were dissatisfied with their democratic institutional arrangements, believing, for example, that elected officials are unrepresentative and often out of touch, and that regular Canadians "do not have any say over what government does" (Howe and Northrup 2000, 8-9).

At the same time, voter turnout in elections was steadily declining. From consistent levels in the 75 percent range, participation rates in the last three elections of the twentieth century dropped dramatically, falling to near 60 percent in 2000 (Courtney 2004, 40). This development was particularly worrisome as it was concentrated among younger voters who appeared to be rejecting traditional forms of democratic participation (Pammett and LeDuc 2003). And those who were voting were turning away from patterns of electoral competition that had defined federal politics in an almost uninterrupted way since Confederation. The two-party domination of the Progressive Conservatives and Liberals was under attack as new entrants were achieving remarkable success, and a marked regionalization of party competition appeared to be taking hold. Observers of electoral politics such as Alan Cairns (1994), Leslie Seidle (1994), and R. Kenneth Carty, William Cross, and Lisa Young (2000) suggested that this was something more than a simple shift in partisan attachments and that it represented a more fundamental dissatisfaction with the state of contemporary democratic practice. Seidle wrote of an "angry citizenry" discontented with long-standing norms of democratic representation and weak institutional responsiveness, whereas Cairns (1994, 229) pointed to the demise of the Charlottetown and Meech Lake constitutional accords as evidence of "changed relations between citizens and governing elites," and as "an attack on brokerage politics, especially of the kind that take place behind closed doors."

This voter displeasure was an impetus for the Audit project, and much of it is still evident today. Voter participation in elections continues to decline, falling below six in ten for the first time ever in 2008. And especially troubling is the finding that young Canadians continue to vote less than any other age cohort and at lower levels than did young voters in earlier generations (Gidengil et al. 2004, 109-10; Gidengil et al., Chapter 5 this volume). Similarly, public confidence in democratic institutions remains low: Canadians are about evenly split between those who are satisfied with their democracy and those who are not, and the majority have less trust in the federal government today than they did a decade ago (EKOS 2005; Angus Reid 2007).

When we began our project, we were aware that similar democratic assessments were being undertaken in other Western democracies such as Sweden, Denmark, Australia, and the United Kingdom. The best known of these are the Democratic Audit of the UK and the work in democratic assessment inspired by it and carried out under the auspices of the International Institute for Democracy and Electoral Assistance (IDEA) (see Beetham 1999). The IDEA and UK projects have sought to create a "universal framework to assess the condition of democracy in any country" (UK Democratic Audit 2009), and indeed under this framework, assessment projects using similar measurement instruments have been carried out "from London to Ulaanbaatar" (Landman 2006).

The Canadian Democratic Audit team decided at the outset that, though we would be mindful of the work ongoing in other Western states, and to some extent we were inspired by it, we would create a methodology allowing us to comment specifically and meaningfully on the state of Canadian democratic life in the first decade of the twenty-first century. Our intent was not to measure the quality of Canadian democratic practice with an instrument constructed for use in countries as diverse as the United Kingdom and Mongolia: rather, we desired to create a framework uniquely relevant to the democratic aspirations and challenges of twenty-first-century Canada. Thus, we decided not to follow the IDEA approach or any other template devised elsewhere as we did not believe that an initial audit of Canadian democracy, which would delve deeply into the workings of our democratic practice, was best conducted via a framework generated for universal use. Of course, this resulted in some loss in the comparative utility of our project; nonetheless, we believe that, for a first audit, it is essential that the measurements used speak directly to the Canadian case.

Indeed, there are already many international league tables of democratic practice - such as the World Audit (www.worldaudit.org). Like others of its type, this project rates Canada relatively highly in comparison with other nations (it tied for seventh place with Norway, just ahead of Australia and Germany, and below New Zealand and the Netherlands). Nonetheless, it tells us relatively little about how our democratic institutions and practices are measuring up to the expectations of Canadians and whether they are evolving sufficiently to meet the changing needs of a dynamic Canadian society (for more on these international comparisons, see Chapter 10 in this volume).

We decided to start from first principles in constructing our project and to make all the important decisions ourselves. These included defining the scope of the Audit, identifying appropriate benchmarks for assessment of contemporary Canadian democracy, and agreeing upon the best measurements of these benchmarks. In addressing these issues, we believe we constructed a methodology that allowed us to comment on the state of democracy today in a way that is uniquely relevant to the democratic challenges that emerge from modern Canada.

An audit conducted elsewhere or at a different time might, and probably should, use different benchmarks and measurements. This reflects our view that democracy is not a static concept. Rather, as an "essentially contested concept," it takes on different meanings depending on time and place. The measures and benchmarks employed in an assessment of democratic life in Canada during the 1920s would differ from ours – and appropriately so – as should those used in a current assessment conducted in a different society. Democratic practices and institutions cannot be one-size-fits-all.

Thus, we faced two key questions: what areas of democratic activity to consider and how to assess them. Although all spheres of life, from quality of education to political economy to public administration to the quality of elections, impact upon the strength of our democracy, examining all of these in a single audit would make the project unwieldy. Given the attitudes of Canadians toward their public decision-making processes, as evident in public opinion studies, as well as the changing nature of democratic values and the changes to civil society discussed below, a first audit focusing on opportunities for participation in public decision making and the relationship between key democratic institutions and civil society seemed appropriate. Thus, we decided to take a largely institutional approach. This is not to suggest that other areas affecting the nature of democratic life are less relevant. Rather, our intent to drill down and conduct detailed examinations of the chosen aspects of democratic experience (in the monograph-length individual studies) dictated that the scope of the investigation could not be exhaustive.

We are cognizant in our work that this is an audit of existing Canadian democratic practice, not an agenda for an idealized version of democracy. Contemporary Canadian democracy is not a blank canvas but rather comes with a largely accepted set of institutional arrangements, many of which are deeply entrenched and not easily changed. Our assessments are based in this reality, and thus we largely restrict our analyses and reform discussions to fit within the contours of responsible Westminster-style parliamentary government, which has defined Canada since Confederation. This does not mean that fundamental reforms (such as electoral system change) are not countenanced but rather that alternative forms of governance such as direct democracy and republican congressional systems are not pursued at length. Instead, we assess Canadian democracy as it is practised today and consider reform proposals that, mostly, are already in play and that fit within the overarching constructs of our governing arrangements.

Setting the benchmarks for evaluation of these practices and institutions necessarily entails substantial consideration of the meaning of democracy. Definitions of democracy are inherently normative, and we are not attempting to agree upon a single one that is applicable to all places at all times. Rather, we are interested in capturing and assessing those principles that allow us to consider how well our democratic institutions are serving contemporary society and that assist in identifying potential reforms that will enable them to do so more fully and effectively.

Our desire to ensure that our assessment is relevant to twenty-first-century Canada means that we are highly cognizant that a significant challenge facing our democratic institutions and practices is that they fully reflect the changing composition of Canadian society, both in terms of who we are and the democratic values we hold. Canadian civil society changed significantly toward the end of the twentieth century, and it is not at all clear how well our existing institutions are able to cope with these dramatic developments and the various democratic aspirations and challenges associated with them.

Canada is one of the world's largest takers of new immigrants. These new Canadians come from differing backgrounds, and their experiences differ from those they join in their new homeland. The 2006 census reported more than 200 different ethnic origins, with 34 of them claimed by more than 100,000 Canadians. The census found that 16 percent of respondents were visible minorities, a growth of 20 percent in just five years, and estimated that this will increase by another 25 percent in the coming decade (Statistics Canada 2008). In 2007, Canada admitted a quarter of a million immigrants, largely from non-European countries (Citizenship and Immigration Canada 2008).

The degree of change from earlier patterns is evident in the list of the most common countries of origin for recent immigrants: China, India, Philippines, Pakistan, United States, United Kingdom, Iran, South Korea, Colombia, and Sri Lanka. The result is a Canada made up of ethnic communities that differ from those of even one generation ago and in which the number of visible minorities is ever-increasing. This change is also evident in terms of mother tongue. Today, there are nearly as many Canadians who claim neither French nor English as their mother tongue as there are native French speakers.

It is also the case that women and visible minorities continue to be under-represented in many of our democratic institutions (see Chapters 3, 4, 7 this volume; Docherty 2005; White 2005; Cross 2004) and that public opinion suggests that many Canadians view this as an important component of a democratic deficit (Howe and Northrup 2000). Given the changing nature of Canadian society and the desire for inclusive representation among Canadians, we conclude that any meaningful assessment of Canadian democracy must consider how well our public decision-making processes and institutions include the many communities comprising the Canadian mosaic. Thus, we identify inclusiveness as one of our central benchmarks. Although many of the assessments focus on inclusion in terms of representing this diversity, issues of political economy and consideration of whether all Canadians have the necessary resources for full democratic participation are also included (see Barney 2005, Chapter 9 this volume; Gidengil et al. 2004; Gidengil et al. Chapter 5 this volume; Greene 2006; Young and Everitt 2004, Chapter 8 this volume).

The democratic values of Canadians are also in transition. Although this is a large and wide-sweeping issue, we identify three general areas in which Canadian values have undoubtedly shifted in recent years: the first is what Neil Nevitte (1996) has called a "decline in deference." Canadians are more willing to challenge authority, have less confidence in public officials, and are less deferential toward public decision making by elite-dominated institutions. The second is the rise of an individual rights-based culture. In a philosophy symbolized by the Charter of Rights and Freedoms, Canadians are encouraged to see themselves as individuals, not solely as members of constituent groups – and if identity is group based, it is no longer limited to the traditional political communities largely formed on region, language, and religion. And third, closely related to the first two, is a desire for more direct participation in public decision making and a rejection of perceived elite-dominated institutions. The results of these are many but are easily observed in increased cynicism regarding elite-driven political compromises, declining rates of participation in traditional political activity such as political parties and voting, and an increase, particularly among young Canadians, in involvement in more direct – unmediated – political activity such as protests and the like. (For more on this, see O'Neill 2007; Chapters 5, 6, 7, 8 this volume.) These findings led us to identify the democratic values of participation and responsiveness as central benchmarks of our investigations.

The challenges presented to Canadian democracy by these changes in demography and values are captured in these three benchmarks: participation, inclusiveness, and responsiveness. A review of public opinion data and of the literature critical of Canadian democratic practice supports a conclusion that Canadians want public institutions and decision-making processes that offer them meaningful ways of participating in their democratic life, that they want this involvement to include all the communities that comprise contemporary Canada, and that they expect democratic outcomes to be responsive to this inclusive participation. Outcomes that do not at least reflect a consideration of the views of participants will not satisfy demands for responsiveness in public decision making.

The challenge is reconciling these evolving democratic norms with traditions of parliamentary democracy, both inherited from the United Kingdom and crafted to serve an earlier, less complex, Canadian society with less demanding democratic aspirations. Canada's traditions of brokerage politics have long been centred on the practices of compromise and accommodation. Elites, committed first and foremost to the maintenance of the federation, have engaged in the brokerage form of national policy making. Whether in the federal cabinet or through the practice of executive federalism, the primary interests to be reconciled were region and language, and participants were often invited to the decision-making table solely as representatives of one dimension of these divides (see Chapters 2, 3 this volume; Smith 2004; White 2005).

These processes, not to be short sold, helped develop and manage a country whose centrifugal forces are often so strong that the unity achieved was nothing short of a monumental accomplishment. Indeed, grand compromises on the most difficult of national questions were often arrived at by our federal ministers and later our provincial first ministers. Whether relating to divisive issues such as conscription or constitutional reform, elite-driven compromises were found possible. Thus, though each of the auditors concentrates on the aforementioned benchmarks, they do so in a nuanced way that acknowledges that more of these may not always be ideal and may come at the cost of other democratic values such as accommodation. Together with a focus on institutions and their interactions with citizens, these benchmarks provide a coherent framework for an initial assessment of Canadian democracy. It is not all-encompassing, and future work on other democratic practices and values, such as equality, efficiency, and accountability, would add to this discussion.

While settling on these guiding principles, we did not impose a strict set of democratic criteria on the evaluations that together constitute the Audit. Rather, our approach allows each author wide latitude in his or her evaluation. Unlike other democratic assessment projects, ours does not use a checklist approach in which a laundry list of democratic attributes is identified and looked for in each institution and practice. We rejected this approach primarily because construction of such a list must reflect the normative perspectives of those who produce it and because its content may have a significant impact on the resulting findings. Instead, our approach reflects an attempt to have a cohesive

project centred on broadly accepted benchmarks while allowing sufficient scope for the authors to shape the assessment in ways they think
best illuminate the democratic strengths and weaknesses of the area
they are considering.

As is consistent with this approach, different investigators discuss
the various aspects of democratic life. Instead of using a small group
to assess all areas, we assembled a rather large team of subject specialists who probe the areas in which they are expert. The result is a richness
in the understanding of the institutions and practices, a diversity of
perspectives relating to the nature of democratic life, and a cohesiveness
achieved through a privileged place given to the three benchmarks.

This approach means that the Audit's perspectives and measurements are not absolutely uniform throughout, something we believe
adds to the value of the project. Democracy is an inherently normative concept, and imposing a single limited set of criteria and having
a small group make the assessments would not capture the depth and
breadth of the debates surrounding democratic practices; nor would it
capture the robustness made possible by engaging a rather large group
of diverse political scientists.

In terms of measuring how democratic performance is consistent
with the benchmarks, the Audit is guided by three general standards:
how well the institution or practice meets the democratic needs of
contemporary Canada, whether positive change has occurred over time,
and where applicable, how Canadian practice compares to that in other
Western democracies. Each auditor determines the weight given to
each measure on the basis of what is most appropriate to the institution
or practice under review. In some instances, reliable cross-national and
over-time data are available; for others, such as emerging communication technologies, the exercise is necessarily more speculative.

Whereas each of the individual monographs in the Audit series
tackles all of these questions, it is not possible to do so in one capstone
volume. For this book, each author considers the greatest strengths and
weaknesses of the area under discussion in terms of the benchmarks.
Each then situates this in a broader context by examining the overall
contribution of the institution or practice to Canadian democratic life

more generally. It is here that other democratic values and imperatives may come into play. Finally, the authors suggest reforms that might improve the contribution of their institution or practice to our democracy.

We do not prioritize these reform proposals; nor do we attempt to reconcile their divergent perspectives on issues such as the advisability of electoral system reform. To a certain extent, these are normative judgments based on how one prioritizes competing, valid democratic concerns. Our objective, as a project, is for individual authors to state their case, outlining their views and the rationale supporting them. The readers' task is to decide for themselves whether such reforms are consistent with their informed view of Canadian democracy.

The Book

The chapters that follow focus on the principal institutions of democratic decision making, the key vehicles for public participation, the capacity of Canadians for democratic citizenship, and the role of emerging technologies in democratic life.

The first three chapters examine institutions that define public decision making: federalism, cabinets and first ministers, and legislatures. These institutions organize the governing structures within which public policy outcomes are determined. Together, they shape the framework within which citizens find opportunity for participation in public decision making, and they significantly influence the degree of responsiveness to citizen interests. These chapters underline the tensions between traditions of elite-dominated decision making, aimed at regional and linguistic accommodation, and demands for increased opportunities for public participation that are inclusive of new and emerging political identities not restricted to old paradigms.

In Chapter 2, Jennifer Smith identifies the complex relationship between democracy and federalism, and the tensions that can arise between the two. She argues that the practice of federalism presents both challenges and opportunities for the enhancement of citizen participation and influence presented by the multiplicity of access points and the overlapping of jurisdictional responsibilities among various levels of government. She highlights both the area of Senate reform as having the potential to significantly change citizens' relationships with their central government and the challenge of adequately representing those elements not formally included in federal structures – such as cities, gender, and ethnicity.

Focusing his attention on cabinets and first ministers, institutions that are increasingly seen to dominate government decision making, Graham White picks up on this theme in Chapter 3, noting Canadian politicians' "hypersensitivity to regional concerns." Although he acknowledges the traditional under-representation of groups such as women, Aboriginals, and visible minorities in cabinets, his focus on the potential role of backbench members in cabinet deliberations and the diversity of information sources available to the executive broadens this discussion beyond mere counting. His analysis also includes a critical examination of the widely held belief that decision making is becoming increasingly concentrated with the first minister, a phenomenon with important implications for the ability of diverse citizen groups to influence policy outcomes.

White notes that, in terms of diversity, the formal composition of cabinets is significantly limited by the government's parliamentary caucus, which, as David Docherty illustrates in Chapter 4 on legislatures, has traditionally been under-representative of groups such as women and visible minorities. In the absence of direct democracy, Canadians look to the elected members of their assemblies, both to represent their interests and to legislate on their behalf. Docherty highlights the centrality of these bodies to both our governing practice and citizens' evaluations of their democracy generally. He also underscores the challenges brought about by the recurrence of minority parliaments and examines the question of coalition arrangements that captured public attention in December 2008.

Chapters 5, 6, 7, and 8 all consider citizen involvement in public decision making, with a focus on the ability of citizens to organize and participate directly in democratic politics. Among other things, they explore the relatively low levels of involvement in voting and political parties. They also suggest a democratic divide, with significantly lower levels of participation and knowledge found among certain cohorts of Canadians. Together, they suggest that, though the formal rules of elections have become significantly more inclusive and liberal, other institutional arrangements favour the participation of particular groups of Canadians.

In Chapter 5, Elisabeth Gidengil and her colleagues assess how well Canadians fulfill their responsibilities of democratic citizenship. Focusing on political interest, knowledge, and activity, they find significant variation among different sets of citizens. They argue that these discrepancies result from a number of factors including both our institutional arrangements and the relative resources, such as levels of education, available to various groups. In considering reforms that might lead to greater levels of political activity and interest, they discuss the importance of engaging young Canadians, of civics education, and of generally improving civic literacy. They also emphasize the importance of integrating new Canadians into the country's democratic culture and ensuring there are access points for them to learn about the political system and participate in it.

Chapters 6, 7, and 8 then examine the key venues for citizen participation: elections, political parties, and advocacy groups. In Chapter 6, John Courtney examines what he calls the "pillars" of Canada's electoral system. These include the franchise, voter registration, electoral districting, election management, and the plurality voting system. Stressing the importance of open, freely competitive, and recurrent elections, Courtney presents a largely favourable evaluation of what he finds to be "a solidly democratic framework" and an ever-expanding franchise that now encompasses almost all adult citizens. His analysis includes a balanced consideration of the single-member plurality voting system and sounds a note of caution for those with unrealistic expectations of what reform in this area might accomplish.

In Chapter 7, William Cross argues that democratically organized political parties are central to a participatory, inclusive, and responsive politics. Accenting the role played by parties in areas such as policy determination and candidate and leadership selection, along with their privileged place in our electoral and legislative institutions, he asserts that parties are essentially the public utilities of our democracy. Nonetheless, he finds relatively low levels of public involvement in parties and uncovers cohort differences similar to those found by Gidengil et al. in Chapter 5, insofar as youth, women, and new Canadians are under-represented within the parties. In considering reform proposals, Cross suggests that parties dedicate more resources for policy study and development among their grassroots activists and open up the candidate and leadership selection processes to make them more accessible and transparent in order to encourage higher rates of involvement.

Although participation levels in parties and elections may be relatively low, advocacy groups are increasingly becoming a vehicle of choice for Canadians who wish to interact with governments and to influence public policy - particularly for those in the younger age cohorts. In Chapter 8, Lisa Young and Joanna Everitt examine the kinds of groups that exist, their relative influence in the public sphere, and the internal democratic dynamics of group organization. This allows them to consider whether groups help to remedy some of the representational deficits found elsewhere. Their conclusions are rather mixed. Although they find that group activity does provide a meaningful method of citizen engagement in public life, they also discover both a disparity in the amount of resources available to different types of groups and that many of the socio-economic representational shortfalls found in organizations such as parties persist in advocacy groups.

In Chapter 9, Darin Barney's consideration of new communication technologies both assesses the policy making involved in establishing a new regulatory framework and considers the possibilities for these new technologies to facilitate greater democratic participation. As he suggests, these are difficult tasks, because the ground is constantly shifting in terms of the relationship between these technologies and our political institutions, and because they are deployed in a wide variety of sites beyond the formal political arena that have potential influence on accessibility and participation in democratic life. His conclusions caution that these technologies do not ensure the democratic panacea often suggested, as he finds little evidence that groups such as governments and political parties consistently use them to expand participatory opportunities for a broader range of Canadians. Barney also points to challenges of political economy that must be addressed in considering the democratizing capacities of these new technologies and decisions relating to their use.

The book concludes with Chapter 10, by R. Kenneth Carty. Carty begins by questioning whether a democratic audit was necessary, considering the relatively healthy state of Canadian society. Though acknowledging that our democratic arrangements have served us well, he points to the ever-changing nature of the Canadian population in arguing that audit-like exercises are important in ensuring that our public and governmental institutions meet the evolving democratic needs and expectations of contemporary Canada. Carty then presents a unified consideration of twenty-one reform proposals found throughout the Audit studies. He categorizes these as ranging from societal changes to major institutional/constitutional reforms to issues of public policy and institutional practice.

Although the Canadian Democratic Audit is an ambitious undertaking, we hope it is but an opening salvo in encouraging others to examine the democratic capacities of various aspects of our public life or perhaps to use other benchmarks and measurements in furthering the assessments that comprise this Audit. Evaluating the state of our democratic practice and considering how it may be improved is not a discrete project but rather is an ongoing obligation of a democratic citizenry. Our hope is that, through this Audit, we have contributed to this task by providing readers with information and analyses that assist them in evaluating their democracy and in considering ways to improve it.

Works Cited

Angus Reid. 2007. Most satisfied with national democracy, but unsure of changing vote process. Angus Reid Strategies/Vision Critical. http://www.visioncritical.com/.

Barney, Darin. 2005. *Communication technology.* Canadian Democratic Audit. Vancouver: UBC Press.

Beetham, David. 1999. The idea of democratic audit in comparative perspective. *Parliamentary Affairs* 52(4): 567-81.

Cairns, Alan. 1994. An election to be remembered: Canada 1993. *Canadian Public Policy* 20(3): 219-34.

Carty, R. Kenneth, William Cross, and Lisa Young. 2000. *Rebuilding Canadian party politics.* Vancouver: UBC Press.

Citizens' Forum on Canada's Future. 1991. *Report to the people and Government of Canada.* Ottawa: Supply and Services Canada.

Citizenship and Immigration Canada. 2008. Facts and figures 2007. http://www.cic.gc.ca/.

Courtney, John. 2004. *Elections.* Canadian Democratic Audit. Vancouver: UBC Press.

Cross, William. 2004. *Political parties.* Canadian Democratic Audit. Vancouver: UBC Press.

Docherty, David. 2005. *Legislatures.* Canadian Democratic Audit. Vancouver: UBC Press.

EKOS. 2005. We're great. Politicians are dirt. News release. http://www.ekos.com/.

Gidengil, Elisabeth, André Blais, Neil Nevitte, and Richard Nadeau. 2004. *Citizens.* Canadian Democratic Audit. Vancouver: UBC Press.

Greene, Ian. 2006. *The courts.* Canadian Democratic Audit. Vancouver: UBC Press.

Howe, Paul, and David Northrup. 2000. Strengthening Canadian democracy: The views of Canadians. *Policy Matters* 1(5).

Landman, Todd. 2006. From London to Ulaanbaatar: Making the state of democracy framework travel. Paper presented at the meetings of the International Political Science Association, Fukuoka, Japan, 12 July.

Nevitte, Neil. 1996. *The decline of deference: Canadian value change in cross national perspective.* Peterborough, ON: Broadview Press.

O'Neill, Brenda. 2007. *Indifferent or just different? The political and civic engagement of young people in Canada.* Ottawa: Canadian Policy Research Networks.

Pammett, Jon, and Lawrence LeDuc. 2003. *Explaining the turnout decline in Canadian federal elections: A new survey of non-voters.* Ottawa: Elections Canada.

Royal Commission on Electoral Reform and Party Financing. 1991. *Reforming electoral democracy,* vol. 2. Ottawa: Supply and Services Canada.

Seidle, Leslie. 1994. The angry citizenry: Examining representation and responsiveness in government. *Policy Options* 15(6): 75-80.

Smith, Jennifer. 2004. *Federalism.* Canadian Democratic Audit. Vancouver: UBC Press.

Statistics Canada. 2008. *Canada's ethnocultural mosaic.* Ottawa: Ministry of Industry.

UK Democratic Audit. 2009. Auditing democracy. UK Democratic Audit, Human Rights Centre, University of Essex. http://www.democraticaudit.com/.

White, Graham. 2005. *Cabinets and first ministers.* Canadian Democratic Audit. Vancouver: UBC Press.

Young, Lisa, and Joanna Everitt. 2004. *Advocacy groups.* Canadian Democratic Audit. Vancouver: UBC Press.

2

FEDERALISM

Jennifer Smith

The Canadian Democratic Audit demonstrates that many institutions and their attendant processes are critical to the quality of democratic life in the country. One such is the federal system of government. Let us recall that, in the federal system, the participating political communities join together to pursue some objectives collectively and other objectives on their own. They establish a central government and empower it to make and administer laws in specified subject areas for the residents of the federation as a whole; and they retain the power to make and administer their own laws in other spheres, laws that apply to the residents within their respective boundaries. Ronald Watts (1999, 1), a leading student of federalism, sums up the federal system as a "combination of shared-rule for some purposes and regional self-rule for others within a single political system so that neither is subordinate to the other."

From the standpoint of democracy, federalism is not a black or white matter. Democracy, simply put, means a government in which the people rule rather than one person or a few. Invariably, the people choose not to govern themselves directly but instead to elect representatives to do so. The federal system of government is the architecture in which the democratic system is housed. More than that, however, it affects the design of the democratic institutions themselves. Generally speaking, the two systems are not incompatible with one another. Thus, the federal guarantee of some degree of autonomy at the local level of government accommodates the self-directing aspirations of participating communities. At the national level, there is always a bicameral legislature that features an elected lower house, the membership of which is more or less proportional to the population of the country, and a second house weighted toward regional representation, the members of which may or may not be elected. The very existence of this second house is an example of the impact of federalism on the structure of the law-making system.

In addition, the federal system is a legal construct characterized by a written constitution, courts that resolve disputes arising under the constitution, carefully defined rules of decision making, and carefully defined roles for the differing levels of government. In other words, it is based on the rule of law. And though the rule of law is not a necessary *and* sufficient condition of democracy, it is nonetheless a necessary condition of it. The reason the rule of law is a necessary condition of democracy is the stability, predictability, and order that it helps to maintain for the members of the society. It is not surprising to find, then, that federal systems of government mostly feature democratic institutions. The odd exceptions, such as the Russian Federation and its predecessor, the Soviet Union, prove the general rule.

Although it is important to appreciate the compatibility between federalism and democracy, it must be stressed that the ramifications of the federal architecture for the democratic system are not entirely positive. In the Democratic Audit volume devoted to federalism, the criteria of participation, responsiveness, and inclusiveness were used to assess the impact of the federal system on Canadian democracy (Smith 2004). The assessment demonstrated that the system serves to strengthen democracy in some ways and weaken it in others. In what follows, the findings under headings representing the Audit's benchmarks of inclusiveness, participation, and responsiveness are reviewed. Next, the changes in the federal system since the 2004 publication of the volume are noted along with projects of reform that have been undertaken since then. Some broader themes of the relationship between federalism and Canadian democracy are explored in the concluding section.

Inclusiveness, Participation, and Responsiveness

INCLUSIVENESS

Does Canadian federalism encourage an inclusive democratic process? At first glance, due to the existence of so many elected governments, it certainly seems to do so. Governments are a positive democratic force in the sense that they offer an array of opportunities for the inclusion of citizens in decision-making processes. In a country the size of Canada, this is no small thing. A highly centralized administration run from the capital in Ottawa would leave vast numbers out in the cold. Nevertheless, the federal system is territorially based, and from that fact flow some constraints on inclusion.

The key territorial unit of Canadian federalism, the very building block of the governing institutions, is the province. The Constitution assigns significant responsibilities to the provincial governments and legislatures in relation to the residents within their boundaries. However, the provinces are also the foundation of the institutions of the federal government. Thus, the way in which people are included in political life at the federal level is organized on a provincial basis too. In the House of Commons, for example, electoral districts are assigned on a province-by-province basis, more or less in accordance with the principle of representation by population. In the Senate, the seats are distributed by region, but "region" turns out to mean either a single province, such as Quebec or Ontario, or a set of provinces, such as the three Maritime provinces of New Brunswick, Nova Scotia, and Prince Edward Island. Under the amending formula, the principal players are parliament and the provincial legislatures. There are even informal conventions signalling the need for broad-based provincial representation in the federal cabinet and the Supreme Court of Canada.

Mention of the Supreme Court immediately raises the question of the position of Quebec within the federation, since it supplies an even more dramatic illustration of the point about the province-based nature of the system. Quebec's distinctiveness, rooted as it is in the historic French-language majority there, is reflected in specific provisions of the Constitution: for example, the guarantee of access to official minority language education for those whose mother tongue is the official minority language of the province in which they reside does not apply to Quebec. Briefly, this means that immigrants to Quebec whose mother tongue is English are not entitled to send their children to English-language schools but instead must send them to French-language schools. The purpose of the exception is to enable Quebec to include English-language immigrants, and especially their children, in its French-language community, thereby securing that community's continuity. The province's distinctiveness is also reflected in federal law, such as in the requirement that three of the nine Supreme Court judges are appointed from the province (and are thereby trained in its tradition of civil law).

These and other such provisions appear both to imply and reflect the special status of Quebec - certainly, many if not most Quebecers hold that they do. On the other hand, in the rest of the country, and notwithstanding such legal marks of distinctiveness, the idea of Quebec having special status is resisted, and the doctrine of the equality of the provinces is adhered to. These two contending views of Canadian federalism lie at the core of the long-standing conflict over Quebec's appropriate relationship with Canada.

In the meantime, however, the point is that the provinces are organized into the federal system. So are the territories in the North. True, they are not provinces: instead, they exercise legislative powers that are delegated to them by the federal parliament. Still, they are territorially based communities with important governing responsibilities, and from time to time, their political leaders remind the country that they aim to become provinces too. Aboriginal peoples with a land base form another set of communities that is formally recognizable under the federal system - some already so in treaties signed with Ottawa, others in process of getting their land and self-government claims recognized. Who is left out of the federal system?

No non-territorially based community - one defined by ethnicity or gender or occupation - is given independent voice under the Constitution. But neither is one very important territorial unit - the city. Cities come under the category of municipalities and as such are the responsibility of the provinces. Great or small, and however the provinces permit them to govern themselves, they simply are not the constitutional equals of the provinces. They have no direct formal institutional relationship with the federal government. They are not vouchsafed seats - as cities - in the House of Commons. Their inferior constitutional status has exacerbated the financial difficulties that cities face in responding to demands for such things as more and better social housing and public transportation. When one weighs this point, it is useful to keep in mind that the ten most populous metropolitan areas contain just over half of Canada's people.

As far as inclusiveness is concerned, the greatest strength of the Canadian federal system, like that of most federal systems, is the fact that citizens everywhere are included in its multi-level governance structure. The greatest weakness flows from the fact that the municipalities are the creatures of the province and therefore lack independent status under the Constitution. The category of municipality comprehends everything from sparsely inhabited rural areas to heavily populated cities. Some argue that the inability of the federal and provincial governments to respond in flexible and creative ways to the problems of the great cities right through to the tiniest municipalities means that the structure of federalism is shortchanging these local jurisdictions - jurisdictions that mean so much to the quality of the daily lives of their residents (Magnussen 2005).

PARTICIPATION

Does the federal system have an impact on the ease with which citizens can participate in political and governmental decision-making processes? It certainly does. On the positive side, it offers many access points of participation - national, provincial/territorial, municipal, and Aboriginal. In law or practice, or both, these governments have some final decision-making authority in relation to specified issues. Therefore, once citizens have targeted the appropriate level of government for the issues in which they are interested, they can pursue their public policy goals there, without having to worry about decisions being appealed to a higher authority. In other words, once citizens have prevailed upon city authorities to make adjustments to traffic policies - usually after a lengthy consultation process with residents - the deed is done.

On the other hand, the federal system is complex, and as a result, it imposes a number of costs on citizens who choose to participate in public life. There is the knowledge cost, or figuring out which level of government (and who in it) is responsible for what subject areas. There is the organizational cost involved in lobbying governments across the country, particularly in relation to provincially controlled matters or, worse, something like the environment, in which all governments are involved in one way or another. These knowledge and organizational costs in turn generate time and expense costs. In short, citizens and organizations need to exert considerable effort to influence the public policy agenda in a federal system. And even if they rise to the challenge, they might encounter still another obstacle - an arena of political life beyond individual governments. This is the intergovernmental arena, or executive federalism, which essentially is reserved to the governments themselves.

Political scientist Donald Smiley (1980, 91) defined executive federalism as "the relations between elected and appointed officials of the two levels of government" that take place in federal-provincial and interprovincial interactions. The reference to elected officials means elected members of the legislature who also serve in the cabinet - that is, the favoured few of the governing party. Most meetings in which public servants from the various levels of government interact with one another are not visible to the public, although hardly the less important for that. Here, bureaucrats beaver away at the necessary work of public policy development and coordination. The showy side features the political leaders who meet to deal with vital issues such as the state of the economy or health care, and sometimes, the constitution.

These meetings of "first ministers" (first ministers' conferences, or FMCs) are uncommon, in part because the prime ministers who call them often find them to be unhelpful. Sometimes the premiers, who are always looking for more money, "gang up" on the prime minister; the media may descend on the event, looking for trouble; and generally, the outcome tends to fall far short of public expectations. During the federal election campaign of January 2006, Conservative leader Stephen Harper promised, if elected, to hold an FMC on the so-called fiscal imbalance, the idea that the provinces have insufficient monies to meet their responsibilities under the Constitution. He was elected but never did hold it. On the other hand, elected again in October 2008, Prime Minister Harper promised immediately to hold an FMC on the global economic crisis, and did. He held another one in January 2009 (Canadian Intergovernmental Conference Secretariat 2009, 1). Back-to-back FMCs are unusual events.

Although no one doubts the importance of executive federalism for the smooth running of the federal system, there is a downside from the standpoint of democratic participation, and it arises from the fact that the meetings are more or less closed to the public. Sometimes, pressure groups are at the table, or if they are not present, they have been consulted by those who are. The general public, by contrast, is reliant on what the officials choose to say about the events and the media coverage of them. Neither is a wholly reliable guide, albeit for different reasons. The officials have an interest in portraying their doings in a bland yet favourable light, whereas the media have difficulty finding out what is going on and therefore lean heavily on speculation. Nor can the public rely on an open debate in parliament or the provincial legislatures on the content of an agreement that might have been reached. For example, after Prime Minister Paul Martin and the provincial and territorial premiers had hammered out the Kelowna Accord in November 2005 – the accord was designed to advance the socio-economic conditions of Aboriginal peoples – they did not return to their respective legislatures to get agreement from them. There was no need to do so. One consequence of the process is the ease with which later governments can change course, which is exactly what Prime Minister Harper did, ignoring the accord, shortly after gaining office in January 2006 (Gordon 2008, 1).

To conclude that the greatest weakness of the federal system from the standpoint of democratic participation is executive federalism is hardly earth shattering. The real issue is whether efficient administration demands closed-door practices. Perhaps it does. Nevertheless, there is something to be said for the idea that legislatures take a role in debating the outcomes (or lack of outcomes) of high-level intergovernmental meetings (Simeon and Cameron 2002). At the very least, such a development would enhance the education of the public about the issues being addressed and exact a degree of accountability for actions taken (or not taken). As with weakness, so with strength. The greatest strength of the federal system for democratic participation is the multiple entry points to the decision-making process afforded by the levels of government. Executive federalism aside, there are still lots of opportunities to get *into* the system.

RESPONSIVENESS

How responsive is the federal system to the public? By "responsiveness" is meant the attentiveness of governments to the preferences of the public. The federal system affects such attentiveness in two ways. One is at elections, which are the key events that compel political parties to seek the support of the public for their candidates and their public policy platforms. The other is between elections, when governments clash over issues, thereby triggering the kind of public debate that, in the end, encourages them to craft policy that is more sensitive to public demand than might otherwise have been the case.

At the federal and provincial levels, elections are fought on the single-member plurality (SMP) system, otherwise known as first past the post. At the federal level, the combination of the SMP system and the federal system has encouraged the development of a multi-party system. The SMP system contributes to this outcome because it rewards regionally based parties. The Bloc Québécois is an example of a success-ful Quebec-based party that routinely wins more House of Commons seats from the province than its percentage of the popular vote would warrant. The federal system contributes to the same outcome by defin-ing and accentuating the differences between the regions of the country. It provides a context in which parties that appeal to regional interests can thrive, thereby enhancing the likelihood of a multi-party system in the first place (for further consideration of the electoral system, see Courtney, Chapter 6 this volume; Cross, Chapter 7 this volume).

Taken together, both the SMP and the federal system also enhance the likelihood that, in terms of the percentage of the popular vote, the leading party will win more House of Commons seats than votes, usu-ally enough to turn a popular-vote minority into a majority of the seats. Of course, the political parties are well aware of this phenomenon. The point is that the leading party in any election can hardly be expected to be as responsive to the electorate as it would if it had to get majority support there. It is true that a coalition government of more than one political party might solve the problem by broadening the basis of voter support to which the government appeals. But Canada has no tradition of this practice. On the contrary, the political leaders have flatly rejected the idea. In the election just past, NDP leader Jack Layton startled reporters by musing about the idea of forming a coalition government with the Liberal Party were he to wind up in the office of prime minister (Benzie 2008, 11), a highly dubious prospect in any event. Initially, Liberal leader Stéphane Dion dismissed the notion out of hand. However, he changed his mind when the Harper government offered its economic statement in November 2008 in the midst of rapidly de-teriorating economic conditions worldwide and in Canada. The oppos-ition parties declared the statement to be utterly inadequate and prepared to band together to form a coalition government to replace the Harper administration, which they sought to vote down by means of a want-of-confidence motion. Facing the prospect of certain defeat in the event of such a vote, the prime minister persuaded the governor general to prorogue parliament and give his government time to prepare a budget for late January 2009 that might pass muster in the House of Commons (Valpy 2008, A6). After consulting broadly about the contents of its budget, the government also undertook a public campaign against coalition government in general and the proposed Liberal-NDP coalition, supported by the Bloc Québécois, in particular (Cheadle 2008, A1). It was positively scathing about the idea, and a number of Canadians were somewhat skeptical about it as well (Valpy, LeBlanc, and Taber 2008, A9). In the event, the Liberal Party, now under the leadership of Michael Ignatieff, signalled its decision to support the budget, thereby putting an end to any immediate prospect of coalition government and solidifying the somewhat negative repute of the idea in the political culture (for more on this general topic, see Docherty, Chapter 4 this volume).

It can be concluded that the greatest weakness of the Canadian federal system in terms of responsiveness to the electorate is that it lowers the threshold of popular support that is needed for a political party to form a government at the federal level. Arguably, however, the system enhances the responsiveness of governments to their publics between elections. In particular, it improves Ottawa's responsiveness to the concerns of its provincial counterparts. This is incredibly important, since provincial governments are the only built-in institutional check faced by a federal governing party with majority support in the House of Commons. Let us recall that, whatever its admirable qualities, the Senate is not an elected body and therefore not a real check on the government of the day.

At any given time, at least one provincial government is carrying on a battle with Ottawa over some issue or other. A good recent example concerns the Atlantic Accords negotiated between Ottawa and Newfoundland and Labrador (NL) in 1985 and Ottawa and Nova Scotia (NS) in 1986 in connection with the administrative and financial management of oil and gas resources off the coasts of the two provinces. Eventually, the offshore resources began to generate substantial revenues for both provinces (as well as the federal government). But this meant that the provinces were no longer eligible for the levels of equalization payments that, as "have-not" provinces, they were accustomed to receiving, and in fact, Ottawa clawed back a portion of these payments. Furious, the provinces argued that the offshore resources were a windfall, and as such, a once-in-a-lifetime opportunity for them to gain entry to the ranks of the "have" provinces, which would never happen if their equalization monies were reduced. The battle between them and Ottawa raged from 1998 to 2007, at which point a settlement of sorts was reached, although it seems to have been a temporary one as far as NL is concerned. The province accuses Ottawa of changing the equalization rules in such a way as to deprive it of some $1.5 billion over three years, and in an interesting development, NL's Liberal MPs, in opposition to their own party, declined to support the Conservative budget of January 2009 in which the controversial measure was contained. Meanwhile, NS cut a deal with Ottawa to reinstate the funding that it stood to lose under the new rules (Stephenson 2009, B1, B5).

At this point, beneficiaries of the dispute might be held to include the members of the public who otherwise would have known next to nothing about subjects as complicated as the relationship between offshore revenue sharing and equalization. Further, one could argue that Ottawa went partway to meet the demands of the provinces and to that extent was more responsive to them than it was prepared to be at the outset. Certainly, neither the opposition parties nor the Senate could have exacted this response. It was the provinces, their role vouchsafed by the federal system, that acted as a serious check on the federal government in relation to this issue. However, the story is not over. And in the end, NS and NL are small provinces in terms of population; between them, they hold only 18 of the House of Commons' 308 seats, not a lot of clout in the face of a federal government determined to get its way.

Reforms

The final chapter of the Audit volume on federalism considered the following four changes that might be made to the federal system so as to enhance its democratic quality: a shift from the appointed Senate to an elected body to make it more inclusive; the establishment of a Council of the Federation that embraces Aboriginal governments, again for the purpose of inclusiveness; a legislative role in the selection of Supreme Court judges in order to broaden the circle of participants in this important institution; and, in the name of responsiveness, virtual regionalism in the Atlantic provinces (Smith 2004, 161). Interestingly, advances have been made on three of these fronts.

Given the roots of the Conservative Party in the short-lived Western-based Reform Party, a proponent of the "Triple-E" Senate (equal, elected, effective), it was hardly surprising to see the Conservative government embark on a campaign to elect the Senate. In *Federalism* (ibid., 161-65), I wrote at length about the difficulty of amending the Constitution to attain this objective and then suggested that nothing prevented the federal government from appointing a provincially elected senator to the Senate. This might even start a trend, in which case it would be "the kind of extra-constitutional development that can force what amounts to constitutional change" (ibid., 165). The first Harper administration appeared to have adopted such a strategy, although with no success. The prime minister introduced bills to establish the machinery to elect senators and to limit their term of office to eight years. The latter specified that, rather than stepping down at age seventy-five, as is currently the case, senators would retire after their non-renewable eight-year term. Neither bill succeeded. Harper also declined to appoint anyone to the Senate who was not elected for the purpose (Flanagan 2007, A19), the exception being Michael Fortier, a Conservative from Quebec, who was expected to resign from the Senate and run for a House of Commons seat in the next election, which he did - and lost. As a result of this policy, the prime minister appointed only one individual, Bert Brown, who won a "Senate election" in the only province that holds such an event - Alberta - and Senate vacancies mounted.

At the outset of his second administration, and in the full realization that, of the rest of the provinces, only Saskatchewan had demonstrated any real interest in establishing Senate elections, Harper announced a change in tactics, proposing instead to appoint (mostly) Conservatives who supported his reform project to fill the Senate vacancies. And he did, beginning with eighteen senatorial appointments made just before Christmas 2008 (Curry and LeBlanc 2008, A1). He appointed another nine senators in late August 2009 (Bailey 2009, A1-A2) and five more in early 2010. His hope is to fill enough Senate seats to ensure eventual passage of his reforms in the Senate itself, which has opposed his reforms. Of course, in making these appointments, something he vowed never to do in the years before he became prime minister, Harper has left himself open to the charge of hypocrisy. And the appointments themselves are not a guarantee of success in the project to establish an elected Senate. However, there is no indication that Harper and his party are not as dedicated as they ever were to the goal, toward which they are advancing. If they get there, would the elected Senate improve the calibre of Canadian democracy from the standpoint of the audit benchmarks of inclusiveness, participation, and responsiveness?

One can only speculate, of course. It seems safe to say that the move from a Senate appointed by the prime minister to one elected by the voters of Canada would mark an immediate leap forward in participatory democracy. It would also manifestly enhance the responsiveness of the institution to the electorate for the obvious reason that candidates would need to appeal to voters rather than curry favour with the prime minister. Inclusiveness is another matter altogether. Given the fact that the political parties currently dominate the conduct of electoral politics, there is reason to think that they would dominate Senate elections too. The government's proposed preferential electoral system, to be used in province-wide elections, might stand in the way of party dominance and enable independents to wage competitive campaigns. Thus, Senate elections could feature a broader array of candidates than do elections to the House of Commons. On the other hand, the government's proposal includes a campaign-finance regime that features no limits on spending and no public funding for election expenses. The impact of such a regime is likely to narrow the field of candidates to those with deep pockets (or access to them), especially in the large provinces in which the campaigns could be costly.

By contrast with the project of Senate reform, the Council of the Federation turned out to be a sure thing. On the instigation of the premier of Quebec, Jean Charest, at the annual premiers conference in Charlottetown in July 2003, the premiers announced their intention to form a new interprovincial council - the Council of the Federation. They did so in Charlottetown in December 2003. The council includes the thirteen premiers of the provinces, the Northwest Territories, the Yukon Territory, and Nunavut. It does not include Aboriginal leaders who do not hold these elected governmental positions. It meets at least twice a year, and each premier in turn assumes the role of chair for a one-year term. Essentially, it is a provincial-territorial coordinating body equipped with a mandate to share the information and experience of the members on issues of public policy, to monitor the impact of Ottawa's actions on the provinces and territories, and to exert a positive influence on the relationship between Ottawa and the provinces and territories.

Since its inception, the council has launched initiatives on a wide range of public policy issues, current examples being climate change, energy strategies, and internal trade. Internal trade, a long-standing issue, is particularly interesting. Within the confines of the council, the premiers appear to have been working on it since 2004. The council's website states that they are taking action in five key areas in an effort to reduce internal barriers to trade: labour mobility, dispute resolution, energy, agriculture, and reconciliation of regulations. One glaring omission is securities regulation (Council of the Federation 2008). With the exception of Ontario, the provinces have shown no enthusiasm to abandon this particular field of jurisdiction, even though the result of their stewardship is a patchwork of securities regulation. By contrast, the federal government, always keen to get the provinces to reduce the various barriers to trade that they have erected over the years, has long been concerned to replace the several provincial regulators of trade in financial securities with one national regulator. The current Conservative government vows to introduce legislation to establish such an institution (CBC News 2009).

It is tempting to see the creation of the council as a step forward in the coordination of intergovernmental relations or, if that sounds too grand, at least a useful and workable body from the viewpoint of its members. Certainly, it does not detract from the democratic state of the federation. Indeed, because it brings all of the premiers together on a regular basis, including those of the territories as well as the provinces, it enhances democratic inclusiveness.

The same cannot be said about the progress made in connection with the appointment of Supreme Court of Canada (SCOC) judges. Essentially, there has been no real progress at all. The appointment of judges to the superior courts, including the SCOC, is in the prime minister's hands. Since the SCOC has the final say on the meaning of the Constitution, including the division of powers between parliament and the provincial legislatures, the provinces have always been sensitive about appointments to it. Indeed, when Mr. Justice Michel Bastarache resigned from the court in June 2008 for health reasons, thereby producing a vacancy to be filled, two premiers weighed in on the matter. Quebec premier Jean Charest said that all the judges should be bilingual. NL's premier Danny Williams said it was time for the appointment of someone from his province. The prime minister simply went ahead and appointed Mr. Justice Thomas Cromwell from the Nova Scotia Court of Appeal. This provoked a brief contretemps, which requires a word of explanation.

As Ian Greene (2006) points out, the incremental changes made to the process of selecting SCOC judges date from the administration of Prime Minister Pierre Elliott Trudeau. The early focus was the establishment of committees to advise the prime minister on the choices that he might make. Recent governments have gone a step further by attempting to integrate the House of Commons into the process, either by including members of the House on the advisory committee or by holding legislative hearings on the nominee, or both. Under Prime Minister Paul Martin, an advisory committee of representatives of the legal community as well as MPs produced a short list of candidates for the Quebec vacancy then in play, but the federal election of January 2006 was set in train before an appointment was made. When Prime Minister Harper took office following the election, he inherited the list and selected from it his appointee, Mr. Justice Marshall Rothstein. Rothstein appeared before an ad hoc committee of sitting MPs and members of the legal community to answer questions about his fitness for the post before the prime minister formally recommended his name to the governor general for appointment to the court.

For the next vacancy - the Bastarache vacancy - the government decided to change the composition of the advisory committee by eliminating the legal community representatives and including only sitting MPs on a five-person committee, two of whom turned out to be cabinet members. The other three hailed from each of the three opposition parties, and they criticized the idea of using cabinet members rather than ordinary MPs. Indeed, in the end, they appeared to have boycotted the committee meetings (Baum 2008). The committee was unable to accomplish anything before the prime minister made the Cromwell appointment, just before calling the election of October 2008. Clearly, there has been no advance on democratic inclusiveness in connection with appointments to the SCOC.

There remains the idea of Atlantic Canada as a virtual region. This arose out of the observation of an economic integrative trend that might be capitalized upon to enhance the responsiveness of the region's provincial governments to the citizens there. Indeed, for some time, Atlantic governments have attempted to respond to the demands of businesses and the professions to streamline and harmonize their respective regulatory systems. Their ongoing efforts to do so, which are recorded on the website of the Council of the Atlantic Premiers (www.cap-cpma.ca), cover public policy areas that range from government procurement to insurance regulation to the availability of venture capital for new businesses. The council institutionalizes the opportunity for the elected political leaders and their officials to get used to conferring among themselves on a regular basis, thereby establishing the lengthening pedigree of common policy initiatives and common administrative activities.

The other side of the virtual regionalism coin is the capacity of the Atlantic provinces to stand politically as a region vis-à-vis the federal government and possibly other provinces. It is logical to think that, by acting together to pursue common negotiating strategies with other governments, they can do more for their citizens than they can if each acts alone. In this respect as well, the ongoing viability and robustness of the council is a positive development because it promotes the sense of Atlantic regionalism. Certainly, the episode of the Atlantic Accords, discussed above in connection with the concept of democratic responsiveness, illustrates the advantage of the common stand – and also how difficult it is to maintain.

One of the oft-noted features of the struggle between Ottawa, on the one hand, and NL and NS, on the other, was the extent to which the two provinces initially managed to cooperate with one another, or at least not undercut each other's efforts. The theme of the first round, launched by NS premier John Hamm, was fairness. He argued that the province was not getting its fair share of the revenues from the offshore petroleum industry as contemplated under the agreement with Ottawa. When Progressive Conservative leader Danny Williams became premier of NL in 2003, he immediately adopted the same argument. The two premiers stood by one another in the increasingly difficult negotiations with the federal government to increase the provinces' share of the resources, and in the end they prevailed in a deal signed with Ottawa in January 2005 (Smith 2008, 89). Stephen Harper, then the federal Conservative opposition leader, was quoted as expressing "great admiration for Premier Hamm in sticking by Newfoundland and not allowing the federal government to play this game of divide and conquer" (Lee 2004, B2).

Harper's comment is ironic, indeed, in light of the fact that his government found itself fighting the same two provinces in the second battle over the accords. In the second round, the issue was the development of a new equalization formula and the impact that it would have on the accords. Under the equalization program, Ottawa transfers funds to the provinces and territories that qualify under the equalization formula in an effort to enable them to offer their residents access to reasonably comparable public services at reasonably comparable levels of taxation. The formula was up for review, and eventually the Harper government chose to change it in a way that was bound to diminish the gains the two Atlantic provinces had made in the earlier round. By this time, Rodney Macdonald had succeeded John Hamm as premier of Nova Scotia.

Macdonald and Williams resisted the federal government's decision and eventually forced it to make some changes to its initial proposal. They hung together, not so tightly as Hamm and Williams but enough to wring some concessions from Ottawa (Smith 2008, 93-94). The advantage of pulling together was revealed again. However, as noted earlier, in the wake of the changes made by the federal government to the equalization formula in the January 2009 budget, the two provinces have gone their own ways. NS made a separate deal with the federal government, whereas, at the time of writing, NL is hung out to dry.

Federalism and the Health of Canadian Democracy

Looking ahead, one feels little doubt that the critical development in Canadian federalism is Senate reform. In *Legislatures,* David Docherty (2005) discusses the issue from the standpoint of the role of the second chamber in the parliamentary system of government. However, Senate reform is also at the nexus of federalism and democracy.

The legislatures of the central government in all federal systems are bicameral, or two-house affairs. Generally speaking, the second house is selected differently from the lower house, often appointed or indirectly elected rather than directly selected by the voters. In addition, the second house always represents the units of the federation, sometimes equally as in the United States, sometimes in a weighted fashion as in Germany. In Canada, the unique twist is equal regional representation. Each of the four regions – the four Western provinces, the three Maritime provinces, Quebec, and Ontario – is assigned twenty-four seats, and then there are add-ons: six for Newfoundland and Labrador, and one each for the Yukon and Northwest Territories and Nunavut.

By definition, the Harper government's plan to elect senators would inject a strong element of democracy into the national parliament. Canadians would find themselves represented twice-over by elected officials, not only on the constituency basis in the House, as is the case now, but also on a province-wide basis in the Senate. It must be stressed, however, that this extra jolt of democracy would have the traditional federal flavour of territorially based representation for the obvious reason that it is designed to advance provincial and territorial representation in parliament. Indeed, the democratic mandate of elected senators would probably intensify the articulation of provincial and territorial views in the national decision-making process. The public policy issues of the day would be refracted through territorially based lenses even more than they are now. Possibly much more. And that is only the start of the observations to be made about such a proposed change. There is also the issue of the relationship between elected senators and provincial and territorial governments. These are uncharted waters.

It cannot be supposed that elected senators would always agree with the governments of the provinces and territories from which they are elected. Disagreements are likely to arise between them, if only for partisan reasons. Canadians are accustomed to the premiers as the only elected spokespersons of the provinces and territories. Should the Harper government's proposal prevail, they will have to get used to other, perhaps competing spokespersons - the elected senators. The possibility of a rivalry between premiers and senators is very real. On the outcome of who wins and who loses in that rivalry, there turns the role of the provinces in the federation.

Canada is widely held to be one of the decentralized federations in which the units - the provinces and territories - are nearly equal players with the federal government. The presence of elected senators with a mandate to articulate authoritatively the interests of their jurisdictions might have the effect of strengthening Ottawa's role vis-à-vis the provincial governments, which could no longer claim to be the sole spokespersons of their residents. Certainly, Ottawa could be expected to exploit competing rivalries whenever it seemed strategically advantageous to do so. On the other hand, it is also possible that the main effect of electing senators is to authorize them to challenge the government of the day, in which case that government must worry about controlling two houses, not just one. Under this prospect, the premiers would emerge stronger than ever. Either way, the adoption of an elected Senate is bound to have significant repercussions for the Canadian federal system.

Conclusion

Do the key developments in Canadian federalism discussed above show promise for the enhancement of the three Democratic Audit benchmarks: inclusiveness, participation, and responsiveness? By definition, an elected Senate would expand the selection committee from the prime minister to the voting citizenry, a step forward in participation and inclusiveness. Less dramatically, the establishment of a legislative role in the selection of Supreme Court judges would do the same thing. Of course, it must be stressed that neither of these two potential reforms is a certain development - far from it.

The establishment of the Council of the Federation is at least a fact. Although the membership is currently restricted to the provinces and territories, it may one day expand to include Aboriginal leaders. Finally, there is the idea of the Atlantic provinces as a virtual region, the thought being that, in acting together wherever it makes sense to do so, these provinces could respond better to the interests of their residents. The ongoing activities of the Council of the Atlantic Premiers are a testament to the validity of the idea. Nonetheless, the stresses involved in regional cooperation are only too evident in an issue that is vital to the well-being of two of the Atlantic provinces - namely, the revenues from offshore petroleum resources.

The conclusion on these four developments is straightforward. Assessing the federal scene from the standpoint of the Democratic Audit plainly reveals that the only solid one is the establishment of the Council of the Federation, and its promise in terms of participation and inclusiveness is still just that – a promise. Meanwhile, in relation to the Democratic Audit benchmarks, the greatest weaknesses remain. The cities are still not included in the federal system in their own right, a point made clear once again when the federal government sketched out its plans for infrastructure spending in the January 2009 budget to meet the challenges of a dismal economy. The funds intended for municipal spending are routed through the provinces. The conduct of federal-provincial-territorial relations continues to take place within the institutions of executive federalism, institutions that are no more open to citizens now than they ever were. Finally, Ottawa's responsiveness to the wide range of opinion and interest within the country continues to be hampered by the low threshold of popular support that is sufficient for a governing party to remain in office – in the general election of October 2008, the minority Conservative government did it with 37.65 percent of the popular vote. Certainly, as long as it can get enough support in the House of Commons for its legislative agenda, it is entitled to govern. Nevertheless, the idea of a coalition government, an obvious remedy for the low-threshold problem, continues to find no traction in the conduct of politics at the federal level.

Works Cited

Bailey, Sue. 2009. Harper sends pals to Senate: PM blasted for rewarding nine Tories with plum jobs. *Halifax Chronicle Herald,* 28 August, A1, A2.

Baum, Eric. 2008. Harper nominates Cromwell for the SCC. The Court (Osgoode Hall Law School). 5 September. http://www.thecourt.ca/.

Benzie, Robert. 2008. Layton opens coalition door. 22 September. http://www.thestar.com/.

Canadian Intergovernmental Conference Secretariat. 2009. http://www.scics.gc.ca/.

CBC News. 2009. Conservatives make plans for national securities regulator. CBC News. 27 January. http://www.cbc.ca/.

Cheadle, Bruce. 2008. Gov. Gen. winging her way back to Canada to deal with turmoil. *Halifax Chronicle Herald,* 3 December, A1.

Council of the Federation. 2008. Internal trade. http://www.councilofthefederation. ca/.

Curry, Bill, and Daniel LeBlanc. 2008. PM does about-turn on stacking Senate. *Globe and Mail,* 23 December, A1, A8.

Docherty, David. 2005. *Legislatures.* Canadian Democratic Audit. Vancouver: UBC Press.

Flanagan, Tom. 2007. Rebuilding the Senate, one block at a time. *Globe and Mail,* 23 April, A19.

Gordon, Sean. 2008. Revive Kelowna Accord, leaders urge. *Toronto Star,* 17 July. http://www.thestar.com/.

Greene, Ian. 2006. *The courts.* Canadian Democratic Audit. Vancouver: UBC Press.

Lee, Pat. 2004. Harper: Get tough with PM – Premiers must force Martin to keep offshore commitment. *Halifax Mail Star,* 10 November, B2.

Magnussen, Warren. 2005. Are municipalities creatures of provinces? *Journal of Canadian Studies* 39(2): 5-29.

Simeon, Richard, and D.M. Cameron. 2002. Intergovernmental relations and democracy: An oxymoron if ever there was one? In *Canadian federalism: Performance, effectiveness, and legitimacy,* ed. Herman Bakvis and Grace Skogstad, 278-95. Don Mills, ON: Oxford University Press.

Smiley, D.V. 1980. *Canada in question,* 3rd ed. Toronto: McGraw-Hill.

Smith, Jennifer. 2004. *Federalism.* Canadian Democratic Audit. Vancouver: UBC Press.

–. 2008. Intergovernmental relations, legitimacy, and the Atlantic Accords. *Constitutional Forum* 17(3): 81-98.

Stephenson, Marilla. 2009. Don't laugh too hard about Danny's equalization dramas. *Halifax Mail Star,* 3 February, B1, B5.

Valpy, Michael. 2008. There's no hint whether prorogation came with strings attached. *Globe and Mail,* 5 December, A6.

Valpy, Michael, Daniel LeBlanc, and Jane Taber. 2008. Ignatieff makes his move. *Globe and Mail,* 8 December, A9.

Watts, Ronald L. 1999. *Comparing federal systems,* 2nd ed. Montreal and Kingston: McGill-Queen's University Press.

3 CABINETS AND FIRST MINISTERS
Graham White

As the Canadian Democratic Audit demonstrates, it is not easy to develop a clear, practical definition of democracy when dealing with a complex political system. Whatever else democracy may be, however, it certainly is not autocracy or dictatorship - political regimes with absolute power held by one person or a handful of people. And yet, knowledgeable, respected observers of the Canadian political scene have charged that, in recent years, political power has become so concentrated in the person of the prime minister and his entourage of political and bureaucratic officials that Canada can, with only slight exaggeration, be described, in the title of an influential book (Simpson 2001), as a "friendly dictatorship."

One facet of the Canadian Democratic Audit involved an attempt to apply the Audit benchmarks to the central institutions of Canadian government - the cabinets and first ministers - in order to evaluate the state of democracy in these key components of the political system. After all, if the country's principal decision-making bodies are highly undemocratic, does it matter how democratic are our elections, political parties, interest groups, and so on? This chapter is a distillation of the key observations and reflections from that study, *Cabinets and First Ministers* (White 2005). (Use of the plural - and the term "first minister" - signified that the book's analysis extended beyond the prime minister to include provincial and territorial premiers. This chapter follows suit.)

After some brief scene setting, the chapter considers how cabinet government in Canada fares in terms of the Audit benchmarks of inclusiveness, responsiveness, and participation. These analyses consider cabinets and first ministers, and thus the institutions and processes at the core of Canadian government, as contributors to or detractors from the health of democracy in this country. The key issue of autocracy on the part of the first minister is assessed under the rubric of participation. This leads to a discussion of possible reforms and a brief conclusion.

Cabinet Government in Canada: Preliminary Observations

Most Canadians know the basics of cabinet government. They know that the cabinet is headed by the prime minister and is the central and most powerful decision-making body in government. They know that ministers are chosen by the prime minister from among elected MPs to head the departments of government and that the prime minister can shuffle and dismiss ministers. They know that cabinet operations and decisions are shrouded in secrecy. Many Canadians are familiar with the names, views, and records of the prime minister and the more prominent ministers. For most people, this level of knowledge is generally sufficient. For a democratic audit of cabinet and first ministers, however, a somewhat more textured appreciation of cabinet government is necessary.

Like the other Anglo-Celtic democracies that have adopted British governmental institutions, Canada follows the principles of the Westminster cabinet-parliamentary system. We lack the space here to enumerate the constitutional precepts comprising British-style "responsible government," but three general observations are in order. First, though the same fundamental elements underpin governance in all Westminster countries, significant variations are evident in its detailed operation across national boundaries. Indeed, noteworthy mutations exist within Canada's fourteen Westminster systems (all provinces and territories, but no municipalities, follow the responsible government model).

Second, the Westminster cabinet-parliamentary system is, by its very nature, characterized by extensive concentration of power. No one "designed" the system; rather, it evolved over the centuries. A key element of that evolution was a gradual transfer of scarcely constrained power from the monarch to parliament and subsequently to the prime minister and the cabinet. Canadian first ministers and cabinets face significant constraints in the exercise of power, but it is well to appreciate that concentrated power is an inherent characteristic of Westminster-style democracies.

Third, it is essential to recognize that Canadian first ministers and their cabinet colleagues are very much components of an unquestionably democratic system. In particular, they are "responsible" to parliament (or the provincial/territorial legislatures) for the use of that power. The fundamental constitutional principle of Westminster-style responsible government requires that they achieve and retain power through continued support - "the confidence" - of a majority of the members of the legislature, who have been elected through free and fair elections. The mere fact that first ministers and their cabinets possess substantial executive power is not inherently undemocratic. To be sure, however, that power represents a potentially serious undermining of Canadian democracy.

The Canadian Democratic Audit benchmarks require recalibration in the case of cabinets and first ministers. After all, by definition, political executives in all systems take and implement decisions and in so doing superimpose their own values and preferences on the advice or instruction they have received, including that offered by elected legislatures. In short, political executives in democracies have power, and they use it. Thus, no one would argue that the central decision-making processes of Canadian government are, or could be, democratic in the same way that elections, party leadership selection processes, or open municipal council meetings can be. Nonetheless, cabinets can be organized and can operate in ways that either diminish or enhance democracy.

Graham White

What does a systematic application of the Audit benchmarks tell us? More so perhaps than in other facets of the Canadian Democratic Audit, the three benchmarks - inclusiveness, responsiveness, and participation - are closely intertwined. This interconnection should be borne in mind in the following application of the benchmarks to the core Canadian executive.

Inclusiveness

If the word is defined literally, the discussion of cabinet inclusiveness is over before it begins, since cabinets surely rank among the most exclusive bodies in Canada. Membership is limited to twenty or thirty people, who gain admission and retain membership only with the first minister's approval. Cabinet meetings are highly secretive affairs, and only the most senior and most trusted officials are permitted to see the documents discussed by cabinet. However, if we adopt an expansive rendering of the concept, the question of cabinet inclusiveness becomes more interesting. In this, we follow the lead of other authors in the Democratic Audit project by focusing on social diversity.

For most of Canadian history, cabinets were anything but diverse, dominated as they were by middle-aged professional males of Anglo-Celtic or francophone heritage. In recent years, far-reaching demographic and attitudinal transformations in Canadian society have been partially reflected in cabinet membership, enhancing the social diversity and hence the inclusiveness of our core decision-making bodies. Yet cabinets necessarily reflect the social characteristics of the legislatures from which they are drawn, and as David Docherty has shown in *Legislatures* (2005), the social composition of Canadian legislatures lags behind societal change. And of course some groups are completely excluded: by definition, there are no poor or unemployed ministers.

At the same time, a distinctive feature of Canadian cabinet government, dubbed the "representational imperative" (Campbell 1985), is the political principle that insists that, so far as possible, cabinet include "representatives" of all regions as well as all important ethnic, cultural, and linguistic groups and various other politically salient groups (such as women and those who hold certain occupations). The other Anglo-Celtic Westminster systems – those of Britain, Australia, New Zealand, and the Irish Republic – certainly value representativeness in their cabinets, but in none is the principle so extensively or formally entrenched as in Canada. This axiom of Canadian politics, which sometimes means that socio-demographic characteristics trump ability in the selection of ministers, clearly enhances inclusiveness in terms of cabinet membership, but does it really ensure that the concerns and perspectives of the diverse groups that make up Canada are represented when important decisions are taken?

To the extent that "group" equates to region, it probably does, given Canadian political leaders' hypersensitivity to regional concerns. At the national level, powerful "regional ministers" (Bakvis 1991) are deeply involved in decision making, promoting the interests of their regions at the cabinet table and in a wide range of government undertakings. Formal systems of regional ministers are less in evidence provincially, but regional concerns are of no less import in provincial politics and thus in provincial cabinet processes. Beyond region, however, the contribution of the representational imperative to cabinet inclusiveness is problematic. In some cases, a minister's appointment to cabinet amounts to little more than window dressing to appease a certain group or region, with the minister holding an insignificant portfolio, sitting on unimportant committees, and wielding little political clout. This is not much of an advance for inclusiveness.

Moreover, by no means does the representational imperative extend to all groups deserving of inclusion in top decision-making processes. Cabinets are not remotely representative in terms of economic status, age, disability, sexual orientation, and other politically salient characteristics. Nor do the broad-brush categories that define cabinet construction necessarily entail genuine inclusiveness – can a minister from one "visible minority community" adequately represent the enormous range of people that phrase encompasses?

All told, then, even when measured by the relatively undemanding criterion of social diversity, Canadian cabinets do not score high on inclusiveness. The root of this shortcoming does not, however, lie so much with cabinets as with the formal and informal processes that produce the members of our legislative institutions. As Docherty's contribution to the Democratic Audit demonstrates (2005, Chapter 4 this volume), on many significant socio-demographic dimensions, our elected representatives are not very representative.

In Ottawa, the prime minister does have the option of appointing senators to cabinet to bolster representivity (the exception here is one essential appointee, the leader of the government in the Senate, a cabinet minister who represents the government in the Senate). However, this happens only occasionally and then only to give cabinet voice to provinces whose voters elected few or no government MPs, never on other representative criteria. In all jurisdictions, the first minister can appoint an unelected person to cabinet (though constitutional convention requires that he or she quickly finds a seat) to fill a gap in representation, but this occurs very infrequently.

Even if we restrict the analysis of inclusiveness to issues of social diversity, cabinets still fare poorly on this dimension, an obvious and overriding weakness. Glimmers of strength may be found in the impulse the representational imperative creates to at least include as wide a range of ministers as possible in cabinet, given the composition of the government caucus, and in the broadening of the socio-demographic profile of ministers in recent decades to somewhat redress the traditional under-representation of groups such as women, Aboriginal people, and visible minorities.

Responsiveness

In a governmental context, responsiveness is primarily about taking action in accord with the wishes of the public: addressing issues of concern to the people and adopting policies that reflect their desires. Responsiveness also carries connotations of capacity to respond quickly. In assessing cabinet responsiveness, two sets of questions are of central interest. The first relates to the quality and extent of information and advice available to cabinet as it considers issues and makes decisions. The second involves the processes by which issues come before cabinet and are discussed and decided upon.

Individual ministers and cabinet collectively receive endless numbers of high-quality analytic background reports, discussion papers, briefing documents, and policy proposals from the permanent bureaucracy. Such documents are essential for thoughtful, informed decision making – though of course the reality is that few ministers have the time and inclination to read and reflect on all the official papers that cross their desks in staggering numbers – but they are not sufficient. Cabinet is pre-eminently a political body – politicians elected by the people to make political decisions – which must necessarily bring more to the table than the technical analysis and policy advice offered by non-partisan public servants, invaluable as these may be. In other words, cabinet needs political intelligence and analysis.

Ministers rely on their own finely honed political judgment, but they also understand the importance of hearing others' views. Ministers are entitled to seek advice and information wherever they wish but have very limited time and capacity to do so directly. Just whom they rely on for political guidance thus relates directly to the question of responsiveness. Two potentially crucial sources of political analysis and advice are the government caucus and ministers' personal political staff.

The roles of the government caucus and of individual backbench members are more fully discussed later in the chapter. For now, suffice it to say that the more extensive and institutionalized the involvement in cabinet processes of individual government backbenchers and of the government caucus collectively, the broader will be the range of political experience and advice available to cabinet as it makes decisions and the more likely that it will accurately reflect the views of the public.

Ministers are not restricted to their elected non-cabinet colleagues for political counsel: they can also call on their personal political staff, who may range in number from two or three, for those holding minor portfolios in small provinces, to two dozen or more, for ministers in the large federal departments. Though paid from the public purse, the political staff in ministers' offices are very different in function and orientation from the politically neutral permanent bureaucrats. Ministers' personal staff are explicitly partisan, and their duties are clearly political. They owe their prime loyalty to their ministers personally, so that, unlike bureaucrats, who remain in their posts when ministers or governments change, political staff usually move with their ministers when they are shuffled and lose their jobs when their ministers leave cabinet. Many of their duties are mundane, but senior political staff wield potentially substantial influence, in part through the "gatekeeper" role they play: deciding which people and organizations the minister meets and which of the enormous number of written submissions from the public and from interest groups the minister reads. Clearly, political staff can contribute to responsiveness by exposing ministers to a broad range of opinion and advice from the public and organized groups, or they can undermine responsiveness by limiting access to the minister to a narrow range of like-minded political supporters, whose views are unlikely to be broadly representative. In all this, it should not be thought that political staff exercise Svengali-like control over hapless ministers; the ministers give general direction as to the types and sources of advice they want, but they must necessarily give their staff considerable discretion. Although we lack much in the way of up-to-date systematic study of ministers' personal staff, especially at the provincial level, on balance, as argued in *Cabinets and First Ministers* (White 2005), ministerial staff enhance democracy by virtue of their contribution to cabinet responsiveness.

It is often remarked, usually by way of pointed criticism, that political staff are unelected. True enough, but they are serving elected politicians, and if they are operating unchecked, this is surely to be held against the elected ministers to whom they are responsible.

At first blush, cabinet's organizational structure and process might seem far removed from the question of how it fares in terms of responsiveness. Over the past few decades, cabinets at all levels in Canada have evolved from somewhat haphazard bodies with minimal formal organization – as late as the 1970s, some provinces lacked formal agendas for cabinet meetings or minutes recording decisions – to highly bureaucratized institutions. Cabinets now have extensive formal procedures for bringing issues before ministers and providing them with professional information and advice; they also have routinized processes for routing proposals through cabinet committees and full cabinet consideration. This is not to say that ministers – most notably the first minister – never circumvent the rules, especially when quick action is needed. The norm, though, is one of comprehensive, formal, routinized processes, supervised and enforced by powerful central bureaucratic agencies.

How does the bureaucratization of cabinet and cabinet processes affect responsiveness? Quite simply, in this instance, order fosters democracy through enhanced responsiveness capacity. The essential purpose of the formalization of cabinet processes is to ensure that ministers are in a position to participate effectively in cabinet decision making. This requires clear priority-setting mechanisms as well as ministers with sufficient information on the issues at hand, time to review the information and reflect on it, and the opportunity to contribute to important decisions. A clear, disciplined process – it matters less what process is followed than that one exists – makes for better, more considered decisions and thus for heightened responsiveness.

From the point of view of responsiveness, the (relatively recent) advent of disciplined, formalized decision-making processes stands out clearly as cabinet's great strength. Its main weakness lies in the hit-and-miss nature of the range of information, opinion, and advice from persons and organizations outside government to which ministers are exposed. Good staff work can ensure that ministers have access to – and are accessible to – broad swaths of diverse people and groups; poor staff work cuts ministers off from information they should have and ideas they should be hearing, thereby rendering them less responsive.

Participation I: Who Takes Part in Cabinet Decisions?

Responsiveness and inclusiveness are important measures of cabinet democracy, but the most fundamental questions relate to the third

Audit benchmark: participation. It ranks as the most important issue because it relates directly to the most basic democratic question arising in contemporary cabinet government: is the first minister a dictator, or autocrat? Public participation in cabinet and other core executive activities is virtually nil, but as noted above, cabinet is a component of a system of representative democratic institutions. Accordingly, it is reasonable to stipulate that, for cabinets, the benchmark should be couched in terms of participation by the representatives of the public. One way to approach the question of cabinet participation is to consider who actually takes part in cabinet decisions and what their involvement entails. Such is the focus of this section. Another approach to the question, however, would suggest that, if power is as concentrated in the first minister and his or her entourage as some would have it, the real issue is whether other participants much matter. The next section explores this crucial concern.

The public does not take part in cabinet or cabinet committee meetings, but in some jurisdictions, interest groups may sometimes be invited to appear before cabinet or its committees. These occasions typically consist of group representatives making a presentation and engaging in discussion with ministers. Rarely, if ever, do such meetings entail actual cabinet deliberations. Nor, save in highly unusual circumstances, are outsiders present, let alone participating, when cabinet makes decisions. Little evidence exists that interest group appearances before cabinet bring about significant results. (Such meetings with full cabinet or with its committees are quite different from the meetings that individual ministers routinely have with a wide range of groups in connection with issues and policies encompassed in their portfolios; these meetings may have substantial impact on government policy.) Overall, the occasional appearance before cabinet or its committees of well-heeled professional interest groups, such as chambers of commerce, labour federations, medical associations, or university presidents, constitutes at best a marginal broadening of participation in cabinet processes.

Of far greater potential, and indeed actual significance, is the participation of government backbenchers in cabinet processes. All ministers engage extensively in formal and informal discussions with their parties' private members on all manner of policy and political concerns, but this is very different from actively engaging them in formal cabinet decision making. Two avenues exist for backbench involvement in cabinet processes: participation in meetings of cabinet or cabinet committees and vetting or approving cabinet decisions by the government caucus.

In Ottawa and some provincial capitals, it is unusual, if not entirely unknown, for government private members to attend or participate in cabinet or cabinet committee meetings. Elsewhere, this may happen occasionally, or it may be an integral part of the process (White 2005, 117-25). It may take the form of representatives of the government caucus attending full cabinet, perhaps on a rotating basis. In some provinces, traditional cabinet committees, composed entirely of ministers, have been replaced by caucus policy committees, some chaired by backbenchers, with as many if not more private members as ministers. If no one harbours illusions that this arrangement gives private members the same clout as ministers, it is nonetheless clear that it does make for significant systematic backbench influence in cabinet processes.

The government caucus plays a role in cabinet decision making in all Canadian jurisdictions, but great variation exists as to the scope and formality of that role - as indeed on the primal issue of actual caucus influence. Caucus will usually be informed in advance of proposed legislation and major cabinet initiatives, but this by no means implies that it is involved in developing policy changes or has the opportunity to modify or even reject them. Moreover, in most jurisdictions, wide swaths of important government undertakings, such as major budgetary initiatives or policy proposals not requiring legislation, are entirely outside caucus' ken.

That said, in some provinces the government caucus is a regular and influential participant in scrutinizing and approving significant new cabinet initiatives, especially if they entail legislative change (White 2005, 125-29). Some jurisdictions have instituted formal procedures for caucus review of policy proposals, though the nature of these procedures and the rigour with which they are enforced are very much up to the first minister – new first ministers are entirely free to significantly alter or entirely scupper their predecessors' practices in this regard. No caucus wields veto power, though doubtless every cabinet has occasionally encountered concerted caucus pressure or opposition that has forced substantial modification or outright rejection of major bills or policy proposals.

Clearly, whether through formal or informal means, caucus involvement in cabinet decision making rates as a potentially important way of enhancing participation. The potential, however, is largely unrealized. Many significant cabinet proposals never come before the government caucus, or come late in the day, with inadequate information and/or time to consider them properly. As well, even when caucus is genuinely involved in government decisions, this almost always takes the form of reaction to proposed cabinet measures; caucus lacks the resources and opportunity to initiate or develop policy change. Moreover, the role of caucus is almost entirely determined by the first minister's willingness to accord it significant influence. Astute first ministers attend caucus regularly and listen carefully to its concerns and advice, but that is not at all equivalent to permitting its formal participation in cabinet processes.

Participation II: The First Minister as Autocrat?

Recognition that it is the first minister's prerogative to decide whether and how the government caucus will participate in cabinet processes brings us to perhaps the most crucial question about democracy in the Canadian core executive: has power become so concentrated in "the centre" that Canadian first ministers have become autocrats, or dictators?

Arguments that Canadian first ministers have become too powerful, especially vis-à-vis parliament and the provincial legislatures, date from at least the 1960s (Smith 1977). The most comprehensive and sophisticated articulation has been made by Donald Savoie, one of the country's leading academics, in an influential book, *Governing from the Centre* (Savoie 1999). Savoie makes a strong case that power has become so concentrated in the Canadian prime minister (his analysis does not extend to the provincial level) and the top political advisors and bureaucratic officials supporting him or her - "the centre" - that not only has parliament been eclipsed but cabinet has been reduced to little more than "a focus group for the prime minister." In terms of the Democratic Audit benchmarks, Savoie questions whether even ministers are fully participating in cabinet decision making.

Nor is Savoie alone in expressing concern about the extraordinary power enjoyed by the Canadian prime minister. Jeffrey Simpson, who ranks among the country's most insightful and prominent political journalists, warns in his book *The Friendly Dictatorship* of "the massive centralization of power in one man's control within the trappings of a parliamentary system" (Simpson 2001, xi). Some academics have questioned aspects of Savoie's analysis (Bakvis 2001; Thomas 2003-04), but none dispute that power is indeed concentrated in the prime minister and what Savoie (2008) calls his "court." A recent systematic comparison by academic experts of prime ministers in twenty-two countries, including all five that feature national Anglo-Celtic Westminster systems, rated the Canadian prime minister not only as the most powerful (on a scale from 1.0 to 9.0, his overall score was 8.24) but the most powerful by a wide margin (the next highest score, for Malta, was 7.16; the rating of the closest Anglo-Celtic system, that of Australia, was 6.98) (O'Malley 2007, table 3).

Savoie's argument is too complex and the evidence he marshals in support of it too extensive to permit full elaboration here; only the briefest of overviews is possible. Savoie builds upon the inherent concentration of power in Westminster systems, enhanced by certain distinctively Canadian traits such as party leadership selection processes. His central emphasis is upon the unprecedented growth over the past few decades in the size, sophistication, and influence of the powerful "central agencies" supporting the prime minister, most notably the Prime Minister's Office and the Privy Council Office. The former is the unabashedly partisan powerhouse of government, whereas the latter is the elite bureaucratic department charged with coordinating and directing government activity; together, they constitute the core of the centre (Savoie 1999). In a more recent book, Savoie (2008, ch. 10) highlights the remarkable extent to which the prime minister and his court - the top political and bureaucratic figures close to him - have rendered the senior bureaucracy more "responsive" to their political agenda as well as the extraordinary measures taken by the Harper government to "manage" the news.

If the prime minister is singularly powerful, what of her provincial colleagues? A recent collection of essays on provincial cabinets and leadership supports the proposition that Savoie's analysis is applicable in the provinces, albeit with certain refinements and qualifications (Bernier, Brownsey, and Howlett 2005). The lesser scale and complexity of provincial government, even in the largest jurisdictions, offers even greater scope than exists in Ottawa for the accretion of power to the centre. Nearly three decades ago, Walter Young and Terry Morley (1983, 54) wrote that "provincial government is premier's government ... The extent of his authority is significantly greater than that of his federal counterpart." Little has changed to challenge their judgment.

Underpinning the exceptional power of Canadian first ministers vis-à-vis their peers in other Anglo-Celtic Westminster systems are the processes for selecting party leaders in this country. Variations abound, but all major Canadian parties, federal and provincial, choose their leaders either at conventions with hundreds, perhaps thousands, of voting delegates or through votes of all party members. This approach permits far greater inclusiveness and participation - and by those standards is more democratic - than the processes still common in other Anglo-Celtic Westminster systems, which limit leadership selection largely or entirely to the party's parliamentary caucus (though that term is not employed outside Canada). Paradoxically, though, it also has the decidedly undemocratic effect of greatly enhancing the first ministers' power, since it largely insulates them from the prospect of being removed from office by caucus or cabinet revolts - if a leader is elected by a convention or a party-wide vote, it follows that he or she can be removed only through similar mechanisms. Since at best these are slow, messy, and uncertain, for all intents and purposes Canadian first ministers can retain power so long as they are prepared to stare down internal dissent. Other Anglo-Celtic Westminster systems have in recent years witnessed the remarkable sight of sitting prime ministers being deposed swiftly and decisively by their parliamentary parties - in Savoie's view (2005, 42) an "unthinkable" occurrence in Canada.

It is true enough that a very few Canadian sitting first ministers, such as Jean Chrétien and even Alberta's Ralph Klein, left office earlier than they might have wished due to party pressure. Their departures, however, reflected party-wide pressure - as opposed to cabinet or caucus revolts - and their leaving was of their choice and timing; they were not formally removed from office as were their opposite numbers in other Anglo-Celtic systems.

Savoie's analysis is nuanced and authoritative; even a skeptic such as Herman Bakvis (2001, 64) calls it "simultaneously compelling and disturbing." No serious observer of the Canadian political scene disputes that our first ministers and their entourages wield formidable power. But are Canadians really living in an autocracy, where their first ministers exercise scarcely constrained autocratic authority? Is the focus on cabinets and ministers in previous sections of this chapter irrelevant since their power has been largely usurped by first ministers? The balance of this section suggests that such dire interpretations are unwarranted - Canadian first ministers are not autocrats, though they are unquestionably very powerful.

In the first place, Canadian first ministers may have great power, but they also face formidable constraints. At the most basic level, they constantly encounter constitutional limits to their authority, most notably the Canadian Charter of Rights and Freedoms, and federalism, which at root is about sharing power among orders of government. Ironically, the power of the prime minister may be constrained by that of a provincial or territorial first minister - and vice versa. (For a discussion of this, see Chapter 2 in this volume.) Other constraints are political rather than constitutional. By way of illustration, first ministers have full and undisputed authority to appoint, shuffle, and dismiss ministers - an enormous power - but find their actual choices hemmed in by myriad political considerations (including the representational imperative), not to mention limited talent pools (the prime minister typically picks about 30 ministers from a caucus of 130 to 180 MPs, but the calculus for provincial premiers is rather less favourable, some having to choose cabinets of nearly 20 from caucuses with barely 30 members). First ministers are also constrained by the need to contend with aggressive, intrusive, and well-informed media.

Within government, a range of constraints substantially circumscribes the first minister's power. As Savoie (1999, 8) notes, the prime minister faces serious overload problems and can focus on only a few key issues at a time. No one person, even supported by a large, expert political-bureaucratic apparatus, can run a government single-handedly. To be effective, first ministers need strong, committed cabinets. But tough, able ministers will not countenance more than occasional instances of being micromanaged or overridden by first ministers or their courts. Savoie (ibid., 86) acknowledges that no prime minister can afford to repeatedly run roughshod over his ministers: "The prime minister's summary and decision on his definition of the Cabinet consensus cannot always go blatantly against the sense of the meeting if he is to retain the confidence of his ministers."

Paul Thomas (2003-04, 80) emphasizes that power relationships within the executive are not simple "zero-sum games" in which one person's gains are another's losses; instead, they reflect complex, fluid interdependencies so that "the Prime Minister needs on most occasions the uncoerced support of his ministers and to a lesser extent his back-bench followers." Thus, first ministers must husband their political resources in dealing with their cabinet colleagues, carefully picking the spots for exercising their undoubted authority – as "the boss" – to call the shots, whether this entails overriding a clear consensus in cabinet, circumventing normal cabinet processes, taking important decisions without consulting affected ministers, or becoming deeply involved in departmental issues. When asked directly whether they were able to get their own way whenever they wanted, a range of former provincial premiers were unequivocal that, even for the first minister, cabinet government is a constant compromise: One remarked that "the premier has a great deal of discretionary authority, but in all cases does seek a genuine consensus of cabinet ... If I had too blatantly misstated the consensus, I would have been challenged." Another commented, "sometimes, as premier, you have to give in one circumstance in order to get in another." A third noted that, "for the premier, getting things done is always an act of persuasion" (quoted in White 2005, 96). And finally, Allan Blakeney and Sandford Borins (1998, 31) point out that "nobody expected to win all the time, not even the premier. A premier has a reserve power to make an opinion stick. But he or she is unwise to exercise that power except in very pressing circumstances."

These former premiers' observations highlight the great difficulty inherent in assessing the "first minister as autocrat" thesis. As researchers, we have no clear, direct way to measure power relations within cabinet; we have no access to cabinet or cabinet committee meetings and only very limited access to cabinet documents less than twenty or thirty years old. Thus, we must rely on what we are told by those involved in the process. Eddie Goldenberg (2006, 75), legendary political fixer for Prime Minister Jean Chrétien, dismissed what he termed "the mythology about excessive centralization or inordinate concentration of power" as a misunderstanding of the crucial need for coordination in a complex modern government. Do we reject this as defensive, self-serving misrepresentation, or do we perceive it as an accurate appraisal by someone intimately familiar with the inner workings of government?

As well, we lack clearly defined benchmarks for establishing whether power is indeed becoming more concentrated. Savoie's critics, for example, argue that he is correct in pointing to the high concentration of power in the prime minister but incorrect in claiming that this is new. As knowledgeable an observer as Stéphane Dion (2007, 178), who was an academic authority on government before becoming a federal cabinet minister, contends that a comparison of present-day Ottawa with that of the William Lyon Mackenzie King era makes it "clearly evident that power at that time was far more concentrated in a few hands than it is today. Perhaps ... it is less a case of increasing concentration of power than increasing sensitivity to and declining tolerance of concentrated power."

In support of his argument, Savoie (1999) points to noteworthy examples of recent prime ministers making far-reaching decisions entirely outside of cabinet processes, sometimes without even informing ministers whose departments are involved. Similar instances of "governing by bolts of electricity," as Savoie terms it (ibid., ch. 10), also dot provincial politics. But does the occasional – perhaps very occasional – exercise of first ministers' unquestioned prerogative to make such "executive decisions" equate with autocratic behaviour? How often must first ministers override or ignore cabinet to be considered dictatorial? How frequently and how extensively must first ministers or their courts interfere in ministers' departments to be considered autocratic? As yet, we have no clear answers to such questions, nor systematic data on the issues they raise (White 2008).

We do know that public image is not a reliable guide to assessing first ministers' exercise of power. Prime Minister Pierre Trudeau was widely viewed as highly autocratic, and some of Savoie's most compelling examples involve him. The judgment of those who sat with him at the cabinet table belie this public image. Eugene Whelan (1986, 195), as plain-speaking a minister as ever was, said of Trudeau, "Contrary to what many people think, Trudeau ran his cabinet with a very loose hand … I always laughed when people described him as a dictator." Veteran minister Mitchell Sharp (1994, 167) wrote that "I never knew him [Trudeau] to anticipate a decision [in cabinet] by giving his opinion before asking the opinions of his colleagues, except, of course, with respect to constitutional questions. He genuinely sought for consensus." Jean Chrétien (1985, 75) recounts thoughts of resigning as finance minister in the wake of a massive shift in economic policy that Trudeau announced without consulting him and yet describes this episode as uncharacteristic, commenting, "In cabinet Trudeau listened more and compromised more than most Canadians imagine … I never subscribed to the notion that Trudeau was a dictator. Often knowing what he thought, I saw him accepting the views of his ministers despite his own wishes."

In sum, important qualifications exist as to just how much power is concentrated in the first minister and his court, and whether the extent of concentration is increasing. Yet, if the "first minister as autocrat" thesis is overstated, no one can doubt that Canadian first ministers do wield remarkable power even by the standards of the Westminster cabinet-parliamentary system. Nor would many disagree on the need for measures to enhance democracy in this country by curtailing that power. The next section briefly addresses this topic.

The greatest weakness in terms of the participation benchmark is obviously the enormous authority of the first minister, which in some instances means that only one person, assisted by a coterie of close advisors, is "participating" in cabinet decision making. This weakness, however, needs to be ranged against the still compelling strength of cabinet government: the capacity of able, experienced elected politicians to work collectively in reaching critical government decisions.

Possible Reforms

Some readers will not be assuaged by my conclusions about the nature and extent of power exercised by the cabinet and, especially, the first minister, and may therefore be drawn to fundamental reforms. In my view, major changes to Canada's political system are neither warranted nor - at least as important - possible. (Of course, much depends on how one defines "fundamental" reform; some might apply that label to my call for a new electoral system.) Still, Canada's political executives do possess unusually extensive powers, and a clear need exists for measures to constrain them.

Fixed Elections

In *Cabinets and First Ministers,* I argued for a minor reform to constrain first ministers' power: legislated fixed elections. Most proponents of this reform see it as a way of levelling the playing field in elections by eliminating the substantial tactical advantage that the governing party holds over its opponents by virtue of the first minister's authority to determine election timing. My advocacy of fixed elections reflected a desire to take away the first minister's ability to bully cabinet and caucus by threatening to call an early election. Since the book was written, Ottawa, Ontario, Prince Edward Island, Newfoundland and Labrador, the Northwest Territories, New Brunswick, Saskatchewan, and Manitoba have all followed British Columbia's lead in passing legislation setting election dates, and others may follow suit. However, Prime Minister Stephen Harper's early election call in September 2008 – ignoring legislation his own government had instituted – makes it apparent that even such a limited reform may be of uncertain value.

Harper was able to exercise his undoubted constitutional prerogative to override the fixed election legislation at little political cost because his was a minority government in a highly confused political environment. Other first ministers, federal and provincial, heading majority governments might well balk at disregarding fixed election laws if they calculated that doing so might cause them significant political problems. Accordingly, fixed election legislation may constitute a modest advance for democracy aside from the levelling-the-playing-field rationale.

PARTY LEADERSHIP SELECTION PROCESSES

As discussed above, a key reason for the extraordinary power of Canadian first ministers is the near invulnerability they enjoy from cabinet and caucus revolts because they owe their position as party leader not to caucus or cabinet but to the party membership as a whole. Neither the leaders nor the rank-and-file members of any political party are likely to countenance giving caucus the authority to depose a party leader on its own. A reasonable measure – requiring action on the parties' rather than the government's part – would see a majority, or perhaps a substantial minority, vote of caucus trigger a formal leadership review within the party. This would retain party members' ultimate power to choose and dismiss leaders yet lessen the first minister's domination of the parliamentary party.

Involving Government Backbenchers in Cabinet Decision Making

As briefly discussed above, several jurisdictions have established ways of involving private members from the government party in cabinet processes, without apparent harm either to the constitutional precepts of responsible government or the political situation of the governing party through leaks of confidential information. To be sure, changes amounting to little more than insubstantial window dressing will do little to widen - and thus democratize - the range of participants in cabinet decision making. Overall, though, jurisdictions that have brought backbenchers into full cabinet or cabinet committee, or have given the government caucus an institutionalized and meaningful role in reviewing cabinet proposals, rate the experience positively. This is an area in which a range of potentially substantial reforms are possible.

Strengthening Parliamentary Institutions

Although this chapter has had little to say of Canada's parliamentary institutions, strong, robust legislatures, with thoughtful, independent-minded members, adequate professional staff, and muscular committee systems, would act as a potent democratic constraint on the power of cabinets and first ministers. Strengthening our parliamentary institutions would entail changes to the formal rules and procedures as well as attitudinal shifts on the part of the members. Neither is easily realized.

As a democratic institution, parliament is clearly at its most effective in times of minority government, though to be sure, legislatures without clear government majorities have problems of their own. In his recent book *Two Cheers for Minority Government,* Peter Russell (2008) argues persuasively that minority governments are our best hope for curtailing prime ministerial government and restoring a modicum of parliamentary effectiveness. Yet, as suggested by the success of the minority Conservative government elected in January 2006 in cowing the opposition, enabling Prime Minister Stephen Harper to operate almost as if he enjoyed a majority, intermittent bouts of minority government will not do the trick.

What we need is minority government as a permanent condition. But that is unlikely to occur in the absence of fundamental structural reform: replacement of the current single-member plurality electoral system with one of proportional representation (PR) or another electoral regime without the bias toward "false" majorities that is inherent in the first-past-the-post system.

The extensive power of Canadian first ministers rests to a substantial degree on their position as leaders of governments enjoying single-party legislative majorities, despite the fact that almost none of them ever wins a majority of the votes at election time. To anyone interested in curtailing executive power in this country, reform of the electoral system – whatever its merits on issues such as fairness – holds the most promise for real results. (Readers are directed to Chapter 6 of this volume, in which John Courtney looks at electoral reform.) A shift to PR is of course a multi-faceted change, generating strong views pro and con that cannot be explored here. Moving to a PR system would entail far-reaching implications, parliamentary and otherwise. Such debates can unfold elsewhere, but there can be little doubt that, since precious few Canadian governments – federal or provincial – would win more than half the electoral seats required to form a majority government, PR would substantially reduce the first minister's power (see Chapters 6 and 7 this volume, for more discussion relating to electoral system reform).

Conclusion

We end where we began, with the recognition and acceptance that, in any democratic political system, the elected executive exercises substantial authority. The mere existence of such power is not inherently undemocratic, but the potential for abuse is nonetheless real, especially in our Westminster system, which is characterized by a strong concentration of power in the cabinet and the first minister. Canadian first ministers arguably wield more power than their opposite numbers in Westminster systems by virtue of the near impossibility of their cabinets or caucuses deposing them from office. At the same time, as is the case with all political executives, Canadian first ministers' powers are circumscribed by a host of constraints, both constitutional and political.

On none of the Canadian Democratic Audit benchmarks do cabinets and first ministers score highly, but this is hardly unexpected. Nor, more importantly perhaps, is it immutable. None of the potential reforms outlined in the previous section (or others proposed in *Cabinets and First Ministers*) is far-fetched or outrageous, which is not to say that they could be easily achieved. None challenges or offends against basic Westminster constitutional precepts; indeed, it is important, in contemplating possible reform of Canadian core executives, to bear in mind that the great genius of British-style responsible government is its flexibility and adaptability. Accordingly, the Westminster system is thoroughly compatible with a wide range of organizational and political arrangements.

To be sure, those with power - ministers and especially first ministers - are rarely keen on giving it up, so more is needed than innovative ideas and strong arguments in their favour. Political leaders with a genuine commitment to democratic reform can bring about serious change, as can clearly articulated and well-organized popular sentiment for reform. Nor should the fortuitous confluence of favourable circumstances be discounted. Reform, in short, is possible.

At the same time, and certainly not denying the unquestioned concentration in this country of power in the centre or the need to constrain it, let us again recall why political systems have executives with far-reaching authority. Provided of course that they attain and retain power through democratic means, political executives in this day and age need the capacity to make important, difficult decisions and to implement them. Many top Canadian political leaders find their time in office marked less by the great power they command than by the difficulty in getting anything of any substance done. Given the need to navigate the rocky waters of federalism, to handle intense media scrutiny and aggressive interest group activity, to overcome enormously complex bureaucratic processes and stringent financial constraints, and to manage overloaded agendas, it is sometimes a wonder that those atop our governments accomplish anything. We need to be concerned about the concentration of authority, but we also need to balance that concern with an appreciation that a democratically elected government needs the power to act. Maintaining that balance is an ongoing task.

Works Cited

Bakvis, Herman. 1991. *Regional ministers: Power and influence in the Canadian cabinet*. Toronto: University of Toronto Press.

–. 2001. Prime minister and cabinet in Canada: An autocracy in need of reform? *Journal of Canadian Studies* 35: 60-79.

Bernier, Luc, Keith Brownsey, and Michael Howlett, eds. 2005. *Executive styles in Canada: Cabinet structures and leadership practices in Canadian government*. Toronto: Institute of Public Administration of Canada and University of Toronto Press.

Blakeney, Allan, and Sandford Borins. 1998. *Political management in Canada*. Toronto: University of Toronto Press.

Campbell, Colin. 1985. Cabinet committees in Canada: Pressures and dysfunctions stemming from the representational imperative. In *Unlocking the cabinet: Cabinet structures in comparative perspective,* ed. T. Mackie and B. Hogwood, 61-85. London: Sage.

Chrétien, Jean. 1985. *Straight from the heart*. Toronto: Key Porter Books.

Dion, Stéphane. 2007. Institutional reform: The grass isn't always greener on the other side. In *Political leadership and representation in Canada: Essays in honour of John C. Courtney,* ed. Hans J. Michlemann, Donald C. Story, and Jeffrey S. Steves, 176-93. Toronto: University of Toronto Press.

Docherty, David. 2005. *Legislatures*. Canadian Democratic Audit. Vancouver: UBC Press.

Goldenberg, Eddie. 2006. *The way it works: Inside Ottawa*. Toronto: McClelland and Stewart.

O'Malley, Eoin. 2007. The power of prime ministers: Results of an expert survey. *International political science review* 28: 7-27.

Russell, Peter. 2008. *Two cheers for minority government: The evolution of Canadian parliamentary democracy*. Toronto: Emond Montgomery.

Savoie, Donald. 1999. *Governing from the centre: The concentration of power in Canadian politics.* Toronto: University of Toronto Press.

–. 2005. The federal government: Revisiting court government in Canada. In *Executive styles in Canada: Cabinet structures and leadership practices in Canadian government,* ed. Luc Bernier, Keith Brownsey, and Michael Howlett, 17-43. Toronto: Institute of Public Administration of Canada and University of Toronto Press.

–. 2008. *Court government and the collapse of accountability in Canada and the United Kingdom.* Toronto: University of Toronto Press.

Sharp, Mitchell. 1994. *Which reminds me ... a memoir.* Toronto: University of Toronto Press.

Simpson, Jeffrey. 2001. *The friendly dictatorship.* Toronto: McClelland and Stewart.

Smith, Denis. 1977. President and parliament: The transformation of parliamentary government in Canada. In *Apex of power: The prime minister and political leadership in Canada,* 2nd ed., ed. Thomas A. Hockin, 309-25. Toronto: Prentice-Hall.

Thomas, Paul. 2003-04. Governing from the centre: Reconceptualizing the role of the PM and cabinet. *Policy Options* 25(1): 79-85.

Whelan, Eugene, with Rick Archbold. 1986. *Whelan: The man in the green Stetson.* Toronto: Irwin.

White, Graham. 2005. *Cabinets and first ministers.* Canadian Democratic Audit. Vancouver: UBC Press.

–. 2008. 'The centre' of the democratic deficit? Power and influence in Canadian political executives. Paper presented at the "Democratic Deficit Conference," Harvard University, 9-11 May.

Young, Walter, and J. Terence Morley. 1983. The premier and the cabinet. In *The reins of power: Governing British Columbia,* ed. J. Terence Morley, Norman J. Ruff, Neil A. Swainson, R. Jeremy Wilson, and Walter D. Young, 45-82. Vancouver: Douglas and McIntyre.

LEGISLATURES
David Docherty

4

As the focal point for democratic representation, legislatures have an important role to play in harnessing support for all of our democratic institutions. If legislators fail to honour the trust Canadians have placed in them, little wonder that Canadians are turned off by the democratic process. Unfortunately, Canadians may be too quick to blame both the players and the arena. We must be careful to distinguish between the failure of legislators and that of legislatures. For example, it may be common to hear both politicians and pundits exclaim that "parliament is dysfunctional," but we might more properly accuse elected officials of creating a legislature that cannot conduct provincial or national business in a collegial or even productive manner.

So how do we distinguish between legislative failures and the inability of legislators to work within proscribed rules of democratic engagement? Within the framework of parliamentary governments, assemblies have three primary functions. First, they are representative bodies. Canadians elect members within constituencies to represent and reflect their interests. Representation of interests can supercede geography. Second, assemblies are charged with keeping the executive accountable for their actions. All members not in cabinet, both government and opposition legislators, are tasked with this scrutiny function. Members also perform an important legislative role. Although all monetary (and thus most significant) legislation emerges from cabinet, members debate, amend, and pass or defeat bills. Finally, it is worth noting that parliamentary legislatures also hold alternative governments within themselves. If an administration is defeated, either in the House or as a result of an election, a new government must be ready to replace it. As will be discussed below, this does not by definition necessitate a new election.

Part of the problem of the so-called democratic deficit rests in a misunderstanding by citizens as to what legislatures are either capable of doing or are supposed to do (for more on citizens' knowledge of their democracy, see Gidengil et al. 2004; Gidengil et al., Chapter 5 this volume). But a great deal of the blame lies in political parties and leaders themselves, who often act in a manner that places their short-term electoral interests ahead of support for our democratic institutions. This chapter provides some reflections on the three benchmarks of democratic governance in Canadian legislatures – namely, inclusiveness, responsiveness, and participation. It does so by drawing specifically on some recent examples from legislatures that have worked well and others in which the opportunities for inclusiveness, responsiveness, and participation have been lacking. In particular, this chapter refers to the 2008 attempt by federal opposition parties to defeat the Conservatives in the House and then form a coalition government without facing the voters. The actions of Prime Minister Stephen Harper to prorogue parliament to avoid a vote of non-confidence mark a sad chapter in parliamentary accountability and transparency.

The chapter argues that legislatures work best when legislators allow scrutiny, representation, and debates on legislation and public policy to take place. A government that takes its lumps on accountability yet provides more support for our institutions should be more highly regarded than one that actively seeks to minimize the proper role of parliament.

Inclusiveness

In the Democratic Audit volume on Canadian legislatures (Docherty 2005), I argued that barriers to entry into office could be either formal or informal. Both types of barriers prevent inclusiveness, or the ability of a legislature to open its membership to any qualified citizen. Canada's elected offices no longer have any significant formal barriers to membership. Citizens over the age of eighteen are entitled to vote and run for public office.

By contrast, those who hold office in the Senate must own $4,000 worth of real property and be at least thirty years old. That the property ownership requirement cannot realistically be considered a bar to office was illustrated when Prime Minister Jean Chrétien appointed Sister Mary (Peggy) Butts to the Senate in 1997. As a nun, Sister Butts had taken a vow of poverty and could not own any real property. The problem was resolved when her religious order effectively transferred ownership of some land to her. In addition, she donated her Senate salary to the poor, continuing a practice that existed prior to her appointment (Catholic New Services 2004). It is therefore hard to argue that the Senate is still the last bastion of propertied male interests when a nun with no property or income can serve in the Red Chamber.

The informal barriers to inclusiveness can be just as detrimental to proper representation and in many ways are more difficult to overcome. At first blush, we might argue that many of the deficiencies in inclusiveness are outside the scope of legislative assemblies. Assemblies, after all, simply meet after the public has elected their members. One cannot blame a legislative assembly for having too many white male attorneys. The assembly did not select them - voters did.

However, this does point to the importance of understanding assemblies as part of a constellation of democratic institutions, each impacting the other. Political parties and the electoral system have a direct influence on questions of inclusiveness inside our elected halls. For it is these two institutions that determine the choices presented to voters and ultimately the types of candidates being placed in front of them.

Political parties can help ensure that the full slate of candidates they offer at election time reflects both the constituencies they hope to represent and the broader Canadian population. Parties must also take pains to make sure that candidates representing this diversity are

Table 4.1

Female representation in the House of Commons:
Women elected in general elections (percentages in parenthesis)

Election	Total candidates	Female candidates (as % of all candidates)		Number of seats won by women (% of female candidates elected)		Total number of seats (% won by female candidates)	
2008	1,601	445	(27.79)	69	(15.50)	308	(22.400)
2006	1,634	380	(23.25)	64	(16.84)	308	(20.700)
2004	1,865	391	(20.97)	65	(16.62)	308	(21.100)
2000	1,808	375	(20.74)	62	(16.53)	301	(20.500)
1997	1,672	408	(24.40)	62	(15.19)	301	(20.500)
1993	2,155	476	(22.09)	53	(11.13)	295	(17.960)
1988	1,574	302	(19.19)	39	(12.91)	295	(13.200)
1984	1,449	214	(14.77)	27	(12.60)	282	(9.500)
1980	1,504	218	(14.49)	14	(6.42)	282	(4.960)
1974	1,209	137	(11.33)	9	(6.56)	264	(0.340)
1968	967	36	(3.72)	1	(2.77)	262	(0.038)

Note: Numbers in column 4 include women who won by-elections.
Source: Heard (n.d.).

nominated in ridings in which they have a realistic chance of winning. Traditionally, this has been one of the informal barriers to increasing gender balance in Canadian legislatures (see Chapter 7 this volume, for more on this point).

Many parties have taken steps to address this problem, by setting targets for the number of women to run or, in the case of Jean Chrétien, simply parachuting female candidates into winnable seats (Docherty 2005, 9). Nonetheless, as Table 4.1 indicates, Canadian legislatures still have a long way to go before they achieve gender balance. Federally, women have had difficulty breaking the one-fifth barrier of all House members (Cool 2006).

Although the figures are impressive on one front, they are a far cry from demonstrating equal gender representation. Women have gone from being less than 4 percent of all candidates for federal office in 1968 to over 25 percent of all candidates forty years later. And with the exception of a decrease from 1997 to 2000, the general trend is a positive one. At the same time, only minor progress has occurred in the five elections held since 1993.

David Docherty

Further, all things being equal, one might expect that the percentage of women winning office should approximately equal the percentage of those running for office. Yet, in each election, the percentage of women who take office is smaller than the percentage who run as candidates. Worse still, the only time the difference was less than five percentage points was in 1968, when only one of thirty-six female candidates won a seat in the federal election and in 1984, when a number of Conservative candidates won seats in ridings traditionally held by Liberals.

Where there has been a bit more progress is in the percentage of women sitting in the House of Commons, from less than 1 percent in 1968, the year after Canada's centennial, to just over 20 percent of all members in 2008. We also find, over time, that women are more likely to be among the candidates running for mainstream competitive parties who have a greater likelihood of winning seats. Nonetheless, it is also clear that women still need to make gains in the nomination process as they are nominated in fewer contests and elected at lower rates than their male counterparts.

Finally, it is worth noting that large electoral swings can produce increases in gender representation. In Pierre Trudeau's final election, that of 1980, only fourteen women won seats, less than one-twentieth of the House of Commons. The huge Mulroney sweep in 1984 saw this number almost double. In this election, women were nominated for seats that might previously have been considered marginal for the Progressive Conservatives (PCs) but that became competitive during the course of the campaign. We see a similar jump between 1988 and 1993, when the PCs were reduced to two seats and the Liberals had a massive resurgence, taking seats previously considered unwinnable.

In terms of demographic minorities, a shift has occurred, though more in attitude than in results. Political parties now actively recruit members of visible minorities, particularly in ridings that are ethnically diverse. Part of this is clearly driven by the parties' hope to broaden their electoral appeal. In Stephen Harper's first government, one MP, Jason Kenny, had specific political responsibility for making connections with multicultural communities across the country. The wooing of ethnic voters takes place among all parties, and this includes an understanding that more diverse representation inside assemblies has payoffs for political parties and substantive benefits for public policy.

At the same time, there still remains a large gulf between Canada's visible minority population outside parliament and the proportion of visible minorities inside the House of Commons. As Jerome Black and Bruce Hicks (2006) describe, the 2004 federal vote produced a House of Commons in which just over 7 percent of MPs described themselves as visible minorities, compared to a federal population of nearly 15 percent. Interestingly, the Black and Hicks study found that visible minority candidates themselves were split on the need for more aggressive policies within parties to increase representation. The split ran along party lines, with New Democrat and Bloc Québécois visible minority candidates far more supportive of affirmative action to increase representation and Green, Liberal, and Conservative visible minority candidates more likely to oppose such a move (ibid.).

Numeric growth in representation has not necessarily translated into substantive representation. Measuring changes in the latter is much more difficult than measuring numeric representation. Jerome Black (2002) has suggested that there are still large advances to be made in substantive representation. Simply put, having a more diverse assembly is a necessary but not sufficient condition for substantive representation. Here, the onus is on political parties to ensure that a diverse caucus is a means to a policy end, not simply a tool for political gain. This also requires providing the assembly with legislative mechanisms to assist in addressing questions of substantive representation. If policies to provide substantive change to Canadians are not placed on the floor of the assembly, opportunities for a diverse legislature to address these questions are minimized.

In sum, Canada has made significant strides toward more truly representative assemblies. Institutional reforms (to party and electoral rules) to quicken this pace seem unlikely. Thus, greater efforts to promote debate and participation among all members of legislatures should be emphasized and encouraged.

Responsiveness

Convincing Canadians that legislatures are responsive can be a hard sell, particularly during periods of majority government. Despite the fact that the model of Westminster parliaments suggests a high degree of responsiveness, the fact remains that legislatures may seem intransigent to public calls for quick action. There are a number of reasons that this is so.

First, though legislatures are the primary responsive democratic institution in Canada, they must work within the framework of the Westminster model. Canadians select a legislature in a series of individual contests (in the 308 federal ridings), and the legislature then selects a government. Perceiving the important difference between a legislature and a government is critical to understanding the often slow pace that large-scale change requires. The Westminster model suggests that the government must respond (or answer) to the legislature and that the legislature is responsible to the public. But this does not necessarily provide the legislature with the tools to directly respond to public demands.

The government (primarily the cabinet and senior bureaucrats) may at times wish to act decisively and with haste. When matters do not require legislative approval, this is often possible (see White 2005, Chapter 2 this volume). But on most larger matters, such as budget issues and policy changes requiring legislation, the process can take time as it requires legislative debate.

Second, this passage of time is required as a result of the institutional hurdles that are in place to temper quick or emotional responses to various issues of the day. In US-style congressional systems, this check is provided by the separation of government branches, whereas, in Canada's system, it is supplied by the institutionalized opposition. Federally, this is assisted by a second chamber devoted to "sober second thought." But in each legislature in Canada, there is an official opposition whose function is to question and hold to account the government of the day.

The opposition often does act to slow down a government's plans. Sometimes, it hopes to open up the process by forcing legislation to committees that can hear from the public. In this sense, such delays can be seen as positive aspects of the democratic process and an attempt to increase opportunities for participation and responsiveness. When the efforts to slow the government process include undue delaying tactics such as filibusters or bell ringing, public resentment is just as likely to be directed at the opposition as at the government. The most infamous of these cases was the 1980s Senate action to delay the GST legislation. Not only did this delay portray the appointed Senate in a bad light for holding up government legislation, it allowed the Mulroney administration to appoint additional senators without facing public resentment for "stacking" the Senate.

Opposition parties can often work with the government to ensure quick passage of legislation in times of emergency, real or imagined. In the spring of 2008, the Ontario legislature passed back-to-work legislation for the Toronto Transit Authority after just a day and a half of a strike (CBC News 2008). The legislature met on a Sunday afternoon to pass the legislation, debated for less than an hour, and unanimously passed the bill requiring mediation and arbitration. Rather than risking the wrath of angry commuters, the institutionalized opposition did not hesitate to cooperate with the government.

Third, Canadian assemblies are marked by high levels of party discipline. The fact that almost all government members desire a cabinet seat means that obedience to the premier or prime minister is a constant more than a variable. As a result, governments effectively speak with one voice, and when that voice (the leader) decides to move in a certain policy direction, there is little room to manoeuvre left or right (see, for example, Simpson 2002; Smith 2007).

This means that members themselves may have a difficult time in being responsive to their own constituents or broader interests that they might wish to represent. Party discipline can be an effective means of keeping one's caucus "on message," but it can suppress responsiveness. But it also requires members to properly use the opportunities for responsiveness that are available to them. For example, the members' statements portion of the daily routine proceedings was meant to allow members to place issues of local or national importance on the floor of the House. Increasingly, these statements have become a forum for personal attacks on other MPs, to the point where Speaker Peter Milliken has cut off individual members from issuing statements (Sotiropolous 2009). One might point to a government and suggest the fault lies with it for encouraging a move away from responsiveness. However, members have a duty to ensure that they are responsive to the representation of their interests.

One venue for this is caucus. The secrecy of caucus should allow members the opportunity to speak freely and (theoretically) to criticize their own party leadership. This should provide some mechanism to make parties more responsive to the needs of Canadians as represented by their elected officials. Yet, even here, larger interests are often replaced by more pragmatic concerns. In the lead-up to the fall 2008 election, the Liberal Party struggled with the public appetite for its environmental "green shift" platform (Diebel 2008). The debate within the party took place both inside and outside of caucus, prompting larger questions about the strength of then leader Stéphane Dion's position in the party. The success of responsiveness in caucus depends on the ability of all party members to keep the debate within caucus and support the leadership once a consensus decision is reached. The necessary secrecy, however, makes it impossible for many Canadians to appreciate the work of their representatives in caucus.

Legislatures can respond to societal needs and wants, but typically not in a rash manner, for that is not their role. Legislatures should ensure speedy passage of legislation when necessary but not bow to the immediate whims of government. At the same time, members themselves need to take more responsibility to ensure that the opportunities for responsiveness that do exist are used appropriately.

Most significant policy changes in Canadian history have required legislative approval. Health care is viewed by most Canadians as an untouchable right, yet, its creation required the approval of all legislatures in Canada. The historic free trade agreement with the United States and the North American Free Trade Agreement were both cabinet initiated but eventually passed through the House of Commons and Senate, and were signed by the governor general. Canadians should be concerned by a government that acts too rashly, without the approval of the legislature or without a strong prior endorsement of policy direction from the public during the previous election. Governments must be able to react to new economic, social, or political situations, and they should also avoid opting for quick fixes to problems rather than working for longer-term structural solutions (see Clarke et al. 1996). But fulfilling electoral promises and addressing new situations can be done with the approval of a sitting legislature, particularly in times of majority government. It simply requires a government that honours the legislative process.

The lack of freedom of individual members, typically the result of strong party discipline, can all too often give the appearance that legislators are "out of touch" with Canadians. This is actually far from the truth, particularly at the constituency level, where members have a keen sense of public sentiment. Changes to some institutional rules, such as a stricter interpretation of standing orders on members' statements, would provide some greater opportunities for responsiveness. But a change in the manner that governments interpret broader rules would be of even greater benefit. Limited use of closure on debates, greater freedom for committees to govern themselves, and a lessening of party discipline would go a long way toward allowing all members greater latitude for responsiveness within the confines of the legislature.

In terms of greater freedom from the shackles of party discipline, the introduction of a British three-line whip should be considered. Under this model, members are free to vote according to their conscience or the desires of their constituents on a "one-line" whip. Two-line whips require members who plan to vote against their party to "twin" with a member of another party or to make sure such a vote does not unduly embarrass the party. Finally, a three-line whip is seen as a matter of confidence in the government (and opposition leaders), and all members are expected to vote with their leadership or face some form of sanction.

David Docherty

On the larger questions, be they long-term planning or reactions to immediate events, governments have the tools to be responsive. Canadians should not confuse legitimate checks on government responsiveness with a parliament's lack of capacity. Rather, mechanisms such as caucus, committees, and the federal Senate have the potential to enhance and not hinder the responsiveness functions.

Participation

In *Legislatures* (Docherty 2005), it was suggested that the ability of a legislature to provide its members with the opportunity to fully participate in the functions of representation, legislation, and scrutiny was dependent upon three factors – namely, size, power, and opportunity. These three factors are critical in determining whether or not a government is required to stand up to scrutiny and defend its policies to the legislative assembly to whom it is responsible.

Small legislatures may provide their members with a greater chance to sit in the front bench, but their small size also means that the opposition is often dwarfed by the governing party and faces an uphill fight in its efforts to keep a well-resourced and well-staffed cabinet accountable for its actions. Large assemblies might not face the same challenges, but if members do not have the ability to force legislation to committees, hear from public witnesses, or engage in their own oversight over departments, they too have limited capacity to properly do their job. Members must have the opportunity and resources to engage in their duties. If they are to scrutinize the government, venues must exist in which this activity takes place. This means not just having question period and opposition days but also regular meetings of the assembly and committees of the legislature.

For many legislators, the problem is not a lack of desire, but, rather, a lack of opportunity. Rules, particularly informal ones that centralize authority around a leader, can dissuade many members from active participation. In some cases, even offices created to assist with legislative oversight can take away from the authority of elected officials.

With limited time, members are more likely to turn to those mechanisms that can produce greater results – namely, constituency service or party-based activities.

Perhaps the greatest reform in terms of participation inside the legislature in the past fifty years was moving to a secret ballot election of the speaker of the House of Commons (Docherty 2005; see also Levy 1986). This reform was eventually emulated by the provinces. In *Legislatures* (2005), I argued that, if the speaker were elected, a single individual would be less likely to serve in the office for consecutive terms. As it turns out, this has not been the case. The first elected speaker, the Honourable John Fraser, served for a term and a half. The next one, Gilbert Parent, was elected twice, and the third, Peter Milliken, has been elected to that post on four separate occasions, once under a Liberal majority, once under a Liberal minority, and twice under Conservative minority governments. As a result, it can now be argued that the election of speakers is no impediment to successive terms.

The election of speakers has not brought with it large- (or even small-) scale electoral reform of assemblies. This was not unexpected among legislative observers but has been a disappointment for legislators who see elections as an opportunity to support someone who will lead an internal reform movement. Unfortunately, these expectations are unrealistic. Many MPs thought that Milliken would be a force for reform. He was generally recognized as an expert on procedure and someone who had a high regard for the chamber and its business. However, Milliken was correct in his assessment that a speaker can lead a reform movement in the House only if the members want to see it come to fruition.

That Milliken is correct in his assessment, but that many members are looking for a different answer, goes to the heart of the problem presently facing legislatures. In order to redeem themselves in the public eye, they must collectively act in a manner that both strengthens parliament and brings back honour to the institution. This is a difficult but not impossible task. Some changes to our institutions have already begun to move in the right direction. The next section of this chapter discusses some of these reforms before turning our attention to the need for leaders to make parliament relevant.

A Change to Strengthen Legislatures

Despite a public desire to strengthen legislatures, or at a minimum to modify how they work, there have been few large-scale changes enacted to strengthen elected assemblies. Of course, governments can, and have, introduced many rule changes to assemblies. The trick for parliamentary observers is to determine whether or not the impact of this will be to strengthen the legislatures or weaken their ability to engage in their three primary functions. One simple way to determine this is to recognize that, though the result is not zero-sum, changes that aid private members and assemblies often take some authority away from the executive.

If we use the measure of whether change provides greater power to the legislature and less to the executive, perhaps the single biggest reform to many legislatures in Canada (since the election of the speaker) is the introduction of fixed election dates. Unfortunately, unlike the election of the speaker, this reform has not been universally implemented by all Canadian assemblies. Nor is it properly applied within some jurisdictions that did adopt it, a fact that further weakens it.

The arguments in favour of fixed election dates are relatively straightforward. First, they prohibit prime ministers and premiers from calling elections when it best suits them. The ability of these leaders to visit the head of state and request an election at any time provides incumbent governments with a clear advantage. It allows them to be better prepared for a general election than are the opposition parties. It further enables them to create conditions that will put them in a more favourable light prior to an election. More than one government in more than one jurisdiction has introduced a budget or economic agenda with which it does not intend to proceed until after an anticipated election.

Fixed election dates should also provide for greater transparency. Voters will know when elections are to be held and can judge a government by its performance leading up the election. In Ontario, the government added to this transparency by having the provincial auditor provide a financial statement on the condition of its books prior to the election. This type of openness should be applauded, and fixed dates make subsequent reforms of this nature easier to implement.

Fixed dates should also provide the legislature a greater opportunity to be more responsive. Although the governing party controls the legislative agenda, all party House leaders have a role in determining the timing of debate on legislation and the scheduling of committee hearings and debate. Too often, legislation that opposition parties deem important can be left to die on the order paper when the prime minister chooses to go to the polls. Fixed dates should provide opposition House leaders the ability to pressure government into moving legislation along or suffering electoral consequences.

The fixed date should also have some positive impact on participation for assemblies and their members. Federally, private members' bills are even more likely than government bills to die when a vote is called. Knowing when elections will occur should allow caucuses and members to prioritize private members' bills that have made it through the initial stages of the legislative process. Although the government may simply choose not to proceed with a vote on such bills, the fact that members know the timetable should provide some opportunity for them to informally influence the government to move ahead on some legislation, particularly if private members on the government side use their voices in caucus effectively.

Finally, fixed dates should bring a better sense of stability to the parliamentary calendar. During the last year of a parliament, delays to the introduction of budgets, or introducing budgets or throne speeches simply as a precursor to a vote, deny parliamentarians the opportunity to scrutinize the wishes of the executive in the appropriate venue – namely, the floor of the legislature. Governments that choose to introduce budgets or throne speeches immediately prior to an anticipated and legislated general vote should suffer the electoral consequences of such a self-serving move. Fixed dates will discourage, though not eliminate, such activity.

There are two arguments against fixed dates. The first is that statutory election dates contravene the principles of Westminster government (See for example Desserud 2005). The second is that these dates will eventually lead to the permanent election campaign as all parties will gear up increasingly early for an election they know will occur. At first blush, there might be some legitimate concern that the introduction of fixed election dates would lead to a congressional form of government that could be less sensitive to the requirements of confidence. The entire concept of Westminster government hinges on the possibility that, at any time, the government might lose the confidence of the chamber and that this may precipitate a general election. To move away from this might seem to actually give the government more authority to ignore *(or be less responsive to)* the will of the assembly. Yet, such actions by a government would effectively cripple its capacity to govern. Should it lose a vote on a major item such as the speech from the throne, a budget, or a motion of non-confidence, it would have no option but to resign. Further, in each jurisdiction that has implemented fixed dates, the legislation explicitly states that the measure is applicable only if the government does not fall and that failure to gain support on matters of confidence would constitute the fall of the government.

Fears of an informal but much longer campaign period have a little more traction than fears of a congressional system. Certainly, in those jurisdictions with fixed election dates, the campaign may appear to be longer. Yet, this is more a problem of election timing than a conscious effort by parties to campaign prematurely. Prior to the adoption of the fixed date, as governments worked their way into the fourth year of their term, informal campaigns have always begun, and the only speculation has concerned the actual date of the vote. Canadians do not see informal premature campaigning only when premiers or prime ministers use their executive authority to call snap and unanticipated elections or when a government unexpectedly loses the confidence of the legislature.

The British Columbia government was the first to introduce fixed election dates, in 2001. Ontario, Newfoundland and Labrador, Prince

Edward Island, the Northwest Territories, New Brunswick, Saskatchewan, Manitoba, and the federal government have followed the BC lead. British Columbia's legislation sets four-year terms with elections in May. The other jurisdictions share the four-year term.

Having fixed election dates and sticking to them can be two different things. Failure to abide by one's own laws may not instill public confidence in a leader. Thus far, only one government has introduced a fixed election date law that it failed to observe, that of Stephen Harper in 2008. The fact that voters did not rebuke Harper for transgressing the spirit (though not the technicalities) of his own law may be more indicative of voter apathy than a disagreement about the direction of the law. However, the fact that the prime minister squandered one of the more significant legislative reforms in recent history marks a sad day for the strengthening of parliament.

Even the timing of scheduled chamber activities can place obstacles in the way of participation. Ontario should be applauded for having the longest question period of all Canadian assemblies. At one hour per day, it is longer than even its House of Commons equivalent (see Docherty 2005, 100). Yet, length of time is only one measure of effective and open participation. Questions (and answers) at Queen's Park tend to be much lengthier than in Ottawa. As a result, more questions can often be posed in forty-five minutes on Parliament Hill than in one hour in Toronto.

Sometimes, changes that are meant to bring more stability to legislatures and encourage a greater sense of inclusiveness can have less desirable results. This is exactly what occurred in 2008, when the Ontario Liberal government revised the legislative timetable in an effort to make Queen's Park more "family friendly" (Leslie 2008). Applying the rationale that eliminating night sittings would improve access for women with young families, Queen's Park became the first legislature in Canada to hold all its question periods in the morning. In the words of the government House leader, the move was made in order to increase accountability (ibid.). Ultimately, however, it did more damage than good. For the opposition, the change was detrimental. A morning question period meant less time to prepare to scrutinize the government, and it afforded the government more time to respond to critical queries outside the assembly prior to press time for the media. Thus, the measure to improve access resulted in a diminution of scrutiny.

Minority Governments

One might be forgiven for thinking that minority governments hold more opportunity than do majority governments for increasing the participation of all members. After all, when a prime minister must negotiate with at least one other party to ensure his or her government's survival, the need for cooperation is by definition present. This is one of many arguments that political scientists have advanced in favour of minority governments, in the hope of convincing Canadians that policy innovation and consensus building outweighs the so-called stability of majority governments (Russell 2008).

Indeed, much can be said in favour of minority governments. The five years of rule under Lester Pearson (1963-68) saw many policy innovations in Canada, including a public pension system (CPP), the new flag, the Canada-US auto pact, the bilingualism and bicultural commission, and the introduction of a national health care system. In working with one other political party, the Liberals managed to embrace the platforms of more than their own party and provide what many analysts have described as a progressive, forward-looking government. Pierre Trudeau's minority of 1972-74 was also active. In attempting to maintain the support of the NDP, the Trudeau Liberals established both a nationalized oil company (PetroCanada) and the Foreign Investment Review Agency (FIRA).

Conservative governments in Canada have had a harder time negotiating minority situations, as there is less likelihood of an ideological ally in the assembly. Joe Clark's 1979 government had just such an ally in the remnants of the Social Credit Party but refused to negotiate with it, and thus Clark's reign was quite brief. The lesson learned from the Clark experience was clear: the governing party must be willing to make parliament work and must reach out to at least one party on the other side of the chamber.

This was a lesson that Stephen Harper accepted to some degree in his first minority government. Harper's victory in 2006 marked a return to Conservative rule for the first time since 1993 and was seen as a vindication for Harper's uniting of the Canadian Alliance and Progressive Conservative Party. Yet, having managed to unite the right in Canada, Harper had a much more difficult time working with other political parties.

On some issues, he seemed to understand the reality of minority governments. Fixed election dates (as described above) should have set a tone of reform. Harper introduced changes to the selection of Supreme Court justices to include a modest role for a parliamentary committee. Parliament managed to force a debate on Canada's role in Afghanistan, though the debate was not as long or open as the opposition would have preferred (Russell 2008, 50). Harper's first year as prime minister may have been a far cry from Lester Pearson's first term, but it did suggest at least a recognition of the need to allow parliamentarians a greater role in public policy debate. In this sense, it did provide some greater opportunities for participation.

Yet, in many other ways, the first Harper government acted very much like a majority. Nowhere was this truer than in the use of committees and the selection of committee chairs. An advocate of secret ballot election of committee chairs while in opposition, the new prime minister had no qualms about announcing his choice of chair for each House of Commons committee and then telling his members to vote accordingly (ibid, 49-50). The not so subtle threat to his own backbench was not lost on members of all parties.

Further, the Conservative administration was not above influencing the direction of committees or providing Conservative chairs with direction on how best to subvert the will of committees with a majority of opposition MPs. In May 2007, opposition MPs released a handbook that had been provided to Conservative committee chairs, outlining methods to disrupt and delay committee proceedings that were not going the government's way. The length of the handbook, two hundred pages, was evidence enough that the government was serious about not letting opposition members steer committees. The actions of some Conservatives on Commons committees, including chairs who cancelled meetings and members who filibustered procedural issues to prevent witnesses from appearing, suggested that government members were taking the executive's advice to heart (Brydon 2007).

Prime Minister Harper was not alone in his iron-fisted approach to committees and the selection of committee chairs. Jean Chrétien may have provided his cabinet ministers more leeway than Harper, but he was equally as adamant that he have a hand in selecting committee chairs. In fact, Chrétien arguably went too far with his authority, to the point that Liberal dissidents and opposition MPs (including Mr. Harper) voted to overturn the open ballot procedure of selecting committee chairs (Docherty 2005). The propensity of prime ministers to interfere in the selection of chairs and running of committees, particularly in minority governments, has not assisted in the strengthening of parliament or in increasing the role of private members in influencing the direction of Commons committees.

The approach by both the Liberal and Conservative executives was a blow to the ability of members to actively participate in their representative duties. How can individual MPs respond to their constituents or other Canadians in the collective setting of a legislative committee when the government sets out to stifle debate? The short answer is that they cannot do so effectively. The committee system can provide members a real opportunity for greater participation only when the executive allows them to control their own internal governance procedures and sees committee chairs as quasi-independent, not as the arms of government strategy.

The release of the handbook for committee chairs foreshadowed a different style to be adopted by the Harper government in the fall of 2007. Having prorogued the House in the spring, Harper set the stage for a more contentious approach to governing. In the days leading up to the new speech from the throne, he indicated that the speech outlined the government's plans for the next session. The speech was a matter of confidence, and should it be defeated, he would have no choice but to ask the governor general for an election. He then extended this to suggest that any vote on any matter coming out of the throne speech must be treated in the same fashion.

Although prime ministers do have the right to treat any matter as one of confidence, such an unusual approach to matters not yet introduced suggested that the prime minister was no longer interested in making parliament work. Taking advantage of a battered official opposition and an even weaker opposition leader, Harper effectively wrote off minority government as unworkable. This also compromised any ability of the legislature to be responsive to changing economic or social conditions when it met to debate and alter legislation. This was one of the more detrimental outcomes of the Harper moves. As a strategy to quash the opposition, it may have been effective but at the cost of a more participatory, responsive House of Commons. Ironically, such an approach to dysfunctional legislatures would come back to haunt the prime minister and force him to revisit the need to work with other parties in the House.

The Case of the Failed Coalition

Perhaps the greatest squandered opportunity for a significant rethinking of stability in minority government came about in the fall of 2008. Soon after breaking his own commitment to a fixed election date, Prime Minister Harper found himself campaigning for a new term during the biggest economic collapse in recent history. The full analysis of the 2008 Canadian election is yet to be written. When it is, it will no doubt describe and analyze a bad campaign full of small errors by the Conservatives, a weakly led Liberal Party, the political emasculation of leader Stéphane Dion, the temporary rise of the Green Party, and an unprecedented number of Canadians voting with their feet and staying away from the polls. When the proverbial dust cleared on election night, the Conservatives had increased their seat total at the direct expense of the Liberals but still fell shy of a majority. In this sense, the election was a major defeat for the Liberals and a serious slap on the wrists for the Conservatives. In the wake of the vote, the prime minister indicated that he was willing to work with the other parties to ensure that the economy was parliament's number-one focus.

Faced with governing under severe economic constraints, Harper chose to address the House with an economic update just after it had convened following the election. The economic update, read to the House on 27 November, was in many ways reminiscent of his previous attempts to distract the House and foster divisions between parties. Among the most contentious parts of the update package was the decision to eliminate public financing of political parties. The reaction of the opposition was swift and vitriolic. Most press analysis echoed the opposition parties' criticism that the package was more about penalizing political parties than addressing the economy. Whether or not the prime minister was hoping for a defeat and a quick election that might deliver him his sought-after majority is speculation. What was clear was that a political game of chicken was being played out, and the opposition was determined not to blink (Chase et al. 2008).

The result was a plan by the three opposition parties to defeat the government in a motion of confidence and then form a coalition between the Liberals and New Democrats with support from the Bloc Québécois. Canada had not had a coalition government at the federal level since the First World War, but the structure of parliamentary government allows for this unusual though not unprecedented arrangement.

Not surprisingly, public debate raged about the undemocratic nature of parties that were willing to take power despite not winning the election versus a prime minister who seemed determined to use an economic crisis to further his political ends. The Conservative government deftly exploited public ignorance on the seemingly arcane constitutional rules of parliament to sow seeds of doubt in the public mind. Most Canadians were siding with the government's position that a coalition was somehow undemocratic, while at the same time taking the prime minister to task for not being more consultative prior to the showdown over power. One poll found that just over sixty percent of Canadians were opposed to the coalition, and just over half of Canadians felt that the Conservatives were to blame for putting forward an incomplete economic stimulus package and/or bullying the opposition (Strategic Council 2008). The result of the call for a coalition was to throw reporters, politicians, and the public into an unnecessary state of confusion. Many decried the move as provoking a constitutional crisis. Nothing could have been further from the truth. Parliamentary government rests on a number of simple rules: first, voters elect MPs, and parliament selects the government; second, the government must have the confidence of the House; and third, without that confidence and without necessarily having an election, an alternative government can be formed, providing that it has the confidence of the legislature. The coalition met all three of these conditions and was thus both constitutionally defensible and well within the spirit of Westminster democracy.

In order to avoid a non-confidence vote that he was guaranteed to lose, the prime minister went to Governor General Michaëlle Jean to ask for a prorogation of parliament. This placed her in a politically awkward position. No prime minister had ever been denied a request to prorogue parliament. However, no prime minister since John A. Macdonald had asked a governor general for a prorogation specifically to avoid defeat on a motion of confidence. Further, the House had sat for only thirteen days, so there was ample reason to avoid an election if the present government could not retain confidence in the legislature.

The governor general gave the prime minister his sought-after prorogation. The House rose, the prime minister avoided defeat, and a new speech from the throne was prepared for late January 2009. In the interim, Liberal leader Stéphane Dion stepped down and was swiftly replaced by Michael Ignatieff. The new Liberal leader was cool to the idea of a coalition but needed to find some reasonable way to support the government. The throne speech was quickly followed by a budget that the NDP and Bloc opposed but the Liberals agreed to support. The budget was very different from the earlier economic statement and contained many measures that appeared more Liberal than Conservative. The so-called crisis passed. The prime minister managed to hold onto power, though much chastened by his brush with near defeat.

David Docherty

Conclusion

Was the governor general correct in allowing for a prorogation? The ruling will be debated for many years by politicians and academics. No matter what decision Michaëlle Jean made, it would set precedent. Although the details of her ruling remain sealed, there is little evidence that limits were set on the prime minister's power during this time. Harper appointed eighteen Canadians to the Senate during this break and moved ahead with an appointment to the Supreme Court. The concerns among academics about the dangers of this precedent are real. Can prime ministers shut down parliament to avoid defeat they know is inevitable? It appears so. Harper's blatant disregard for the rule of the country's elected assembly is disconcerting to say the least.

If there is a silver lining to this saga, it is this: in coming so close to defeat, the prime minister realized that governments play just as crucial a role in making parliaments function as do opposition parties. His attempt to use the economic crisis as a political weapon in a minority government backfired. The coalition might have been avoided, but there was no avoiding the lesson learned by the government. Not only can parliament be relevant, but it must be.

Perhaps the best evidence that both major political parties had learned this lesson came in the early summer of 2009. With the NDP and the Bloc ready to vote against the government to force an election, the new Liberal leader, Michael Ignatieff, met with the prime minister to look for common ground on several issues and avoid an election. The fact that neither wanted an election (nor did the Canadian public) suggests that self-interest was front and centre. Nonetheless, the fact that these individuals met over two days and agreed to a series of measures (most notably a re-examination of changes to employment insurance) suggested that leaders can be responsive to the public and thus allow parliament to be responsive. It was a strong positive signal for the House of Commons as a whole.

This chapter began by suggesting that a successful legislature is a necessary prerequisite to encouraging public support for all democratic institutions. If the best electoral and party systems in the world can create a legislature that cannot function, support for all three institutions will diminish.

The fact that most Canadians did not understand the parliamentary nuances of prorogation or the ability of governments to be formed in the absence of a public vote may be a reflection of our lack of a good civics education (for more on this, see Gidengil et al., Chapter 5 this volume). But blame can and must also be laid at the feet of those politicians who have treated our legislative assemblies with disrespect. Until such time as politicians see their profession as noble, and see the institutions in which they serve as providing the necessary conditions for good government, the prospects of strong representation, scrutiny, and legislation are bleak.

The present parliamentary system in Canada has the flexibility to provide innovative and transparent government. It also holds the opportunity to be more responsive and participatory. Whether one liked or disliked the idea of a Liberal-NDP coalition backed by a Bloc opposition, such a move would have been both more responsive and responsible than an immediate election. The initial Harper economic update showed a government at its most unresponsive. The idea of proroguing the House to avoid defeat was an attempt to deny all members the ability to participate in the legislative process. The desire to remain in power is a natural one for all prime ministers and government parties. However, it cannot override the need for parliament to meet its obligations of representation and legislation; nor can it supersede the benchmarks that affect all democratic institutions in Canada.

Leaders of all stripes have offered some strong reforms that help strengthen the system. It is unfortunate that such good measures are more than offset by the desire to control their caucus of elected officials and avoid the legislature as much as possible. Some simple reforms should provide parliament and parliamentarians with greater latitude to make the assembly function and meet basic democratic benchmarks.

First, Commons committees need to be more independent. Allowing members more freedom in choosing which committees they serve on and allowing committees complete freedom in selecting chairs without threat of removal from the government would signal an amplification of the role of committees. It would also foster greater participation from members and from the public who may appear before committees. And it would negate some of the ill effects of a government that encourages chairs to engage in obstruction over consensus.

Speaker Milliken's move to cut off members' statements that were attacks on other MPs was correct as he tried to emphasize the original purpose of these statements. Statements by private members should focus on issues of representation and inclusiveness. These statements afford an occasion for members to represent constituent or group interests that are often absent from government deliberations.

Greater opportunity should be provided for private members' bills to reach the third-reading stage of the legislative process. Recent parliaments have taken some steps to furthering more private members' bills through the Commons, including requirements that bills that pass second reading go to committee with a time limit for reporting back to the full chamber. This could be enhanced by specifying a set number of private members' bills to be voted on at third reading. Such bills cannot be "money bills" or require dedicated generation and expense of tax dollars. Thus, allowing more private members' bills the chance to make it to final reading should encourage members to think creatively and constructively about the legislation they propose.

Fixed election dates should be more closely adhered to by governments that introduce or support them. Both federally and provincially, fixed dates strengthen assemblies by reducing the power of the first minister. But such a reform works only when the head of government bows to the spirit of the legislation.

Finally, parliament is at its best when party leaders allow parliamentarians to do their job. During periods of minority government, this means setting aside some of the theatrics of the legislature to ensure that parliament can function. Canadians may be more willing to embrace minority government if they are exposed to minority administrations that work and are not under a constant threat of collapsing, due either to opposition threats or a government throwing down the gauntlet. When party leaders on both sides of the speaker's dais recognize that scrutiny and representation are the distinguishing features of legislatures, and that proper access to responsiveness and participation is the key to achieving these, legislatures have the greatest likelihood of flourishing. This is no guarantee of a functional parliament. But, at the very least, it would allow Canadians a greater opportunity to distinguish between the failures of legislators and legislatures.

Reforms

If legislatures are to better meet the three Audit benchmarks of inclusiveness, responsiveness, and participation, the following seven reforms could be implemented. First, Canadians cannot respect parliamentary institutions that leaders treat with disrespect. Governments must honour the valid and valued role of accountability and scrutiny provided for by Westminster parliaments.

Second, changes to increase diversity within our legislative bodies best lie with changes to internal party rules and reforming the electoral system. However, legislatures can afford opportunities for members to provide substantive representation by allowing greater freedom for members in their committee work and in the introduction of private members' legislation. Improvements to substantive representation can be addressed inside assemblies.

Third, party discipline must be implemented in a manner that allows governments to respond to larger public policy questions but provides individual members with greater flexibility to participate and represent local interests. The introduction of British-style three-line whips, where members can vote against some government initiatives free of fears of a vote of non-confidence, would provide such opportunities.

Fourth, changes to committees to allow for a greater degree of self-governance can afford better scrutiny and greater participation in the legislative process.

Fifth, a tighter interpretation of rules on members' statements would force all members to use this parliamentary tool to represent constituents and provide immediate responses to critical topical issues.

Sixth, rules governing fixed election dates will be effective and increase support for parliamentary institutions only if prime ministers and premiers follow both the letter and the spirit of the law. Fixed date laws should also be coupled with a more stable parliamentary calendar, where proposed dates of prorogation can be laid out well in advance.

Seventh, Canadians need to be shown by example that minority governments can be just as functional (and indeed, can provide for greater accountability and participation) as majority governments. Governments should approach minority parliaments with a greater degree of willingness to embrace a more open style of governance. This should include regular meetings with opposition leaders, greater flexibility (and autonomy) for committees, and a willingness to let the legislature sit without resorting to frequent prorogations. Opposition leaders must also respect such changes and not seize upon every opportunity to challenge the government with the threat of an election.

These reforms would underscore the need for all members of parliament (and provincial assemblies) to place the institutional good ahead of short-term partisan interests. Canadians will have greater faith in our Westminster systems when our politicians treat parliament with the respect it deserves. Political leaders must not only understand the capacity of Westminster assemblies to properly address the long- and short-term problems facing Canada, but they must also allow parliament to reach that capacity. Too strong an emphasis on party discipline and the centralization of authority weakens the ability of legislatures to allow for proper accountability, representation, and effective legislation.

Works Cited

Black, Jerome. 2002. Ethnoracial minorities in the House of Commons. *Canadian Parliamentary Review* 25(1): 24-28.

Black, Jerome, and Bruce Hicks. 2006. Visible minorities and under-representation: The views of candidates. *Electoral Insight*. December. Elections Canada. http://www.elections.ca/.

Brydon, Joan. 2007. Opposition handbook leaked. *Toronto Star*, 18 May.

Catholic News Service. 2004. Sister Peggy Butts, Canadian activist, senator dies at age 79. *Georgia Bulletin,* 10 March. http://www.georgiabulletin.com/.

CBC News. 2008. Weekend walkout over, Toronto transit returns to normal. 27 April. CBC News. http://www.cbc.ca/.

Chase, Steven, Brian Laghi, Jane Taber, and Gloria Galloway. 2008. Harper delays confidence vote. *Globe and Mail,* 28 November.

Clarke, Harold, Jane Jenson, Lawrence LeDuc, and Jon H. Pammett. 1996. *Absent mandate: Canadian electoral politics in an era of restructuring.* Scarborough, ON: Gage.

Cool, Julie. 2006. Women in parliament. Parliament of Canada, Political and Social Affairs Division. February. http://www2.parl.gc.ca/.

Desserud, Don. 2005. Fixed election dates, improvement or new problem? *Electoral Insight,* 2005. http://www.elections.ca/.

Diebel, Linda. 2008. Dion ignored green shift warnings. *Toronto Star,* 17 October. http://www.thestar.com/.

Docherty, David. 2005. *Legislatures.* Canadian Democratic Audit. Vancouver: UBC Press.

Gidengil, Elisabeth, André Blais, Neil Nevitte, and Richard Nadeau. 2004. *Citizens.* Canadian Democratic Audit. Vancouver: UBC Press.

Heard, Andrew. N.d. Canadian election results by party, 1867 to 2008. Simon Fraser University. http://www.sfu.ca/.

Leslie, Keith. 2008. Ontario Liberal government wants morning question period, no night sittings. *Canadian Press,* 11 February. Equal Voice. http://www.equalvoice. ca/.

Levy, Gary. 1986. A night to remember. *Canadian Parliamentary Review* 9(4) (Winter): 10-14.

Russell, Peter. 2008. *Two cheers for minority government: The evolution of Canadian parliamentary democracy.* Toronto: Emond Montgomery Press.

Simpson, Jeffrey. 2002. *The friendly dictatorship.* Toronto: McClellend and Stewart.

Smith, David E. 2007. *The people's House of Commons: Theories of democracy in contention.* Toronto: University of Toronto Press.

Sotiropolous, Evan. 2009. The use and misuse of member's statements. *Canadian Parliamentary Review* 32(3). http://www2.parl.gc.ca/.

Strategic Council. 2008. *A report to the Globe and Mail: Harper's Conservatives versus the Liberal/NDP coalition.* 4 December. http://www.thestrategiccouncil. com/.

White, Graham. 2005. *Cabinets and first ministers.* Canadian Democratic Audit. Vancouver: UBC Press.

CITIZENS

Elisabeth Gidengil, Richard Nadeau,
Neil Nevitte, and André Blais

5

An audit of democratic citizenship is as much – if not more – an evaluation of the performance of Canadian democracy as it is a judgment on the extent to which Canadians fulfill their responsibilities as citizens. The degree to which citizens involve themselves in the country's democratic life is a function in part of the opportunities that democratic institutions afford for meaningful participation, as well as the amount of time, money, and skills that individual citizens possess. Institutional arrangements work to the benefit of some citizens while disadvantaging others, just as structural inequalities in Canadian society affect the political resources at citizens' disposal. Auditing democratic citizenship can thus cast important light on both the inclusiveness and the responsiveness of Canadian democracy.

It is important at the outset to delineate the scope of the Audit upon which this chapter is based. Democratic citizenship is underpinned by important norms and values, including empathy, egalitarianism, tolerance, respect for minorities, and justice. These could be the subject of an audit in themselves, and so, important as they are, they are not treated here. Instead, the focus is on political interest, political knowledge, and political activity, both electoral and non-electoral.

Participation

Elections are at the very core of representative democracy. They are essential mechanisms for ensuring that governments are held account-able, and they afford one of the main opportunities for exercising democratic citizenship. As such, elections provide a litmus test of the vitality of the relationship between citizens and their political system. With turnout in the 2008 federal election at the lowest level ever re-corded in Canada's history, Canadian democracy appears to be achiev-ing only a bare pass on this basic test. Although other established democracies have also experienced diminishing voter turnout, the Canadian decline has been particularly steep (see Figure 5.1), and the slide has shown little sign of reversing. As a result, Canada now ranks near the bottom on this indicator among the Anglo-American, Nordic, and West European democracies (see Figure 5.2).

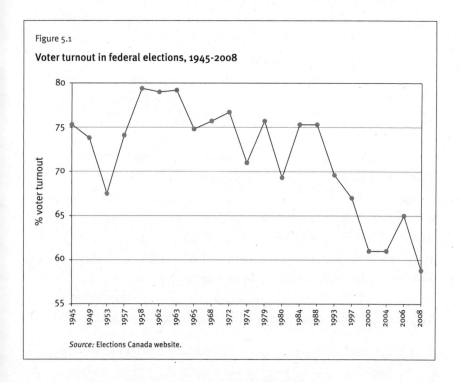

Figure 5.1

Voter turnout in federal elections, 1945-2008

Source: Elections Canada website.

Elisabeth Gidengil, Richard Nadeau, Neil Nevitte, and André Blais

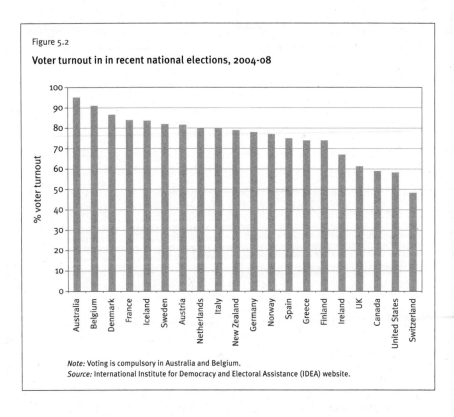

Figure 5.2

Voter turnout in in recent national elections, 2004-08

Note: Voting is compulsory in Australia and Belgium.
Source: International Institute for Democracy and Electoral Assistance (IDEA) website.

Declining turnout is the most striking sign of disengagement from traditional electoral politics, but it is not the only indication of weakness in Canada's democratic fabric. Few Canadians play an active part in election campaigns, and the number of campaign activists is shrinking. This is worrisome since it means that fewer citizens are actively engaged in mobilizing their fellow Canadians to go to the polls. Although the level of party membership is not particularly low by international standards, Canadians are quite skeptical about the potential for effecting meaningful change by working through a political party, and relatively few of them have ever belonged to one (see Cross 2004).

These trends would be less troublesome if there were compelling evidence that Canadians are turning to other forms of action to express their political voice. However, little suggests that they are abandoning political parties and joining interest groups instead. Canadians *are* more sanguine about the possibility of working for change by becoming members of an interest group (by a margin of about three to one over political parties), but they are even less likely to have actually belonged to one.

A more intriguing possibility is that citizens are abandoning traditional vehicles of political participation, such as voting or joining a political party, in favour of more unconventional modes of political action. When it comes to signing petitions and supporting boycotts, Canadians are actually more active than citizens in several other established Western democracies. According to the 2005-07 World Values Survey, Canada ranked fifth out of thirteen countries for signing petitions (72 percent) and tied with Norway in second place, just behind Sweden, for joining in boycotts (24 percent). When it comes to more assertive acts, though, Canada slips down the list to seventh place: at 26 percent, Canada ranked well behind France (38 percent) and Spain and Italy (36 percent) for attending peaceful demonstrations. Moreover, Canadians are only a little more likely to have supported a product boycott than they are to have been a party member (19 percent), even though joining in a boycott, like signing a petition, takes little time or effort. More importantly, those Canadians who are most likely to vote are often most likely to participate in these other forms of political action. Indeed, the extent to which different types of political activity tend to go together is one of the more striking findings to emerge from the audit of democratic citizenship in Canada (see Gidengil et al. 2004, ch. 5). Affluent and well-educated Canadians are the most likely to have signed a petition, taken part in a boycott, or attended a peaceful demonstration, just as they are the most likely to vote or to have belonged to a political party.

This is not to underplay the existence of citizens who are turned off by traditional electoral politics and prefer alternative vehicles for exercising democratic citizenship and working to effect change. It is, though, to caution against being too optimistic about the country's democratic health. The fact that voter turnout is declining while participation in less conventional forms of political action is increasing does not necessarily mean that the latter is substituting for the former. Many Canadians are simply disengaged: they do not vote in elections

Elisabeth Gidengil, Richard Nadeau, Neil Nevitte, and André Blais

and they do not sign petitions, take part in demonstrations, or boycott products, either.

At the same time, though, a core of politically engaged Canadians does participate in all of these activities. For them, new ways of engaging in politics, such as Internet activism and political consumerism, signify a broadening of their political action repertoire rather than a retreat from traditional electoral politics, and this is a positive sign. Like petitions and demonstrations, Internet activism may target either public institutions or private corporations. Political consumerism, on the other hand, is entirely market oriented. Nonetheless, using purchasing power to pressure multinational corporations to respect human rights, engage in fair trade, or adopt environmentally friendly business practices can be construed as a political act (Micheletti, Follesdal, and Stolle 2003). Political consumerism now goes beyond refusing to buy a product due to ethical or political considerations to include product *buy*cotts that reward socially responsible behaviour on the part of producers of goods and services.

The common denominator underlying all these different forms of political action is political knowledge. Whether casting a ballot or boycotting a product, people need to be informed about what is going on. Indeed, "political information is to democratic politics what money is to economics; it is the currency of citizenship" (Delli Carpini and Keeter 1996, 8). The more informed people are about politics, the more likely they are to participate. A significant number of Canadians, however, lack basic knowledge. They cannot name prominent political actors such as the federal finance minister or the leaders of the federal political parties. Some do not even know the name of the prime minister or the premier of their province. If they knew what they need to know when it comes to making political choices, such knowledge deficits might not matter. It turns out, though, that many Canadians cannot correctly identify the policy positions of political parties, and they have little or no understanding of terms, such as "left" and "right," that routinely figure in political discourse. These deep pockets of ignorance would be less troubling if election campaigns closed the knowledge gap between low- and high-information voters. But the evidence seems to be that campaigns often have the very opposite effect (Nadeau et al. 2008).

The inability of significant numbers of Canadians to answer simple questions about their country's politics speaks to a basic lack of political awareness. These Canadians have little interest in politics, here or abroad. They pay little, if any, attention to news about current affairs. For them, politics is a low priority and only an occasional topic of conversation. There is little to suggest that the Internet is changing this. It does offer unprecedented access to information about politics, but those who are most likely to go on-line in search of it are typically already tuned in to political affairs.

To end on a more positive note, as mentioned above, Canada has among the highest levels of participation in activities such as signing petitions and taking part in boycotts. However, the most important area of strength lies in a type of activity that Robert Putnam (2000) has highlighted as underpinning successful democracy. Democracy works best, he argues, when dense networks of connection between citizens and norms of social trust make for large stocks of social capital. According to Putnam, voluntary associations play a vital role in the accumulation of social capital. When citizens are active in these associations, "their individual and otherwise quiet voices multiply and are amplified" (ibid., 338). Equally importantly, citizens learn to accept the give-and-take and the need to accommodate opposing points of view that characterize democratic decision making. They also acquire skills that enhance active engagement in public life. To the extent that this is so, Canada's relatively high level of associational involvement compared to other established Western democracies suggests that the essential foundations of democratic citizenship remain strong (see Young and Everitt 2004, Chapter 8 this volume).

Inclusiveness

If the disengaged were randomly distributed throughout the population, political disengagement would be less cause for concern. However, this

Elisabeth Gidengil, Richard Nadeau, Neil Nevitte, and André Blais

is clearly not the case. The deeper roots of democratic malaise lie in the disparities in income and education, and in the differences in the power and status of groups such as women and visible minorities that characterize Canadian society. These structural inequalities contribute to some profound democratic divides in Canada's political life.

Turnout rates among Aboriginal people are low, on average, in both federal and provincial elections. However, this simple statement masks significant, and largely unexplored, differences in the behaviour of on-reserve and urban Aboriginal people, as well as dissimilarities across nations and localities (Ladner and McCrossan 2007). Variations in Aboriginal voting behaviour, Kiera Ladner and Michael McCrossan suggest, reflect differing perceptions of the effectiveness of elections and varying ways of understanding both citizenship and nationhood.

Differences between women and men have received much more attention, though they are still not well understood. Women are typically less interested in politics than men are, and they have less confidence in their political abilities (Gidengil, Giles, and Thomas 2008). They also pay less attention to news about politics and know less about the subject than do their male counterparts (Gidengil et al. 2006). These gaps have proved remarkably persistent in the face of the social forces that have transformed women's lives in Canada. Women have made huge advances over the past forty years in terms of both education and participation in the paid workforce, yet these gender gaps continue to exist. They cannot be explained by the feminization of poverty or by the demands of combining full-time employment with caregiving activities in the home. Their persistence may well be attributable to a combination of factors such as the perceived remoteness of politics from women's daily lives, the lack of women in elected office, and the media emphasis on partisan squabbling. Whatever the explanation, women's stronger sense of civic duty, combined with their greater involvement in religious organizations, appears to mitigate the effects of a lack of interest in politics on women's propensity to be politically active (O'Neill 2006). Women in general are as likely as men - or not - to vote, to participate in protest activities, and to join voluntary associations and interest groups. And they are only marginally less likely to have been party members. Questions necessarily remain, though, about the effectiveness of their participation. Simulations demonstrate that, if women were as well informed about politics as men are, gender gaps in political opinion would actually widen (Gidengil et al. 2004). The implication is that information shortfalls are compromising some women's ability to give political expression to their needs and wants.

Unequal participation in Canada's political life is apparent along a number of other social divides. Whether Canadian-born or foreign-born, members of certain visible minorities (notably citizens of Chinese, South Asian, and African ancestry) are less likely than other Canadians to vote (Tossutti 2007). They also tend to be less informed about politics and less likely to belong to voluntary associations. The same holds for recent immigrants, even allowing for differences in age and socio-economic status (ibid.; White et al. 2008). This is hardly surprising, since settling into a new environment and becoming acquainted with the workings of an unfamiliar political system takes time and energy. On a more encouraging note, immigrant status per se does not necessarily entail a participation disadvantage.

Democratic divides defined by socio-economic status cut across ethno-cultural lines and country of birth. On almost every indicator used to audit democratic citizenship in Canada, affluent Canadians qualify as being more active and engaged in politics than their fellow citizens who are struggling to make ends meet. This is even true of protest activities. Low-income Canadians are not necessarily lacking in civic spirit: when it comes to charitable giving, they are actually much more generous relative to their means than are affluent Canadians (Hall, McKeown, and Roberts 2001). Rather, these democratic divides between the haves and the have-nots in Canadian society reflect a lack of resources. People living on low incomes may simply not have the funds to subscribe to a newspaper, hire a babysitter, or travel to a meeting, and the sheer effort entailed in making ends meet may leave little time or energy for politics, especially if the stakes are perceived to be low. Education does not offset the effects of poverty. Nor does material advantage compensate for lack of education: low literacy skills are a serious impediment to political involvement (Prince 2007).

Elisabeth Gidengil, Richard Nadeau, Neil Nevitte, and André Blais

Perhaps the most important, and in some respects worrying, demo-cratic divide is generational. Much of the decline in voter turnout in federal elections since 1988 is the result of generational replacement. Today's young Canadians are less likely to vote than their parents or their grandparents were at the same age. There is nothing new about age differences in turnout: people typically become more likely to vote as they move from young adulthood to middle age, with turnout falling off only as physical infirmity takes a toll. However, young people today are less likely to vote to begin with, and they are much more likely to become habitual non-voters than were their counterparts in the early 1970s (Howe 2007). Part of the explanation may lie in "delayed matur-ity" (ibid., 14): witness the number of young adults still living with their parent(s). The root causes may go deeper, though. The shift to a knowledge-based economy has resulted in a profound marginalization of those young people who are not equipped to compete. Turnout has dropped thirty points or more among young Canadians with less than a high school education while remaining much the same among their university-educated counterparts. The difference in turnout between these two groups is estimated to be a massive fifty percentage points (Gidengil et al. 2004).

An Elections Canada (2008) study of estimated youth turnout in the 2006 federal election provides some grounds for optimism. The slight increase in turnout in that election proved to be concentrated in the younger age groups. But turnout fell in the following election, so it may be premature to assume that the pattern of low voter turnout among young Canadians is reversing. Indeed, even in 2006, the gain among first-time eligible voters was less than three percentage points, and turnout among those in the eighteen to twenty-four age group remained nineteen percentage points below average.

The generational divide is not confined to voting. Young Canadians rank lowest on every indicator of political engagement, including pol-itical consumerism and participation in protest activities. The only exception is using the Internet to get information about politics, but even this activity is marked by a deep educational divide: the less formal schooling young Canadians have, the less likely they are to go on-line in search of information about politics (for more on this digital divide generally, see Barney 2005).

Responsiveness

That a substantial number of citizens fail to take an active part in the country's political life raises questions about the responsiveness of the political system. If the propensity to participate – or not – were equally distributed across the population, there might be less cause for concern, but, as we have seen, democratic citizenship in Canada (as in other established democracies) is characterized by systematic social biases. And clearly, "when there are disparities across social groups in political knowledge and participation, democracy is at least a little less democratic" (Eveland and Scheufele 2000, 216).

On a more positive note, there is some evidence that voters and non-voters hold fairly similar opinions on a wide array of policy questions. To the extent that this is so, election outcomes would probably not be very different if everyone voted (Rubenson et al. 2007). However, this assessment does not factor in the effects of gaps in civic literacy. Citizens can choose their representatives wisely only if they know where the political parties stand on the issues. And citizens can hold their elected representatives accountable for their actions only if they know what those representatives have been doing. As long as citizens lack basic information about the issues of the day and government performance, elections will be less effective in fulfilling their fundamental role as mechanisms for ensuring responsiveness.

At stake here is citizens' ability to make an "enlightened choice," the choice that they would make if they knew all the relevant facts. The optimistic assumption is that the "magic of aggregation" (Page and Shapiro 1992) and the use of information shortcuts (Popkin 1991; Sniderman, Brody, and Tetlock 1991) can compensate for information deficits. The opinions expressed by those who know little or nothing about the matter at hand are likely to be random and thus to cancel each other out, whereas information shortcuts help those who know at least a little to get it right. An information shortcut can be as simple as deferring to the opinion of a trusted friend who is better informed or voting for a party whose leader shares a similar social background (Cutler 2002).

Simulating the effects of informed opinion, however, suggests that neither aggregation nor the use of information shortcuts necessarily corrects for shortfalls in information (Althaus 1998; Gidengil et al. 2004). Public opinion on some important social and fiscal questions would shift if information levels were higher, and it would shift in a systematically liberal direction. Indeed, opinion on the death penalty would actually reverse.

To understand why, we must return to the question of inclusiveness. As we have seen, the social distribution of political knowledge is very uneven. Older affluent men tend to know more about politics, and consequently, their views are most likely to be accurately reflected in collective expressions of public opinion. This is not just because those who are younger, poorer, and/or female are more likely to be *un*informed: it is because they are also more likely to be *mis*informed. Misinformation about policy-relevant facts skews opinion in predictable ways (Kuklinski et al. 2000; Gidengil et al. 2004). People who overestimate the amount of crime are the most likely to favour a get-tough approach; people who underestimate the gap between the rich and the poor are less likely to favour increased welfare spending. The net result is that a "relative deprivation of knowledge may lead to a relative deprivation of power" (Donoghue, Tichenor, and Olien 1973, 4).

Enhancing Democratic Citizenship

To borrow from Cameron Anderson and Elizabeth Goodyear-Grant (2008, 697), "antidotes remain elusive" when it comes to finding ways to enhance democratic citizenship. Humility is also in order in undertaking such a task. Policy prescriptions or institutional reforms are no match for vibrant candidates, such as Barack Obama, Ségolène Royal, or Nicolas Sarkozy, capable of energizing voters and bringing them back to the polls as they did in the recent US and French presidential elections. That said, some solutions aimed at re-engaging young citizens, creating a more informed citizenry, and narrowing the democratic divides can be suggested.

The Youth Option: From High School to the Polling Booth

Many scholars believe that, if citizens are to participate in their democratic institutions, the time to take action is during the pre-adult years. As Anderson and Goodyear-Grant (2008, 697-98) note, because "voting and abstention are habit-forming ... greater attention to immediate pre-adult years is necessary." Perhaps the strongest argument for "plant[ing] the seeds of democratic engagement in the formative years" (Howe 2008, 5) is the dramatic gap in voter turnout between newly eligible voters who have attended university and those who have not. This suggests that the place to start is in high school when *all* future potential voters are easily reachable. Trying to involve young adults when they first become eligible to vote is "too little, too late," if the purpose is to decrease the structural inequalities in political engagement, since many youngsters have already left the school system. Strategies aimed at re-engaging young citizens must begin in their formative years. The "youth option" advocated in this chapter consists of a series of interventions, starting in adolescence and ending when young adults become eligible to vote. It comprises civics education, community service, and reducing the start-up costs of youth voting.

Civics Education

Research in the United States and elsewhere (Campbell 2008; Niemi and Junn 1998; Niemi and Finkel 2006; see also Putnam 2000) shows that civics education encourages students to acquire knowledge, skills, and values that are likely to produce more engaged citizens (Zukin et al. 2006) as well as enhancing the formation of social capital (Print and Coleman 2003). Although certain scholars remain skeptical (see, for example, Lewis 2008), a growing body of evidence suggests that these

conclusions also apply in the Canadian context (see particularly Anderson and Goodyear-Grant 2008; Llewellyn et al. 2008; Howe 2008).

Efforts to implement a civics education strategy in Canada raise two
key questions. The first concerns the universality of the civics education to be offered to young Canadians in a federal system where education comes under provincial jurisdiction. The "opting-out" formula
could be part of the solution to this problem. The impetus to guaranteeing equal access to civics education could come from the federal government and take the form of unconditional financial support to enable
the provinces to establish their own programs. The guidelines for using
this funding should be loose, with the provinces being encouraged to
adopt the Ontario model: a universal compulsory civics course, offered
no later than grade 10. The second question concerns the content of the
civic knowledge to be transmitted. Civics education should teach students not just "how a bill becomes a law" but how they "can participate
effectively in the public life of [their] community" (Putnam 2000, 405;
see also O'Neill 2008; Westheimer and Kane 2004a, 2004b). A group of
Canadian scholars recently reached the same conclusions. After extensively interviewing students and teachers in four Ottawa schools,
Llewellyn and her colleagues (2008, 1) concluded that "education programs for civic literacy should teach students to make informed, active
choices about policies that affect their lives and to engage with their
community in efforts for social change."

Community Service

Community service is another important device for stimulating civic
involvement among adolescents. To be effective, these community experiences should be available on a universal basis and must possess
certain characteristics. To quote Putnam (2000, 405), a "mounting body
of evidence confirms that community service programs really do
strengthen the civic muscles of participants, especially if the service is
meaningful, regular, and woven into the fabric of the school curriculum"
(see also Niemi, Hepburn, and Chapman 2000; Stolle and Cruz 2005,
88-89). Mandatory community service is currently limited to certain
provinces and remains an isolated episode rather than an integrated

part of the high school experience (see Howe 2008; Brown et al. 2007). A recent study by Ellen Claes, Marc Hooghe, and Dietlind Stolle (2009, 613), based on a large sample of young Canadians aged fifteen to seventeen, underlines the potential of this "new form of civic education." According to these authors (ibid.), volunteering, an activity on the rise among young Canadians mostly because of mandatory high school programs (see Stolle and Cruz 2005, 89; McClintock 2004), "fosters political knowledge and conventional future participation." These results suggest that mandatory community service forms another promising avenue to enhance democratic citizenship among young Canadians.

Reducing the Start-Up Costs of Voting

The developmental theory of turnout suggests that voting, like non-voting, is characterized by a strong inertia component: once people have paid the start-up costs, they are likely to become habitual voters (see Plutzer 2002). Reducing the start-up costs for young voters is crucial from this perspective. One very simple strategy would be to launch a take-your-children-to-vote campaign. This could be initiated by Elections Canada or one of the grassroots organizations that is committed to enhancing electoral participation in Canada.

Efforts to facilitate voter registration should be pursued as well, including on-line registration as is now the case in British Columbia (Archer 2003). A more radical measure should also be considered. Borrowing from similar experiences in the United Kingdom and Australia, where registration is allowed at ages sixteen and seventeen, respectively, Canadians should be allowed to register to vote at age sixteen (Elections BC 2001; Howe 2007, 32). There are two reasons to choose sixteen years of age. On practical grounds, a lag between registration and voting eligibility allows extra time to ensure that young voters are on the permanent list by election day. Second, and more importantly, education is compulsory to age sixteen, meaning that all young people would still be in school and thus easily reachable when they are added to the permanent list. With the assistance of Elections Canada and voluntary groups, the school system could be responsible for ensuring that all students are on the permanent electoral list when they leave high school. Once they are registered, the challenge is to bring young voters to the polling booth. Canvassing efforts by a large array of non-partisan groups have proven to be fruitful (see Green and Gerber 2004, in particular) and should be conceived of as a complementary strategy to increase turnout among young voters.

CIVIC LITERACY: CREATING A MORE INFORMED CITIZENRY

According to Henry Milner (2002, 107), "levels of civic literacy are not immutable; they can be altered by deliberate policy choices." Milner's strategies can be divided into broad categories. First, taking inspiration from the Scandinavian countries, efforts should be made to encourage citizens to look for information in print form; innovations here could include subsidies to daily newspapers and measures to stimulate the reading of books. Second, civic literacy should be promoted through adult education. This form of education is neglected in Canada in general, and civic literacy is no exception. Finally, significant reinvestments should be made in media of public-service information.

This last point deserves attention. Despite the recent decrease in the quality of informational programs in the public broadcasting sector, it remains a crucial reference for the journalistic profession in general and continues to set the standards for the tone and content of the coverage of politics (Nadeau and Giasson 2005). Two changes appear particularly important for improving this coverage. First, journalists should undertake serious efforts to shift political coverage from a depiction of the partisan motivations of politicians to the presentation of information about issues and policies. In doing so, they should encourage citizens to perceive the relevance of these issues and policies to their own well-being and that of their families and communities. The amount of press attention given to a policy proposal clearly affects how many people get to know about it: when coverage is intense, even those who are generally poorly informed about politics are able to learn where a political party stands (Nadeau et al. 2008). Second, a wider range of perspectives should be offered to readers and viewers (see Entman

2004). The bulk of media coverage of elections currently consists of discussions among journalists about party strategies. Experts, as well as politicians themselves, should be given greater visibility, especially during election campaigns.

Finally, at a time when politics and political coverage are increasingly virtual, every effort should be made to limit the digital divide between Canadians. New communication technologies such as the Internet have profound implications for the quality of the democratic process (Barney 2005, Chapter 9 this volume). The Internet provides party strategists with a novel opportunity to bypass the traditional media and to communicate directly with voters. At the same time, it presents citizens with new avenues for political engagement. Citizens vary, though, in their capacity and motivation to take advantage of these new opportunities. Enhancing access to the Internet is still in order, but the most significant digital divide nowadays lies in the differential ability of citizens to take advantage of the Internet for political ends. Internet literacy is the next frontier to reach so that Canadians may be equipped to fully engage in the political process (Norris 2001; Blumler and Coleman 2009).

INSTITUTIONAL REFORMS: RECONNECTING CANADIANS WITH THEIR POLITICAL SYSTEM

A third approach to curing democratic malaise is institutional. According to Paul Howe, Richard Johnston, and André Blais (2005, 11), "there is now a significant mismatch [in Canada] between the political institutions and the citizenry they are meant to serve ... And in seeking to reconnect Canadians with their political system, institutional remedies are likely to be the simplest and the most effective."

The institutional approach has been very influential at both the federal and provincial levels over the last few years. Innovative deliberative mechanisms, including both large consultative processes (such as citizens' assemblies and *états généraux*) and more traditional commissions of enquiry, have been put in place in five provinces to examine the possibility, among others, of implementing various changes in the workings of the electoral system. The adoption of Bill C-24, which set new rules for party financing, and the holding of coast-to-coast public consultations on Canada's democratic institutions and practices (Privy Council Office 2007) reflect the same impulse at the federal level.

Despite the large amount of time and resources allocated to these initiatives, actual changes at the provincial and federal levels remain limited. Proposals for infusing a larger dose of proportionality into the first-past-the-post voting system have been rejected by voters or abandoned by provincial governments. The conclusion in a report handed to the Harper government in 2007, that "Canadians express strong satisfaction with our first-past-the-post or plurality electoral system" (ibid., 79), might well contribute to maintaining the status quo at the federal level.

Two significant changes have nevertheless emerged from these efforts. The first, and most important, is the federal government's adoption in 2003 of new rules that strictly limit donations from corporations and trade unions, and that provide public financing to political parties based on their level of support (Nadeau 2002; Cross 2004). The second is the adoption of four-year fixed-term mandates by the federal government, as well as several provincial governments.

It is too early to reach any conclusions about how the institutional reforms adopted so far have affected Canadians' involvement in the political process. But despite the rejection of electoral system change in British Columbia and Ontario, the innovative consultation processes put in place in both provinces have much to commend them and have already produced significant results, such as fixed-term mandates and the efforts in Ontario to implement a universal civics education program for all adolescents.

Are there other changes that could produce positive results? One potential reform can be rejected at the outset: compulsory voting. This is alien to Canadian political culture, and its beneficial effects remain to be proven (Loewen, Milner, and Hicks 2008). More technical adjustments to facilitate registration and voting (such as on-line registration and extended voting periods) should be pursued. But perhaps more importantly, a last round of consultations should be devoted to settling two key issues: the adoption of new rules for the selection of senators and the inclusion of a dose of proportionality in the voting system at the federal level. Richard Nadeau (2002) expressed the view that these two changes, along with the adoption of the new rules for party financing inspired by the legislation passed in Quebec during the late 1970s, represent the most significant reforms to be considered in order to increase Canadians' relatively low level of satisfaction with democracy in their country. The adoption of Bill C-24 represents a positive first step. Enhancing the legitimacy and representativeness of both Houses of the Canadian parliament might be another useful measure to consider in the future.

Citizens and the Health of Canadian Democracy

The "youth issue" is central to any discussion of the future vitality of democracy, both in Canada and abroad. Cliff Zukin and his colleagues (2006, viii) express a common view when they write that "the generational chain of engagement has been broken, at least in the electoral realm." If there is a consensus about the disengagement of younger generations from traditional forms of politics, the meaning of this disengagement is a matter of debate. Are young Canadians tuning out of politics altogether, or are they turning to new forms of political action? Some believe that the younger generations are leading the way in transforming political engagement in contemporary democracies (Cain, Dalton, and Scarrow 2003; Dalton 2008). Russell Dalton, for instance, has titled one of his recent books *The Good Citizen: How the Young Are Transforming American Politics* (2007), and in an even more provocative title, Martin Wattenberg asks *Is Voting Good for Young People?* (2008). Globalization and the changing balance between the state and the market mean that the targets of political engagement extend beyond the traditional political arenas to multinational corporations and supranational organizations.

But even if young adults are resorting to alternative forms of political action, such as Internet activism and political consumerism, there would still be reason for concern. The fragmentation of political action into separate spheres is not good news for the quality of the deliberative process in electoral democracies, the more so if generational replacement exacerbates this tendency. Whatever view one takes about the evolution of youth involvement in politics, there seems to be no more pressing challenge in the task of making Canada a more vibrant democracy than reconciling new voters and forms of engagement with more traditional, but still essential, forms of political participation.

A second pressing challenge relates to the political integration of newcomers. As Livianna Tossutti (2007, 7) notes, "Immigrants and ethnocultural minorities are likely to constitute increasingly larger segments of the electorate in the 21st century, and thus, their importance to maintaining Canadian democracy cannot be underestimated." It is encouraging that, once established, foreign-born citizens participate at similar rates to those of their Canadian-born counterparts. However, more needs to be done to facilitate the political adaptation of recent arrivals (Bloemraad 2006). It is easy to overlook the difficulty of learning how politics works in an unfamiliar setting, especially for immigrants coming from countries with very different political regimes.

The third major challenge is narrowing the democratic divides that characterize Canada's political life. As we have seen, these are not confined to the traditional arenas but pervade other political spaces as well. Citizens who are politically disengaged can be found in every walk of life, but they are clearly most numerous among certain segments of the population. Differences in power and socio-economic status translate into unequal participation in politics. The implication is clear: deeply rooted structural inequalities mean that some citizens are less likely than others to be able to make their voices heard and their preferences count.

These democratic divides also raise important questions about the performance of our democratic institutions. As Ronald Lambert and his colleagues (1988, 360-61) observe, "the overall level and distribution of political knowledge within a population is no less revealing of the political system that generates it than is knowledge of the individual who possesses it." If significant numbers of citizens are disengaged, we must ask why. There is no shortage of possible explanations for citizens' eroding faith in the effectiveness of democratic elections as mechanisms of accountability. The Canadian federal system is becoming an increasingly complicated network of intergovernmental relationships that is difficult even for experts to disentangle (Smith 2004, Chapter 2 this volume). The complex divisions of responsibility encourage credit taking and blame shifting, making it difficult for citizens to assign responsibility. The resulting confusion and uncertainty may reduce governments' incentives to pursue policies that satisfy citizens and deepen social inequalities by muting some citizens' voices and amplifying others. Meanwhile, political parties fail to provide clear alternatives on the issues that are most salient to voters, and distortions in the translation of votes into seats (Courtney 2004) encourage some citizens to believe that their votes simply do not matter. The net result is representative institutions that systematically under-represent certain parts of the population (Cross 2004, Chapter 7 this volume; Docherty 2005, Chapter 4 this volume). Finally, the pervasive game frame employed in media coverage contributes to a sense that politics is simply not that important to people's lives.

That perception was encouraged in the 1990s: globalization compromised governments' ability to fulfill their primary role of ensuring the well-being of their citizens, and neo-conservative rhetoric proclaimed that governments govern best when they govern least. However, the new millennium is causing many to reappraise the role of governments as terrorist attacks threaten personal safety and economic crises jeopardize material well-being. If governments prove equal to the task, we may well witness a renewed sense that politics matters. In the meantime, the democratic deficits in participation, inclusiveness, and responsiveness should not cause us to lose sight of the fact that the fundamental underpinnings of democratic citizenship in Canada remain strong.

Elisabeth Gidengil, Richard Nadeau, Neil Nevitte, and André Blais

Works Cited

Althaus, Scott L. 1998. Information effects in collective preferences. *American Political Science Review* 92: 545-58.

Anderson, Cameron D., and Elizabeth Goodyear-Grant. 2008. Youth turnout: Adolescents' attitudes in Ontario. *Canadian Journal of Political Science* 41: 697-718.

Archer, Keith. 2003. Increasing youth voter registration: Best practices in targeting young electors. *Electoral Insight* 5: 26-30.

Barney, Darin. 2005. *Communication technology.* Canadian Democratic Audit. Vancouver: UBC Press.

Bloemraad, Irene. 2006. *Becoming a citizen: Incorporating immigrants and refugees in the United States and Canada.* Berkeley: University of California Press.

Blumler, Jay C., and Stephen Coleman. 2009. *The Internet and democratic citizenship.* Cambridge: Cambridge University Press.

Brown, Stephen D., Agnes Meinhard, Kimberly Ellis-Hale, Ailsa Henderson, and Mary Foster. 2007. *Community service and service learning in Canada: A profile of programming across the country.* Draft research report to the Knowledge Development Centre Imagine Canada. Laurier Institute for the Study of Public Opinion and Policy, Working Papers Series. http://www.wlu.ca/.

Cain, Bruce E., Russell J. Dalton, and Susan E. Scarrow. 2003. *Democracy transformed? Expanding political opportunities in advanced industrial democracies.* Oxford: Oxford University Press.

Campbell, David E. 2008. Voice in the classroom: How an open classroom climate fosters political engagement among adolescents. *Political Behavior* 30: 437-54.

Claes, Ellen, Marc Hooghe, and Dietlind Stolle. 2009. The political socialization of adolescents in Canada: Differential effects of civic education on visible minorities. *Canadian Journal of Political Science* 42: 613-36.

Courtney, John. 2004. *Elections.* Canadian Democratic Audit. Vancouver: UBC Press.

Cross, William. 2004. *Political parties.* Canadian Democratic Audit. Vancouver: UBC Press.

Cutler, Fred. 2002. The simplest shortcut of all: Socio-demographic characteristics and electoral choice. *Journal of Politics* 64: 466-90.

Dalton, Russell J. 2007. *The good citizen: How the young are transforming American politics.* Washington, DC: CQ Press.

–. 2008. Citizenship norms and the expansion of political participation. *Political Studies* 56: 76-98.

Delli Carpini, Michael X., and Scott Keeter. 1996. *What Americans know about politics and why it matters.* New Haven: Yale University Press.

Docherty, David. 2005. *Legislatures.* Canadian Democratic Audit. Vancouver: UBC Press.

Donoghue, G.A., P.J. Tichenor, and C.N. Olien. 1975. Mass media and the knowledge gap: A hypothesis reconsidered. *Communication Research* 2: 3-23.

Elections BC. 2001. *Report of the chief electoral officer: 37th provincial general election, May 16, 2001.* http://www.elections.bc.ca/.

Elections Canada. 2008. *Estimation of voter turnout by age group at the 39th federal general election, January 23, 2006.* Working Paper Series. Ottawa: Elections Canada.

Entman, Robert M. 2004. *Projections of power: Framing news, public opinion, and U.S. foreign policy.* Chicago: University of Chicago Press.

Eveland, W.R., and D.A. Scheufele. 2000. Connecting news media use with gaps in knowledge and participation. *Political Communication* 17: 215-37.

Gidengil, Elisabeth, André Blais, Neil Nevitte, and Richard Nadeau. 2004. *Citizens.* Canadian Democratic Audit. Vancouver: UBC Press.

Gidengil, Elisabeth, Janine Giles, and Melanee Thomas. 2008. The gender gap in self-perceived understanding of politics in Canada and the United States. *Politics and Gender* 4: 535-61.

Gidengil, Elisabeth, Elizabeth Goodyear-Grant, Neil Nevitte, and André Blais. 2006. Gender, knowledge, and social capital. In *Gender and social capital,* ed. Brenda O'Neill and Elisabeth Gidengil, 241-71. New York: Routledge.

Green, Donald P., and Alan S. Gerber. 2004. *Get out the vote! How to increase voter turnout.* Washington, DC: Brookings Institution Press.

Hall, Michael, Larry McKeown, and Karen Roberts. 2001. *Caring Canadians, involved Canadians: Highlights from the 2000 national survey of giving, volunteering and participating.* Catalogue no. 71-542-XIE. Ottawa: Statistics Canada.

Howe, Paul. 2007. *The electoral participation of young Canadians.* Working Paper Series on Electoral Participation and Outreach Practices. Ottawa: Elections Canada.

–. 2008. Engendering engagement among young Canadians: A holistic approach. Paper presented at the Civic Education and Political Participation Workshop, Montreal, 17-19 June.

Howe, Paul, Richard Johnston, and André Blais, eds. 2005. *Strengthening Canadian democracy.* Montreal: Institute for Research on Public Policy.

International Institute for Democracy and Electoral Assistance (IDEA). 2010. Voter turnout. http://www.idea.int/.

Kuklinski, James H., Paul J. Quirk, Jennifer Jerit, David Schweider, and Robert F. Rich. 2000. Misinformation and the currency of democratic citizenship. *Journal of Politics* 62: 790-816.

Ladner, Kiera L., and Michael McCrossan. 2007. *The electoral participation of Aboriginal people.* Working Paper Series on Electoral Participation and Outreach Practices. Ottawa: Elections Canada.

Lambert, Ronald D., James E. Curtis, Barry J. Kay, and Steven D. Brown. 1988. The social sources of political knowledge. *Canadian Journal of Political Science* 21: 359-74.

Lewis, J.P. 2008. Is civic education the answer? The futile search for policy solutions to youth political apathy. Paper presented at the Civic Education and Political Participation Workshop, Montreal, 17-19 June.

Llewellyn, Kristina R., Sharon Cook, Joel Westheimer, Luz Alison Molina Girón, and Karen Suurtamm. 2008. School-based programs to promote democratic and political participation. Paper presented at the Civic Education and Political Participation Workshop, Montreal, 17-19 June.

Loewen, Peter John, Henry Milner, and Bruce M. Hicks. 2008. Does compulsory voting lead to more informed and engaged citizens? *Canadian Journal of Political Science* 41: 655-72.

McClintock, N. 2004. *Understanding Canadian volunteers: Using the national survey of giving, volunteering and participating to build your volunteer program.* Toronto: Canadian Centre for Philanthropy.

Micheletti, Michele, Andreas Follesdal, and Dietlind Stolle, eds. 2003. *Politics, products, and markets: Exploring political consumerism past and present.* New Brunswick, NJ: Transaction Press.

Milner, Henry. 2002. *Civic literacy: How informed citizens make democracy work.* Hanover, NH: University Press of New England.

Nadeau, Richard. 2002. Satisfaction with democracy: The Canadian paradox. In *Value change and governance in Canada,* ed. Neil Nevitte, 37-70. Toronto: University of Toronto Press.

Nadeau, Richard, and Thierry Giasson. 2005. Canada's democratic malaise: Are the media to blame? In *Strengthening Canadian democracy,* ed. Paul Howe, Richard Johnston, and André Blais, 229-67. Montreal: Institute for Research on Public Policy.

Nadeau, Richard, Neil Nevitte, Elisabeth Gidengil, and André Blais. 2008. Election campaigns as information campaigns: Who learns what and with what effect? *Political Communication* 25: 229-48.

Niemi, Richard G., and Steven E. Finkel. 2006. Civic education and the development of civic knowledge and attitudes. In *Developing cultures: Essays on cultural change,* ed. Lawrence E. Harrison and Jerome Kagan, 77-93. New York: Routledge.

Niemi, Richard G., Mary A. Hepburn, and Chris Chapman. 2000. Community service by high school students: A cure for civic ills? *Political Behavior* 22: 45-69.

Niemi, Richard G., and Jane Junn. 1998. *Civic education: What makes students learn?* New Haven: Yale University Press.

Norris, Pippa. 2001. *Digital divide.* Cambridge: Cambridge University Press.

O'Neill, Brenda. 2006. Canadian women's religious volunteerism: Compassion, connections, and comparisons. In *Gender and social capital,* ed. Brenda O'Neill and Elisabeth Gidengil, 185-211. New York: Routledge.

–. 2008. Assessing the 'education' in civic education. Paper presented at the Civic Education and Political Participation Workshop, Montreal, 17-19 June.

Page, Benjamin I., and Robert Y. Shapiro. 1992. *The rational public: Fifty years of trends in Americans' policy preferences.* Chicago: University of Chicago Press.

Plutzer, Eric. 2002. Becoming a habitual voter: Inertia, resources, and growth in young adulthood. *American Political Science Review* 96: 41-56.

Popkin, Samuel L. 1991. *The reasoning voter: Communication and persuasion in presidential campaigns.* Chicago: University of Chicago Press.

Prince, Michael J. 2007. *The electoral participation of persons with special needs.* Working Paper Series on Electoral Participation and Outreach Practices. Ottawa: Elections Canada.

Print, Murray, and David Coleman. 2003. Towards understanding of social capital and citizenship education. *Cambridge Journal of Education* 33: 123-49.

Privy Council Office. 2007. *Public consultations on Canada's democratic institutions and practices.* http://www.democraticreform.gc.ca/.

Putnam, Robert. 2000. *Bowling alone: The collapse and revival of American community.* New York: Simon and Schuster.

Rubenson, Daniel, André Blais, Elisabeth Gidengil, Neil Nevitte, and Patrick Fournier. 2007. Does low turnout matter? Evidence from the 2000 Canadian general election. *Electoral Studies* 26: 589-97.

Smith, Jennifer. 2004. *Federalism.* Canadian Democratic Audit. Vancouver: UBC Press.

Sniderman, Paul M., Richard A. Brody, and Philip E. Tetlock. 1991. *Reasoning and choice: Explorations in social psychology.* Cambridge: Cambridge University Press.

Stolle, Dietlind, and Cesi Cruz. 2005. Youth civic engagement in Canada: Implications for public policy. In *Social capital in action: Thematic policy studies,* 82-114. Ottawa: Policy Research Initiative.

Tossutti, Livianna. 2007. *The electoral participation of ethnocultural communities.* Working Paper Series on Electoral Participation and Outreach Practices. Ottawa: Elections Canada.

Wattenberg, Martin P. 2008. *Is voting good for young people?* New York: Pearson Education.

Westheimer, Joel, and Joseph Kahne. 2004a. Education and the 'good' citizen: Political choices and Pedagogical goals. *PS: Political Science and Politics* 37: 241-47.

–. 2004b. Introduction – The politics of civic education. *PS: Political Science and Politics* 37: 231-35.

White, Stephen, Neil Nevitte, André Blais, Elisabeth Gidengil, and Patrick Fournier. 2008. The political resocialization of immigrants: Resistance or life-long learning? *Political Research Quarterly* 61(2): 268-81.

Young, Lisa, and Joanna Everitt. 2004. *Advocacy groups.* Canadian Democratic Audit. Vancouver: UBC Press.

Zukin, Cliff, Scott Keeter, Molly Andolina, Krista Jenkins, and Michael X. Delli Carpini. 2006. *A new engagement? Political participation, civic life, and the changing American citizen.* Oxford: Oxford University Press.

6

ELECTIONS
John Courtney

Canada's electoral system is constructed on six pillars, or building blocks. Five of these - the franchise, voter registration, electoral districting, election management, and the plurality voting system - are the focus of this chapter. The remaining pillar - the financing of political parties, candidates, and campaigns - is examined in the Democratic Audit volume *Political Parties* (Cross 2004).

This chapter, which is divided into three sections, employs the benchmarks common to the Audit project: participation, responsiveness, and inclusiveness. The first section examines the changes that have been made to the first four of the electoral building blocks over time and argues that, collectively, they ensure a solidly democratic framework within which to conduct elections in Canada. The next section describes the arguments advanced in favour of or in opposition to replacing plurality voting with some form of proportional vote, and it cautions against unrealistic expectations about what can be accomplished through electoral reform. It also questions the appropriateness to the Canadian electoral system of the voter identification requirement adopted by parliament in 2007. The final section is devoted to an overall assessment of the institutional and operational framework within which elections are conducted in Canada. It places elections squarely at the heart of Canadian democracy and suggests that, without open, freely competitive, and recurrent elections, a citizen's vote is of little value, and any claim to legitimacy on a government's part could not be accepted at face value.

Two caveats should be noted at the outset. First, the term "electoral system" can be used in two different ways. In its narrowest sense, it means a method of voting – that is, how votes are cast, counted, and converted into legislative seats. This view of the electoral system pervades political science literature, classroom discussions, and press accounts of elections. It is less usual to talk or write of an electoral system in its broader sense, as including *all* of the components of electoral machinery – from the franchise and electoral registration to districting and method of voting. It is in this wider, more inclusive sense that "electoral system" is used in this chapter.

Second, the following analysis is devoted to a study of electoral institutions at the federal level. Important though it is in a country such as Canada to describe and assess the federal and provincial frameworks for the conduct of elections, it is not feasible in a chapter of this length. Where possible, however, appropriate references will be made to the experience of the provinces. That is especially the case for the transference of electoral institutions from one jurisdiction to another and where important electoral reform debates at the provincial level might help to inform the larger issues of governance and representation at both the federal and provincial levels.

A Changed Electoral System

The evidence to date powerfully demonstrates that four of the five components of the electoral system (the franchise, voter registration, electoral districting, and election management) have changed extensively from the time of Canada's first post-Confederation elections. In response to shifting social values, judicial rulings, and public pressures, Canada's electoral system has become both more participatory and more inclusive. Canada now ranks as the most populous country among the top 11 "full democracies" in a 167-country comparison of democracy worldwide (Economist Intelligence Unit 2008, 1-4). The plurality vote system stands as the exception to the 140-year pattern of gradually altered electoral institutions. That building block will be considered separately, in the second section of this chapter.

Canada's electoral system has many unquestioned strengths. Several of these, such as a universal adult franchise, a virtually complete electoral registry, and an impressive array of independent election officials at both the federal and provincial levels, set Canada apart from many other liberal democracies. Nowhere is that more the case than by comparison with the United States. From the fiasco over the vote counting in Florida, which occurred during the 2000 presidential election, to the arrantly partisan gerrymander of congressional districts in a number of states, to the questionable application of electoral laws by some election officers who obtained their jobs solely because they were adherents of one party or another, the American electoral experience in the past decade stands in stark contrast to the Canadian. (On the contested American election of 2000 and partisan electoral administration, see Rakove 2001. For a recent study of gerrymandering and electoral redistricting in the United States, see Persily 2005.)

The current strengths of the Canadian electoral system have taken decades to achieve. At the time of Confederation, elections were so markedly different from what they are today that contemporary voters would scarcely recognize them. With only short exceptions between 1867 and 1917, determining who could vote and creating the voters' lists for federal elections both came under the control of the provinces. Four criteria establishing voter eligibility were common to all provinces: electors had to be British subjects by birth or naturalization, as well as male, property owners, and at least twenty-one years of age. By definition, that excluded non-British subjects, females, the propertyless, and those under twenty-one. In addition, government employees, government contractors, judges, court officials, and election officials were denied the vote in many provinces on the basis that they depended on the government for their livelihood. The poor, or those who received social assistance, were barred from voting since they did not meet the criteria of either independence or of having a stake in the community. Criminals were also denied the vote.

Still others could not vote because of their race or national origin. Status Indians were denied the franchise on the grounds that their treaty rights made them dependants of the government. British Columbia refused to enfranchise Orientals, a group defined initially as Chinese but later widened to include Japanese and other East Asians. In the early twentieth century, Manitoba introduced a "literacy test" that denied the vote to residents who had recently emigrated from Ukraine or another central European country, even though many had become naturalized British subjects through immigration. The restrictive nature of the franchise is demonstrated by the fact that, in the twelve federal elections between 1867 and 1911, an average of only about 20 percent of the *total* Canadian population was entitled to vote.

Restrictions on the right to vote were gradually removed through the twentieth and early twenty-first centuries. The initial shift came at the end of the First World War when parliament, following the lead of the three Prairie provinces, enfranchised women. This effectively doubled the size of the electorate. Under the Dominion Elections Act 1920 (now the Canada Elections Act), property restrictions were abandoned as a criterion to vote. Oriental Canadians were added, in stages, to federal and provincial electoral rolls after the Second World War, as were the Inuit and status Indians, who were granted the federal franchise in 1950 and 1960 respectively. In 1970, parliament lowered the voting age from twenty-one to eighteen, thereby adding an additional 2 million Canadians to the voters' list in the largest increase since women received the vote a half century before.

Progressively more liberal social values and participation of organized interests regarding vote entitlement (especially in the case of women's groups in the first decades of the twentieth century) account for these developments. The Canadian Charter of Rights and Freedoms, adopted in 1982, added yet another instrument for change. According to section 3 of the Charter, "every citizen of Canada has the right to vote." The courts have interpreted this section generously. In 1988, the Federal Court of

Canada ruled that the prohibition on judges voting clearly violated section 3 of the Charter. In a 1988 case launched by the Canadian Disability Rights Council, the same reasoning applied to the exclusion of mentally challenged Canadians. Anticipating a possible Charter challenge by expatriate Canadians, parliament amended the Canada Elections Act in the 1990s to extend the franchise to Canadian persons living abroad for up to five years who intend to return to Canada. Prisoners were the single remaining group prohibited from voting. A series of cases and appeals over a protracted period ended in 2002 when the Supreme Court of Canada, in a five-to-four decision, ruled that all prisoners eighteen years of age and older holding Canadian citizenship were entitled to vote. (For court cases accepting Charter challenges to franchise restrictions, see *Muldoon v. Canada* 1988; *Canadian Disability Rights Council v. Canada* 1988; *Sauvé v. Canada (Chief Electoral Officer)* 2002.)

The inclusiveness of the franchise is now without question. The cumulative effect of more than a century of changes to the franchise is seen in the fact that the share of the *total* Canadian population now eligible to vote in a federal election has grown to its highest level ever: over four and a-half times what it was in 1867 (70 percent versus 15 percent). (The 30 percent ineligible to vote are Canadian citizens under eighteen years and persons residing in Canada who are not citizens of the country.)

Canada and the provinces have used two different methods to construct the lists of electors in advance of elections. In the past, enumerations were conducted door-to-door by one or two enumerators named by local party officials soon after an election was called. The enumerators were selected from lists supplied by the two candidates receiving the highest number of votes in the preceding election. This bipartisan element of the process was intended to serve as a check against possible registration fraud. Because enumerators were paid on a per voter basis, there was a built-in incentive to ensure a complete and accurate list of voters. Door-to-door enumeration was premised on the idea that the state plays a significant role in making certain that the voters' lists are as inclusive of eligible electors as possible.

The advantages of enumeration were obvious. The lists were prepared and updated (through revisions) mere weeks in advance of voting.

This process ensured that voters' lists were current, complete, and (because they were drawn up only as needed every three or four years) cost-effective. The lists captured between 95.0 and 97.5 percent of Canada's eligible electorate, which is a remarkable figure by any comparative standard (Courtney and Smith 1991, 365, 451; Elections Canada 2001, 67).

Designed to record the names of voters in a country with elections, on average, once every four years, and whose population was both smaller and more rurally based than it is now, enumeration was found wanting in the 1980s. Canada experienced a record number of elections – twelve – between 1957 and 1988; over that time, the electorate doubled in size (from 8.9 to 17.6 million); urban growth vastly outpaced that of rural Canada, with metropolitan populations that were ethnically, linguistically, and culturally mixed; and enumerators were more difficult to find and train than had been the case in the past. These developments combined to place enumeration under stress.

Door-to-door enumerations had worked well when elections were less frequent than they became in the last half of the twentieth century and when voters were fewer in number. For several reasons, constituency returning officers found it difficult to recruit and train enumerators. The pay scale was low; the increasingly mixed linguistic composition of Canada's population made it difficult to find the right "linguistic match" of enumerators and polling districts; and election officials voiced concerns for the safety and security of enumerators in some large urban areas. The cracks that had appeared in the enumeration process were flagged by Elections Canada and accepted by the Chrétien government as sufficient reason for fundamentally changing the method of voter registration.

The National Register of Electors replaced door-to-door enumeration in 1997. It serves as a database of qualified electors and contains each person's name, address, sex, and date of birth. Information to maintain the register continuously is received by Elections Canada from several government sources, including Citizenship and Immigration Canada (for the names of new Canadian citizens), Canada Customs and Revenue Agency (for tax filers who consent to share basic demographic information), and such provincial agencies as vital statistics, election authorities, and motor vehicle registration bureaus.

The register is not without its critics. Maintained 365 days per year regardless of whether or not there is an election that year, it may in the long run prove to be less cost-effective than election-generated enumerations. That remains to be seen. It is known that the register is marginally less comprehensive than enumeration lists. Ninety-three percent of eligible voters were registered for the 2000 and 2008 elections, a slippage of between two and four and a-half percentage points over enumerated elections (Black 2002; Elections Canada 2008).

Those most likely to be left off the register or to experience difficulties getting on it tend to be the young, poor, mobile, tenants, and those with limited language skills. These are "precisely [the] groups that are most in need of assistance from the state in exercising their democratic rights" (White 2002, 4). (They are, incidentally, also the groups least likely to vote when they *are* registered.) The register is blamed for contributing to "increasing participation inequality" among potential voters (Black 2000, 20; see also Black 2003). Moreover, what has been lost with the replacement of door-to-door enumerations by the register is a personal reminder of a pending election through "the human contact that occurs between the potential voter and the compiler of the voters' list" (Smith 1991, 37). Human contact has the potential to positively reinforce a civic good – that is, taking part in an election. A positive correlation between voter contact by parties and candidates and the propensity to vote in federal elections has been established (Pammett and LeDuc 2003, 24-28), and it is reasonable to assume that the same relationship would exist between voter contact by election officials through door-to-door enumeration and voting. One can only speculate whether the shift to the register, possibly as a demonstrated instance of the law of unintended consequences, has contributed to the decline in voter turnout about which so much has recently been written.

Early in 2009, the privacy commissioner of Canada and the auditor general of Canada took the unprecedented step of issuing a joint report on the voter registration system. They found fault with a number of aspects of the new system including data gathering, protection of voters' personal information, and dissemination of information. Voter lists were found to have made their way into the hands of a Toronto Tamil Tiger cell (classed by Canada as a terrorist organization), and it was determined that paper and electronic copies of voter lists had been widely circulated to candidates and political parties, none of whom are subject to the Privacy Act's provisions governing protection of privacy. Elections Canada responded to the commissioners' criticisms by agreeing to bring, where suitable, the information gathering and dissemination processes in line with the relevant statutes. Even so, some improvements to the registration process can be made only by parliament through approval of appropriate legislative amendments (Auditor General 2009; Privacy Commissioner 2009).

Canada and the provinces have completely overhauled the way in which electoral districts are designed. With House of Commons MPs elected from geographically defined districts, and with the district boundaries redrawn following every decennial census according to the shifts in population, much rests on the configuration of the districts for parties, candidates, MPs, voters, and, ultimately, public policy.

Elected politicians remain keenly aware of that fact, but the historical record shows that two remarkably different approaches have been taken to the constitutionally mandated redistributions of each decade. From 1872 to 1952, redistributions were carefully managed by the government of the day (Conservative or Liberal) in its own interest. The great majority of the redistributions were partisan and blatantly self-serving affairs. In none of the nine redistributions over that period was the public invited to participate; nor was it formally consulted. For the better part of a century, Canada's boundary readjustments were totally partisan in-house exercises that, by design, excluded the public.

Such redistributions were regularly subjected to editorial and public criticism. By 1964, parliament had responded to pressures to replace the politically charged process by adopting the Electoral Boundaries Readjustment Act (EBRA). Modelled on a plan instituted a decade earlier by Manitoba for its own provincial redistributions, the EBRA requires that a three-member independent electoral boundary readjustment commission be named in every province following every decennial census. A judge chairs the commission, and the remaining two members are selected from the general public (often from universities) by the Commons' speaker.

Each commission is to construct the province's federal districts according to two important principles. First, constituency populations must not vary by more than 25 percent of that province's average per district population unless there are "exceptional circumstances." Second, consideration should be given to community of interests or identity, historical pattern of a constituency, and a manageable geographic size for sparsely populated or isolated regions of a province. Moreover, the public is encouraged to participate in the process by presenting written briefs and making representations at public meetings of the commissions.

The introduction of independent commissions has dramatically altered the electoral boundary readjustment landscape in Canada. Determining the size and shape of an electoral district is no longer the exclusive preserve of elected politicians. Districts are now far more equal in population within each of the ten jurisdictions than had previously been the case, which represents an important advance for those who support Canada's moving toward acceptance of the principle of "one person, one vote." The new process encourages public participation, and as it is federally structured (with one commission for each province), it rests on the premise that, in a diverse federal system such as Canada's, differences of communities, regions, and geographic size deserve consideration when electoral districts are designed (Courtney 2001).

At the time of Confederation, electoral machinery was firmly in the hands of the governing party. Those chosen to conduct elections were known partisans, and the party in office saw electoral administration as an institutional mechanism easily manipulated for its own benefit. Countless examples of unscrupulous behaviour and of blatantly partial decision making by election-day officers have been recorded. The ballot was open and public, not secret. Voting took place over an extended period of time (six weeks in 1867 and three months in 1872), an individual could stand as a candidate in more than one constituency in the same election, and election expense limits were either non-existent or unenforceable. Intimidation and bribery of voters were not uncommon, and money and liquor often played an instrumental part in determining election outcomes in a number of constituencies (Ward 1950, part 4).

None of the corrupt or blatantly partisan practices of conducting elections in the nineteenth-century has survived. An expanding population, a widening franchise, a better-informed electorate, strict enforcement of election laws, and honest and trustworthy election officials have combined to make widespread electoral "manipulation and corruption impracticable" (ibid., 277).

There are two significant dates in the democratization of Canada's electoral system. In 1874, parliament approved the secret ballot and same-day elections, and in 1920, it created the Office of the Chief Electoral Officer. Both were responses to, in the first instance, early post-Confederation corrupt electoral practices and, in the second, partisan manipulation of the franchise and the electoral process in 1917. The chief electoral officer (an officer of parliament whose independent agency is now widely known as Elections Canada) has brought legitimacy and credibility to the management of elections. The professionalism in the administration of federal and provincial elections (agencies similar to Elections Canada exist in every province and territory) is unquestioned. Possibly the best measure of the strength of Canada's electoral machinery comes from the fact that international agencies and emerging democracies regularly call upon Canada to provide either impartial election observers or expert assistance in running fair and open elections.

In all, these four pillars of electoral democracy in Canada stand as proof of the institutional change and improvement. As now constituted, they are exemplars of the three benchmarks common to the Democratic Audit series. The franchise has been expanded to *include* all Canadians eighteen and older. The voter registration system, although it captures a slightly smaller share of eligible voters than does enumeration, is nonetheless impressively *comprehensive.* Electoral districting by independent commissions charged with redrawing constituency boundaries is *participatory* and stands in marked contrast to the partisan, self-interested dealings of the past. And the management and operation of the electoral machinery, in *response* to the earlier manipulated processes, have been turned over to legitimated and authoritative bodies that brook no political interference. In all, the Canadian electoral system has many impressive strengths.

That said, however, some unresolved questions hang over these building blocks. Voter participation has declined at an alarming rate in recent elections, both federally and provincially. This cannot be laid at the feet of either a limited franchise or a glaringly incomplete voter registry. The fault lies elsewhere. Declining individual and group interest in the political and electoral process? A growing distrust of politicians, combined with a heightened cynicism about the value of elections? Newly created outlets, such as Internet social-networking sites, offering alternative venues for citizen participation? An educational system that, from primary to post-secondary schooling, places less value on electoral participation than it previously did? Whatever the combination of factors accounting for the decline in voter turnout, there remains a challenge to civic, educational, and electoral authorities to direct even greater resources than has so far been the case to resolving the issue (for more on this, see Gidengil et al., Chapter 5 this volume).

As responsive as Canadian policy makers and courts have been to gradually more liberal and generous social values, and as inclusive as such electoral pillars as the franchise and voter registry are, the fact remains that legislative authorities have made some unexpected (and, arguably, unwarranted) intrusions aimed at "fine-tuning" Canada's election machinery. As will be discussed below, the 2007 statutory recasting of voter identification requirements for federal elections was underlain by a questionable rationale and may already have had a deleterious effect on voter turnout. The new statutorily defined voter identification requirements are at odds with the spirit of the massively expanded and inclusive franchise, and the tradition of a substantial measure of *mutual trust* between electoral officials and voters that characterized Canadian elections for decades.

As noted earlier, the introduction of federal independent electoral boundary commissions has opened the redistribution process to public participation and has the merit of encouraging commissions to take economic, social, and group differences into account when they design parliamentary districts. This is in keeping with the time-honoured Canadian practice of accepting differences within the country's political fabric. But the acceptance of differences has come at a cost. Critics of the current redistribution process point to two of its features that work against equality of the vote in Canada.

First, it is noted that permitting variances in average federal district populations within a province (of greater or less than 25 percent) allows commissions to construct seats with markedly disparate populations. In reality, there is far less to support that criticism than might on the face of it seem to be the case. The record shows that the overwhelming majority of federal seats have been constructed to contain populations that are only 10 percent greater or lesser than the provincial average. This is a distinct improvement over the redistribution record prior to the introduction of the EBRA in 1964, and by most international standards, it is judged to be quite satisfactory (Courtney 2001; Handley and Grofman 2008).

Second, although there has been a demonstrable move toward *intra*provincial population equality, *inter*provincial differences in average district populations have unquestionably increased. This has been the result of differential growth rates among the provinces in recent decades (the growth in Ontario, British Columbia, and Alberta has greatly outpaced that in the remaining provinces) and the application of the senatorial and grandfather clauses to the allocation of seats to the provinces every ten years. With continued uneven population growth among provinces, interprovincial variations in district size will persist as a dominant feature of redistributions in Canada so long as the current formula remains in place. In 2007, the Harper government introduced a bill to grant additional Commons' seats to Ontario, British Columbia, and Alberta. By early 2010, the legislation, which had gone through different iterations over the course of three parliaments, had not been approved. (For an additional criticism of the current redistribution formula, see Pal and Choudry 2007.)

Plurality Voting and Voter ID

PLURALITY VOTING

Plurality voting or, more commonly, first-past-the-post (FPTP) voting, stands as the exception to the other electoral building blocks, for in no major respect does it differ now from what it was in 1867. A voter marks a single "X" on a ballot paper opposite the name of a chosen candidate. At the end of the day, election officials in each geographically designed electoral district count the ballots and, in turn, declare one candidate elected. The winner receives either a clear majority of the valid votes (as was the case in the early post-Confederation period when, typically, only two parties contested each district) or a plurality of the valid votes (as is more usual now, with a greater number of parties competing in every constituency). The fact that the plurality vote is still employed federally, and in all provinces and territories, is in some measure a function of the varied and sporadic expressions of competing political and representational interests calling for either its replacement or its retention. Unresolved as the debate over FPTP remains, the plurality vote survives alone among the pillars of Canada's electoral democracy in essentially the same manner as it existed at the outset.

FPTP voting is claimed by its supporters to have several strengths. It is undoubtedly the easiest electoral system for the voter to use and to understand. Nothing could be much simpler than marking an "X" for a single candidate and having all the "Xs" counted at the close of polls to determine the winner. As a rule, FPTP elections in Canada have produced single-party majority governments. This is seen as an advantage insofar as majority governments tend to last longer and to bring greater stability to the political system and the economic order than do minority governments. Of Canada's forty federal elections to the end of 2008, three-quarters produced majority governments. They lasted, on average, two and a-half times as long as minority governments: 4.0 years compared to 1.6 years. (These figures exclude the extraordinary parliament of 1911-17, whose life was extended by constitutional amendment for one year beyond the constitutionally defined maximum of five years.)

John Courtney

In the past, FPTP has been conducive to broadly based, accommodative, centrist parties that succeeded in gaining sufficient support from the various regions, religious and linguistic groups, and ethnocultural minorities to win office. These parties (the Liberals and Conservatives) drew their strength from the fact that they were *intraparty* coalitions composed of socially and regionally diverse interests. That has long been considered an important stabilizing element of the party system in a country with as many potently centrifugal forces as Canada.

Finally, because majority governments are more likely to result from FPTP elections than from more proportional methods of voting, ultimate political responsibility and accountability is easier for voters to establish at election time. By contrast, multi-party coalitions make it more difficult for voters at election time to assign blame or give credit to individual parties for a government's record.

Those who favour replacing FPTP with some variant of proportional representation cite several weaknesses of plurality voting. FPTP is faulted for acting in seemingly capricious ways when the popular vote is converted into parliamentary seats. From the beginning of Canada's moving away from its classic two-party system at the conclusion of the First World War to the recent parliaments in which four or five parties have been present, there are many examples of the "unfair" manner in which votes are translated into seats. These include the following:

- The party forming a majority government has rarely been elected with the support of a majority of the popular vote. In only three of the twenty-seven federal elections since 1921 has a majority government also won a majority of the popular vote: 1940, 1958, and 1984.
- The party forming a government may receive fewer votes but more seats than its principal adversary. During this period, this has happened three times: 1957, 1962, and 1979. A twist was added to this in 1925 when the Liberal government of William Lyon Mackenzie King continued in office in spite of having won both fewer seats and fewer votes than the Conservatives in the election that year.

* A party winning approximately the same share of the popular vote as another party may end up with considerably fewer Commons seats. For example, in 1997, the Reform Party and the Progressive Conservatives were less than one percentage point apart (19.4 to 18.8 percent respectively), but Reform elected forty more MPs than the Tories.

Judged from the perspective of majoritarian democratic theory, these results illustrate a perverse tendency of Canada's FPTP system to reward regionally strong parties, penalize weak national ones, and discriminate arbitrarily among some parties in converting votes into seats. FPTP can also give an inaccurate portrayal of a party's actual level of support. In 2000, for instance, the Alliance Party received 23.6 percent of the vote in Ontario, yet it elected only 2 of the province's 103 MPs.

A variety of other criticisms have been levelled at FPTP. Women, visible minorities, and Aboriginals have never gained seats in the Commons commensurate with their share of the total population. It is argued that they would fare better with a proportional vote scheme. Plurality voting does not take a voter's order of preference into account, as do preferential electoral systems such as the alternative vote and the single transferable vote (STV). At the provincial level, where legislative assemblies are much smaller than the House of Commons and where two-party systems are more usual, a party can sweep every one of a legislature's seats. That happened, for example, in New Brunswick in 1987, when 60 percent of the popular vote gave the Liberals all fifty-eight seats in the legislature; the pattern recurred four years later in British Columbia, when the Liberals won all but two of the seventy-seven seats with 58 percent of the vote.

The results of several federal and provincial elections of the past decade prompted an assortment of editorialists, pundits, academics, and politicians to call for the replacement of FPTP with a more "proportional" electoral system. It comes as no surprise that electoral reform has surfaced as an issue at the provincial level. Federalism lends itself to a measure of "test-tube" experiments conducted by its component units, for provinces are, by definition, less heterogeneous, less complex, and smaller in both population and territory than the country as a whole. Accordingly, they have a greater capacity to innovate and, should they so wish, to change some of the fundamentals of their system of government. With time, the successful innovations are often adopted by the other jurisdictions. Canada's provinces have a demonstrated history of having been the first order of government to initiate fundamental changes to several key elements of their electoral systems. Manitoba led the pack in granting the vote to women in 1916 and, forty years later, in passing legislation guaranteeing that independent commissions would redraw electoral districts. In 1964, Quebec became the first Canadian jurisdiction to adopt election expenses legislation, and several of the provinces granted the vote to status Indians well before Ottawa did in 1960.

In the past few years, five provinces have undertaken investigations of various kinds to explore alternative methods of election. To date, none of the calls for a different voting method that were made by the provincial commissions, committees, or citizens' assemblies (the types of investigatory bodies varied among the provinces) has led to any changes. Electors in Prince Edward Island and Ontario voted against replacing FPTP with a mixed member proportional (MMP) scheme. In British Columbia, voters in a 2009 province-wide referendum opted to retain the plurality vote instead of adopting STV as recommended by the province's citizens' assembly. This was BC's second referendum on the issue in four years. In the first (2005), a majority of the voters endorsed the plan to replace FPTP with STV, but at 57.4 percent, the approval rate fell short of the 60 percent needed to adopt the change. Proposals to implement a variant of MMP elections in Quebec and New Brunswick have not proceeded to province-wide votes. This no doubt reflects both the uncertainty and diffidence of the government and opposition parties about electoral change and the absence of a strong, organized, and vocal campaign capable of mobilizing public support behind a demand for a different method of voting (Carty 2004; Seidle 2007).

Together, the assorted weaknesses of the plurality vote are seized upon by critics of FPTP as evidence of an electoral institution that contributes to lower voter *participation,* is less *responsive* than more proportional systems as a means for converting votes into seats, and results in legislative assemblies that are less *inclusive* of the range of expressed voter preferences and parties competing in an election.

But as compelling as the arguments may be for replacing the plurality vote with a proportional electoral scheme, it is important to bear in mind that a complicated relationship exists between institutional change and presumed outcomes. The benefits claimed on behalf of electoral change can create unrealistic expectations. For example, it is a commonplace to assert that voter turnout will increase with the switch, and that more women and minorities will be elected under a non-plurality system. Evidence from abroad and from some of the Canadian provinces is mixed on both turnout and gender/minority representation under different election methods, which confirms that improvements cannot be assured solely by modifying an electoral system. Social, cultural, and political variables count every bit as much as institutional ones in changing voter behaviour and legislative representation.

As counterintuitive as this may seem, one can plausibly argue that a proportional electoral scheme would diminish both the ability and the capacity of national party leaders in Canada to fashion broadly based, accommodative, and centrist parties. Parties could see an electoral advantage in becoming more regionally or sectionally based in their support than they are now. If that were the case, the major parties in the national political arena would no longer play the integrative role that they have tried to take throughout Canada's history.

In all, the presumed benefits that would accrue to Canadian politics and government from changing electoral methods cannot be considered, in current jargon, a "slam dunk." (Questions about the possible implications of electoral reform for Canada's national parties are raised more fully in Courtney 1980, 2004, 2005.)

Voter ID

In 2007, after considerable debate in the House of Commons, the Senate, and the Commons Standing Committee on Procedure and House

Affairs, parliament amended the Canada Elections Act to establish a new voter identification requirement for federal elections. For the first time in the history of Canadian elections, voters must now prove their identity and residential address by providing one piece of government-issued photo identification showing both name and home address. Failing that, two pieces of identification authorized by the chief electoral officer are acceptable, so long as both establish the voter's name and one establishes the voter's address. A third option allows the voter to swear an oath and to be vouched for by a registered elector from the same polling division.

In introducing the proposal in the Commons, the minister argued that the change was needed to "bring Canada into line with the system in the province of Quebec" (another illustration of institutional transference in a federal system), to provide "consistency and clarity" in the election law (widely interpreted as code for ensuring that anyone with a concealed face, such as veiled Muslim women, would be required to bare it), and to "reduce the opportunity for electoral fraud" (Canada 2006).

This change amounts to a retrograde move and seems oddly out of keeping with the country's earlier history of gradually more expansive and generous electoral institutions and practices. The record shows that, throughout the twentieth and early twenty-first centuries, there have been few instances in Canada of electoral fraud in the form of electoral impersonation or of voting by non-eligible individuals. Officials from Elections Canada noted that fact in the parliamentary committee examining the voter ID proposal, but to no avail. By international standards, Canada fares well in comparisons of false or illegal voting.

When the new requirement was debated, many of its critics anticipated that it would inflict a hardship on some voters. Elections Canada pointed out that, in most provinces, a driver's licence is the only form of government-issued ID containing name, address, and photo, which would mean that in the order of 15 percent of eligible electors (roughly 3.4 million) would have to fall back on the second or third identification options if they were to vote. For a number of them, these alternatives would not always be practicable. For example, as no elector will be able to vouch for more than one person, it is now impossible for directors of nursing homes, senior citizens' residences, and homeless shelters to vouch for a number of eligible electors at one time, as they had done in the past.

For those reasons, the new voter ID requirement can be called into question by virtue of its potentially negative impact on voting. It is reasonable to assume that, with such additional hurdles to overcome in the voting process, some citizens (it is impossible to know precisely how many) will opt out of the electoral process completely. If so, voter participation rates can be expected to continue their decline.

Once approved by parliament, the new requirement was challenged by several individuals and advocacy groups in British Columbia. The plaintiffs included senior citizen, disabled, homeless, and drug user groups as well as First Nations citizens living in rural reserves or other rural areas without residential addresses. Their challenge was launched under section 3 of the Charter ("right to vote"), and their claim alleged that the new regulation would predictably result in eligible Canadian citizens being refused a ballot (Supreme Court of British Columbia 2008).

The 14 October 2008 federal election confirmed many of the misgivings of the critics. Lacking proper identification papers, or without a registered voter from the same poll to vouch for them, a number of eligible voters who presented themselves at polling stations were unable to cast a ballot. Following the election, Elections Canada admitted that, across the 308 federal constituencies, there had been "inconsistent application" of the new voter identification provision as well as a degree of confusion among local election officials over which pieces of identification entitled electors to vote (Elections Canada 2009, 41-45).

The exact number of Canadian citizens who were adversely affected by the new rule is unknown, as election officials did not keep records of those who were "turned away" at the polls. In a survey conducted after seven federal by-elections held prior to the October 2008 election but after the approval of the new voter ID provision, Elections Canada found that 4.5 percent of voters did not vote, because they lacked proper documentation or were unable to swear an oath and be vouched for at the polls (Elections Canada 2009, 42). Accounts carried by the media and on the Internet in the days following the 14 October general election suggested the numbers were not insignificant. Residents of nursing homes, university students, homeless individuals, and those living temporarily in shelters were among those refused a ballot (CBC News 2008). As voter turnout in the 2008 federal election fell to a new low (58.8 percent), some observers pointed to the voter ID requirement as a possible contributing factor. Parliament would be wise to revisit the issue of voter ID, with the goal of establishing less onerous regulations.

A record number of Canadians were registered to vote in the 2008 election (23,677,639, or 600,000 more than in 2006). Even so, 1 million fewer votes were cast than in the previous election. The 2008 election was the latest in a string in which turnout rates declined. Although participation did rise slightly in the 2006 election (which ended thirteen years of Liberal government and put Stephen Harper's Conservatives in office), voter turnout rates have dropped steadily in Canada since 1988. The 1988 figure (75.8 percent) had been in line with the post-war (1945-84) average turnout of 74.8 percent, but the downward slope since then suggests that a fundamental shift has taken place among the Canadian electorate. (See Figure 5.1 in Chapter 5 for voter turnout levels.)

Declining voter turnout is not unique to Canada. Other Western liberal democracies have experienced much the same phenomenon and for much the same reasons. Lack of interest in politics has become widespread, particularly among younger eligible voters, who, compared with older voters, routinely prefer alternative (often Internet-based) forms of social or civic engagement rather than election participation. But there are a number of "country-specific" reasons in Canada that can be suggested for the drop in turnout. These include the collapse of the Progressive Conservative vote in 1993, the subsequent fragmentation of the national party system and electoral dominance of the Liberals, the widespread public disaffection with federal and provincial politicians, the skepticism among potential voters that their vote is "worth much" and that parties, once in office, will deliver on their promises, and the "decline of deference" to public authorities that has been detected in Canada since the 1990s. (There is a considerable literature on voter turnout in Canada, including Blais, Dobrzynska, and Massicotte 2003; Gidengil et al. 2004; Gidengil et al. Chapter 5 this volume; Pammett and LeDuc 2003.)

Conclusion

Elections in Canada perform a number of essential tasks. They play a central and crucial role in the operation of government and in defining the institutional framework within which day-to-day governing takes place. Both are described by David Docherty (2005, Chapter 4 this volume) and Graham White (2005, Chapter 3 this volume) in their contributions to the Democratic Audit series. Elections ensure that differing political and social views can be organized and expressed, which in turn helps to contribute to a country's political stability and social cohesiveness. The flip side, however, is sometimes all too apparent. Free and democratic elections may work against stability and cohesiveness if certain interests – regional, linguistic, or religious – find that they offer no satisfactory way of expressing their views, of advancing their cause, or of converting electoral support into legislative presence.

Democratic elections do more than flesh out the institutional skeleton of government or enable individual and collective interests to be aggregated and represented. They contribute to the number and configuration of political parties, as William Cross' (2004) contribution to this series reminds us. Parties, having chosen leaders and candidates, are called upon to compete periodically in democratic elections under a set of rules. Ostensibly, the stated intent of most parties is to win office and form the government. But realistically, the best that the great majority of them can hope for is to gain sufficient support to influence the political agenda and public policy. Many parties do not realize even that goal.

When elections operate as theory suggests they should, they contribute to a sense of citizenship. Having cast a vote in a free and democratic election, a citizen should, when an election is over, believe that he or she has made a contribution to society. This is the most elusive and intangible of purposes served by democratic elections, for it clearly involves several calculations, both personal and group, about the meaning that the election results convey to citizens. Yet, it is also the most critically important purpose that elections can serve, which makes the decline in recent federal and provincial voter turnout a cause for concern.

No electoral system is neutral. Canada's current franchise laws distinguish between residents of this country according to age and citizenship. District boundaries create communities of interest, which differ from those that would have been created had the lines been drawn another way. Voter registration systems vary in their ability to capture eligible electors. The way in which votes are converted into seats affects the composition of governing institutions, the concept of representation, the number and type of political parties, and ultimately, the content of public policies. In the final analysis, how the institutions of our electoral system are configured directly affects our understanding of democracy. Thus, it is critical for the health of a democratic regime such as Canada's to create a set of election laws and regulations that safeguards citizens' electoral rights and at the same time ensures regular and open competition between the parties and candidates.

An election has been described as a game "designed to constrain the action of its players" (Massicotte, Blais, and Yoshinaka 2004, 158). That only partly describes what democratic elections are about, as Canada demonstrates. This country has come a considerable distance at both the federal and provincial levels in designing a game in which the major players (parties and candidates) are constrained. But it has also made great strides in ensuring that the participants (voters) are able to make their choices within a set of institutional arrangements that are inclusive, responsive, and independent of outside influence. Of the five pillars, or building blocks, of Canadian elections discussed here, four have gone through a major transformation from what they were at Confederation. By any comparative standard, Canada has established a set of prized electoral institutions and practices: a universal franchise free of arbitrarily disqualified categories of voters, a widely inclusive registry of electors, a non-partisan and participatory method for redistributing parliamentary districts, and an enviable cadre of election officials capable of managing largely faultless elections and of responding to the variable requirements of an increasingly diverse population.

The plurality vote, as contentious as it remains as a means of aggregating votes and converting them into legislative seats, is the clear outlier of the five building blocks. Little has changed about FPTP since 1867, and perhaps as a result plurality voting has a demonstrated capacity to generate considerable debate among observers and participants over the presumed benefits of alternative methods of voting. Thus, there is no agreement among critics and supporters on a common solution to the readily identified problems of the plurality vote. Without agreement, FPTP will remain the unreformed electoral building block in Canada.

In the voter ID requirement adopted in 2007, parliament may have created an unnecessary impediment to voter participation by otherwise eligible electors. Detailed and reliable counts of voters who were turned away at polling stations because they lacked the necessary documentation are unavailable, but post-election media accounts point to a problem with the current law. Parliament, as was suggested earlier, may want to revisit the issue. As matters now stand, the 2007 ID requirement provides an odd contrast to what has marked the development of the Canadian electoral regime since Confederation – increasingly accessible, supportive, and inclusive electoral institutions.

Works Cited

Auditor General of Canada. 2009. *Managing identity information.* Ottawa: Office of the Auditor General of Canada.

Black, Jerome H. 2000. *The national register of electors: Raising questions about the new approach to voter registration in Canada.* Montreal: Institute for Research on Public Policy.

–. 2002. The permanent voters list vs. voter enumeration. Paper presented at the "Transparency, Disclosure and Democracy Conference," Ottawa, 27 February.

–. 2003. From enumeration to the national register of electors: An account and an evaluation. *Choices* (Institute for Research on Public Policy) 9(7).

Blais, André, Agnieszka Dobrzynska, and Louis Massicotte. 2003. Why is turnout higher in some countries than in others? Elections Canada. http://www.elections. ca/.

Canada. 2006. Debate on 2nd reading of Bill C-31, An act to amend the Canada Elections Act and the Public Service Employment Act. *House of Commons debates* (7 November). (Rob Nicholson, MP).

Canadian Disability Rights Council v. *Canada,* [1988] 3 F.C. 622 (T.D.).

Carty, R. Kenneth. 2004. Doing democracy differently: Has electoral reform finally arrived? Twentieth annual Timlin Lecture, University of Saskatchewan, Saskatoon, 1 March.

CBC News. 2008. New ID rules cause confusion at polls. CBC News. http://www.cbc.ca/news/.

Courtney, John. 1980. Reflections on reforming the Canadian electoral system. *Canadian Public Administration* 23(3): 427-57.

–. 2001. *Commissioned ridings: Designing Canada's electoral districts.* Montreal and Kingston: McGill-Queen's University Press.

—. 2004. *Elections.* Canadian Democratic Audit. Vancouver: UBC Press.

—. 2005. Is talk of electoral reform just whistling in the wind? In *Strengthening Canadian democracy,* ed. Paul Hose, Richard Johnston, and André Blais, 149-58. Montreal: Institute for Research in Public Policy.

Courtney, John C., and David E. Smith. 1991. Registering voters: Canada in a comparative context. In *Democratic rights and electoral reform,* ed. Michael Cassidy, 343-461. Vol. 10 of *Research studies for the Royal Commission on Electoral Reform and Party Financing.* Toronto: Dundurn Press.

Cross, William. 2004. *Political parties.* Canadian Democratic Audit. Vancouver: UBC Press.

Docherty, David. 2005. *Legislatures.* Canadian Democratic Audit. Vancouver: UBC Press.

Economist Intelligence Unit. 2008. *Index of Democracy 2008.* New York: Economist Intelligence Unit.

Elections Canada. 2001. *Report of the chief electoral officer of Canada on the 37th general election held on November 27, 2000.* Ottawa: Elections Canada.

–. 2008. Information provided on 17 November 2008 to the author by Elections Canada. Estimates based on the preliminary list of electors for the October 2008 federal election.

—. 2009. *Report of the chief electoral officer of Canada on the 40th general election of October 14, 2008.* Ottawa: Elections Canada.

Gidengil, Elisabeth, André Blais, Neil Nevitte, and Richard Nadeau. 2004. *Citizens.* Canadian Democratic Audit. Vancouver: UBC Press.

Handley, Lisa, and Bernard Grofman, eds. 2008. *Redistricting in comparative perspective.* New York: Oxford University Press.

Massicotte, Louis, André Blais, and Antoine Yoshinaka. 2004. *Establishing the rules of the game.* Toronto: University of Toronto Press.

Muldoon v. *Canada,* [1988] 3 F.C. 628 (T.D.).

Pal, Michael, and Sujit Choudry. 2007. Is every vote equal? Visible minority vote dilu-tion in Canada. *Choices* (Institute for Research on Public Policy) 13(1).

Pammett, Jon H., and Larry LeDuc. 2003. Explaining the turnout decline in Canadian federal elections: A new survey of non-voters. Elections Canada. http://www.elections.ca/.

Persily, Nathaniel. 2005. Forty years in the political thicket: Judicial review of the redistricting process since *Reynolds v. Sims*. In *Party lines: Competition, parti-sanship, and congressional redistricting,* ed. Thomas E. Mann and Bruce E. Cain, 67-91. Washington, DC: Brookings Institution Press.

Privacy Commissioner of Canada. 2009. *Privacy management frameworks of selected federal institutions.* Ottawa: Office of the Privacy Commissioner of Canada.

Rakove, Jack N., ed. 2001. *The unfinished election of 2000.* New York: Basic Books.

Sauvé v. *Canada (Chief Electoral Officer),* 2002 SCC 68.

Seidle, F. Leslie. 2007. Provincial electoral systems in question: Changing views of party representation and governance. In *Canadian parties in transition,* 3rd ed., ed. Alain-G. Gagnon and A. Brian Tanquay, 303-34. Peterborough: Broadview Press.

Smith, David. 1991. Federal voter enumeration in Canada: An assessment. In *Regis-tering voters: A comparative perspective,* ed. John C. Courtney, 35-40. Cambridge, MA: Center for International Affairs, Harvard University.

Supreme Court of British Columbia. 2008. Writ of summons and statement of claim between Rose Henry, *et al.* and the attorney general of Canada and the chief elec-toral officer of Canada. Vancouver Registry. 30 January.

Ward, Norman. 1950. *Canadian House of Commons: Representation.* Toronto: Univer-sity of Toronto Press.

White, Graham. 2002. Sandbagging the permanent voters' list. Paper presented at the "Transparency, Disclosure and Democracy Conference," Ottawa, 27 February.

–. 2005. *Cabinets and first ministers.* Canadian Democratic Audit. Vancouver: UBC Press.

POLITICAL PARTIES

William Cross

7

Canada's political parties exist to enhance the democratic capacity of a large geographically dispersed society. There are too many Canadians, living too far apart, to routinely allow for unmediated citizen participation in the governing and legislating enterprises. Instead, Canadians elect representatives whom they charge with fulfilling these tasks on their behalf. Political parties are the glue that structures our electoral politics, unites parliamentarians from the regions, and provides a bridge between regular citizens and their governing institutions and elites.

In terms of the Democratic Audit, our primary interests are in determining how successful parties are in facilitating the participation of Canadians in the country's democratic life and in organizing disparate interests into a national concern. The Audit's benchmarks of responsiveness, inclusiveness, and participation are used to organize a discussion of the parties' strengths and weaknesses. Concerns for more responsive, inclusive, and participatory parties are balanced with traditional demands for Canadian parties to privilege an accommodative and brokerage style of politics. The latter approach is typically presented as necessarily exclusive and elite dominated, and thus is often viewed as an obstacle to a more democratically organized party politics. I return to this theme in the concluding section, arguing that it is a false dichotomy.

The emphasis here is on the extra-parliamentary parties. Legislatures and governments are considered in David Docherty (2005, Chapter 4 this volume) and Graham White (2005, Chapter 3 this volume).

Responsiveness

Like so many of Canada's political institutions (such as parliament, cabinet, and federalism), political parties are organized to provide voice to Canada's regional interests. Responding to the imperatives of a geographically organized electoral system, all of Canada's parties use local constituency associations as their organizational building blocks (Carty and Eagles 2005). As far as responsiveness is concerned, their greatest strength lies in their recognition of regional interests.

Partisans join and participate in parties through locally organized constituency associations, and the parties' internal structures ensure representation of geographic constituencies in important party decision making. For example, the vast majority of delegates to party conventions represent local associations. A smaller number may be chosen to represent "identity" interests such as a party's female and youth members, but these groups too are often organized territorially. The result is that regional interests are well represented within each of the extra-parliamentary party's decision-making processes.

This is consistent with the traditional brokerage nature of Canada's governing parties, the Liberals and Conservatives. As the governing task has almost always been consumed by the challenge of knitting together divergent regional demands into a common national interest, these parties have always been keen to ensure that regional voices are heard. Thus, both parties have representation from each province on their national decision-making bodies enshrined in their constitution. At party conventions, each local constituency association is represented by an equal number of delegates. In leadership contests, each constituency receives an equal share of the vote. The result is that each geographic component of the federation has a proportionate voice in party decision making even at the expense of equality among members.

All parties have their regions of strength and weakness, which results in dramatically different numbers of members in local constituencies. A local Conservative Party association in Alberta, for example, may have three thousand members, whereas its Quebec cousin may have a few dozen. Similarly, an Alberta Liberal association may have fewer than one hundred members, whereas its Toronto counterpart has several thousand. In both parties, weak and vibrant local associations are provided equal voice in party decision making to ensure that regional voices from areas of party weakness are not drowned out by those from areas of electoral strength. This is manifest in party leadership selection processes. Although the two parties have used differing processes, one common element is the allocation of an equal number of votes to each constituency association regardless of how many individual members actually participate in the leadership vote. The result is that a constituency with twenty partisans has equal voice to that with two thousand (Stewart and Carty 2002).

From time to time, the main parties have been challenged by the emergence of parties that do not share this strength of commitment to regional representation and are not committed to the brokerage principle. The most enduring of these is the New Democratic Party; other recent examples include Reform and the Canadian Alliance. The New Democrats calibrate representation at party conventions according to the number of members in a local party association, which results in significant regional disparities (Archer and Whitehorn 1997). Similarly, in leadership contests, all members' votes count equally, so the association with few members has less influence than the one with many. The Bloc Québécois organizes only in Quebec and makes no pretence of being responsive to concerns from outside the province.

At times, voters in some areas of the country have argued that their interests are not well represented by the established parties. Parties devoted to the interests of the Western provinces and to Quebec nationalists have arisen in response to these criticisms. Examples here are the Progressives in the 1920s, Reform in the 1990s, and the current Bloc Québécois. The regional impulses of the electoral system facilitate the success of parties articulating regional interests (Cairns 1968;

Courtney, Chapter 6 this volume; Carty, Cross, and Young 2000). Thus, though individual parties may not always fully reflect the panoply of regional interests, the party system as a whole typically does.

If regional representation is one of the strengths of our extra-parliamentary parties, a weakness is the absence of any institutional opportunity for activists to exert meaningful influence over the parties' policy directions. Canada's governing parties have traditionally taken the position that policy making is a function of the parliamentary party, with only a weak advisory role assigned to the extra-parliamentary membership. Citing their brokerage function, the Liberals and Conservatives have long argued that, because they are national parties wishing to govern, their primary task is to conciliate among regional and provincial concerns in seeking a national interest that transcends the cleavages dividing Canadians. This, they assert, can be accomplished only by restricting policy making to small groups of elites who can engage in the kinds of closed-door bargaining required to reach these accommodations.

Parties in government, arguing that they represent all voters and not solely their partisans, have traditionally been the most distant from their members in terms of policy making; both the Liberals and Conservatives have been largely consistent in this regard. For example, the latest incarnation of the Conservative Party was created, chose a leader, and waged an election campaign all before holding any policy consultation with its members. Similarly, when the Liberals were removed from office in 2006 and long-time party activists such as Tom Axworthy suggested that a major rethinking of Liberal policy was overdue, the party mostly ignored these views and instead sought rejuvenation through selection of a new leader (for a longer discussion of this subject, see Axworthy 2009). When the parties have engaged in policy consultation processes, these have often resulted in increased cynicism among their members as, invariably, the parliamentary leadership has moved to distance itself from the recommendations of the activist party (see, for example, Clarkson 1979; Cross 2007).

Unlike their equivalents in many European states, none of the Canadian parties has a policy foundation; nor do they have an ongoing commitment of resources to policy development. Their extra-parliamentary branches are essentially campaign service operations meant to support the parliamentary parties' electoral efforts. The parties' central offices do not routinely employ policy analysts; nor do they spend any substantial time between election campaigns considering and developing new policy alternatives. Party policy platforms are written by small groups of advisors surrounding the leader and often take on the appearance of being crafted late in the day during the run-up to an election campaign. Emblematic of this was the Conservative Party's release of its platform just days before the 2008 vote, a month after the election call was precipitated by its leadership. Despite controlling the timing of the election, the party appears to have entered the campaign without a set of policy prescriptions to offer voters and without engaging its supporters in any dialogue about future policy direction.

There is evidence that this lack of opportunity for partisans to exercise policy influence results in a decline in activism within parties. Surveys of party members indicate that they are dissatisfied with their opportunities to discuss policy within their parties and with their lack of collective clout in influencing policy direction (Cross 2004). Similarly, they believe their parties to be overly hierarchical, with leaders and their entourages of campaign professionals exercising too much control over decision making. This sentiment may be strongest among the youngest cohort of voters. In unprecedented numbers, these voters are turning away from political parties and choosing to participate through advocacy groups and in other forms of direct, less traditional political involvement such as protest marches (O'Neill 2001).

Although membership in political parties among those younger than thirty is dramatically lower than that for older cohorts and appears to be declining over time, the same cannot be said for youth activity in other types of political participation. For example, young Canadians are the only group of voters more likely to belong to an interest group than to a political party. When the attitudes of young Canadians who reject parties in favour of more direct advocacy are probed, it becomes clear that they see parties as hierarchical institutions with little opportunity for regular members to exercise any meaningful policy influence.

The most stark example of this is found in a study by William Cross and Lisa Young (2008) in which university students who belonged to advocacy groups ranked the effectiveness of various types of activity in achieving political change. These young activists ranked joining a political party as the least efficacious of the six activities they were offered, placing it below signing a petition and supporting a boycott. In large part, this reflects their perception that rank-and-file members have little opportunity to influence the policy directions and priorities of parties.

Inclusiveness

The representation of various constituent groups of Canadians in our democratic institutions has both symbolic and substantive importance (Pitkin 1967). From a symbolic perspective, greater legitimacy attaches to policy decisions when voters see themselves reflected in their democratic institutions, allowing them to feel that their interests are represented in the decision-making process. From a substantive perspective, there is compelling evidence that the inclusion of representatives from various groups brings different styles, life experiences, and priorities to democratic decision making (see, for example, Arscott and Trimble 1997). In short, diversity in democratic institutions ensures that varying perspectives are heard and that issues of concern to all Canadians are raised at the decision-making table.

Our political parties have not been particularly successful in representing the diversity of Canadian society. To illustrate this point, I briefly examine the cases of ethnicity and gender by considering the representation of these groups within party memberships and their inclusion among the candidate pools offered by the parties in general elections. On both these counts, the parties are found wanting.

Party memberships are disproportionately male and under-representative of new immigrant communities. In terms of gender, though women make up a majority of the population, William Cross and

Lisa Young (2004) found that approximately six in ten party members were male; these findings are consistent with surveys of the general population, which report that significantly more men than women have belonged to a political party (Howe and Northrup 2000). Lisa Young and William Cross (2003) suggest that this is consistent with women's expression of greater confidence in interest groups than in political parties as vehicles for achieving meaningful change. In part, this reflects their views of parties as overly hierarchical and partisan, resulting in their preference to channel their political and community activism through advocacy groups in which they find a more egalitarian and less partisan environment.

Not only do fewer women than men belong to parties, they also tend to be less active and are less likely to hold positions of influence. Female members spend considerably less time engaged in party activity than do their male counterparts and are significantly less likely to hold a party office (at the constituency or national level) and to have sought their party's nomination to stand as a candidate in a general election. The findings of Young and Cross (2003) are consistent with those of Sylvia Bashevkin (1993), which led her to conclude that female party activists were overrepresented in positions of low prestige and influence (such as local association secretaries) and under-represented in influential positions (such as party executive committees, general election candidates, and campaign managers). The situation does not appear to have changed dramatically in the intervening years.

The shifting demographics of Canadian society, resulting from ever-diverse patterns of immigration, are not reflected in the parties' activist base. The 2006 census found that 16 percent of Canadians were visible minorities and that among the most common countries of origin for the millions of immigrants admitted in recent years were China, India, the Philippines, Pakistan, Iran, South Korea, Colombia, and Sri Lanka (Statistics Canada 2008). Formally, the parties encourage the participation of new arrivals as none of them requires citizenship for membership. Nonetheless, Cross and Young (2004) found that 99 percent of members were Canadian citizens, that the vast majority (nine in ten) were born in Canada, and that very few were drawn from the ethnic minority community. For party members, the most common countries of ancestry are Britain, Ireland, France, Germany, Austria, Russia, and Scandinavia; very few members come from the homelands of many recent immigrants, including Africa and Asia.

The under-representation of women and Canadians from new immigrant communities is also apparent in the pools of candidates nominated by the parties. The most recent comprehensive data on the nomination of visible minorities are found in Jerome Black and Bruce Hicks' (2006) study of the 2004 election. They reported that, though visible minorities made up 15 percent of the general population, only about 9 percent of the candidates nominated by the major parties came from this demographic. On the positive side, they found that, generally speaking, visible minorities were not ghettoized to unwinnable ridings but were as likely as other candidates to be nominated in a riding where their party had a chance of electoral success. This partially results from the parties' perception that, in communities with large numbers of new immigrants, visible minority candidates are potential vote getters. Black and Hicks (2006) and Livianna Tossutti and T.P. Najem (2002) found that parties were more likely to run minority candidates in ridings with significant visible minority communities.

The situation is both similar and different for female candidates. Although their numbers increased somewhat in the 2008 election, women continue to be dramatically under-represented in the candidate pools of all the parties, ranging from 37 percent of Liberal candidates to just one in five Conservatives. These numbers can be deceiving, however, as unlike visible minorities, women tend to be nominated disproportionately in ridings where their parties have little chance for success. For example, in Alberta, a province in which the Liberal Party had no real prospect of winning any seats, fifteen of the twenty-eight Liberal candidates were female. Overall, slightly more than one-third of Conservative female candidates were elected, compared with half of their male counterparts, and 16 percent of female Liberal candidates won a seat, whereas more than one-quarter of their male equivalents did so.

Both the Bloc and New Democrats have done a better job in recent elections of nominating women in equal numbers with men in winnable ridings.

The evidence suggests that, when women seek political office, neither party members, who choose nominees, nor voters, who exercise the franchise, discriminate against them (Cross 2004, 69; Carty and Erickson 1991, 147). Rather, their under-representation seems to result from the relatively small numbers of women seeking nominations in winnable ridings. Of course, this may well reflect more subtle patterns of discrimination among local and national party elites in terms of not aggressively encouraging and recruiting female candidacies in these constituencies. The under-representation of women in local party executive associations may influence the low numbers of female candidacies as these party elites often run themselves or play an important gate-keeping role by seeking out potential candidates and encouraging them to stand.

That parties have not done a satisfactory job of recruiting female candidates in the constituencies where they are most competitive can be illustrated by examining the thirty-seven ridings in the 2008 election where an incumbent MP was retiring. Eleven of these retiring incumbents were women. If the parties truly were committed to increasing the number of female MPs, incumbent parties would have nominated more women in these ridings in 2008 since all were guaranteed to produce a new MP, and the incumbent party was almost certain to be competitive. Instead, the number remained static at eleven. Sixteen MPs elected as Liberals in 2006 were retiring (five of them women) and they were replaced with ten male and six female Liberal candidates. Thirteen MPs elected as Conservatives in 2006 retired (two of them female) and the party replaced them with three female and ten male candidates. Perhaps most telling was the situation in the five ridings where a female Liberal MP was retiring. In all five of these ridings, the party nominated a man for the 2008 election. Given this, it is not surprising that, though the overall number of female candidates nominated by the parties increased significantly in 2008, the number of female MPs remained static, as it has for the past two decades.

Participation

In the absence of meaningful opportunity to contribute to policy making, personnel recruitment contests draw the largest numbers of partisans to party activity. Tens of thousands of Canadians take part in contests to choose the party candidates for general elections and to select their leaders. Evaluating levels of participation in these events presents the classic "is the glass half full or half empty" conundrum. Although, as far as party involvement is concerned, more Canadians participate in this form of activity than in any other, I have elsewhere been highly critical of the parties for establishing rules and norms that limit accessibility and unnecessarily restrict the numbers who can take part in these most consequential contests (for example, Cross 2004).

These are the most important events carried out by our political parties. In selecting leaders, parties are choosing the two or three individuals from among whom Canadians will select a prime minister. And in some instances, these contests directly result in the selection of a prime minister, as in the relatively recent cases of John Turner, Kim Campbell, and Paul Martin. Similarly, in choosing parliamentary candidates, parties significantly narrow the options open to Canadians as virtually all MPs are first nominated by one of the major parties (Cross 2006, 2008). Because Canada uses the single-member plurality electoral system, voters in a general election have no choice in the selection of a candidate from their preferred party – the decision is fully made at the nomination stage. This explains why many Canadians who never before (and often never again) have involved themselves in party affairs are drawn to one of these events.

A picture of party membership levels in Canada typically shows low, flat lines interrupted by sharp, short-lived spikes, which are followed by steep decline and another flat line – the spikes represent recruitment during leadership and candidate selection races (Carty, Cross, and Young

2000). It is not uncommon for a party's membership to increase by two or three times during a leadership contest, and local party associations with a hundred or fewer activists can find themselves swamped with several hundred or even a few thousand members in the most contested local nomination battles. Inevitably, membership dramatically declines afterward, returning to its typically low levels. And, as noted by Elisabeth Gidengil et al. (Chapter 5 this volume), Canadian parties are not unique in attracting low levels of members: this is a common fate of parties in many contemporary Western democracies (Dalton and Wattenberg 2000).

The peak membership numbers sometimes attracted to leadership and candidate selection races can seem impressive, but it is important to remind ourselves that they represent a very small percentage of voters. Although there is no obvious way to calculate participation rates in these contests, the best method is to compare the proportion of voters who generally support a particular party with that which votes in one of these competitions. As individual Canadians never universally publicize their party preferences, we require a proxy for this information. Voter behaviour in the prior federal election is perhaps the best indicator of general support for a party. For example, we can estimate that the pool of potential partisans available for involvement in a party leadership race is roughly equal to the number of voters who supported that party in the prior election. Obviously, this is not a perfect estimate, but it allows for a benchmark approximation of how many of a party's supporters are attracted to participation.

When calculated in this manner, participation rates in party leadership contests are abysmally low. Although, from party to party, the numbers who take part in leadership races range from fewer than 50,000 to more than 125,000, the percentage of each party's voters in the prior election who participate is remarkably consistent (Cross and Crysler 2009). For illustrative purposes, consider the most recent leadership contest that resulted in the direct selection of a prime minister – that of 2003, which was won by Liberal Paul Martin. This is not the case of an opposition party choosing a leader who may never become prime minister, but rather of a long-time governing party, well ahead in the polls, selecting a leader who was certain to become prime minister and likely to remain so for some time. Nonetheless, the participation rate was dismally low. The party highlighted the fact that its membership levels grew dramatically in the lead-up to the vote, as candidates and would-be candidates recruited supporters to party membership. Indeed, the levels rose to slightly more than half a million, what may be an all-time high. Nonetheless, only one-quarter of these members voted in the contest, which represented 2.5 percent of the total votes received by the party in the 2000 election and 2.6 percent of those it garnered in the 2004 election. The Liberals' 2003 experience is consistent with that of all the federal parties whose participation rates in recent leadership contests have consistently been in the 2 to 3 percent range (Cross 2004).

By contrast, we find significantly higher participation rates in US presidential primaries. In 2008, 58 million Americans voted in a presidential primary election for one of the two major parties. This represents approximately 46 percent of that year's general election voters. The US case illustrates how the rules governing accessibility of the process affect participation rates. Individual states have the option of holding either a primary or caucus election. Primaries are similar in format to general elections, whereas caucuses are party-organized meetings that partisans must attend in order to vote. Caucuses typically take place at a specific time (as opposed to day-long voting) and require a greater commitment from the voter than does voting in a primary. This is reflected in participation rates: as is illustrated by the 2008 data from Iowa and New Hampshire, states that hold primaries realize significantly higher turnout than those using the caucus method. Both Iowa and New Hampshire were hotly contested by candidates for the Republican and Democratic presidential nominations, and their votes were held just days apart. New Hampshire has one of the country's most accessible primary processes, whereas Iowa uses the caucus method. Approximately 53 percent of eligible voters participated in the New Hampshire primary, compared with 16 percent in the Iowa caucuses, a difference that is typical of those found between primary and caucus states (Pew Center 2008).

This is relevant to Canada as our parties use leadership nomination processes that are more restrictive and less accessible than any employed in the US. The hurdles to participation are made apparent by reviewing the 2006 Liberal case, in which Stéphane Dion was chosen as leader. Those who wished to participate in the process were required to join the party by 4 July 2006, even though the selection itself occurred some months later, during a party convention in December. Anyone joining the party after 4 July, perhaps attracted by media attention to the race, was not eligible to vote. Those joining by 4 July were required to pay a membership fee and travel to a single location in their constituency to cast their ballot. Many constituencies are geographically large, often requiring significant travel. We can contrast this situation with general election voting in which the state takes on the obligation of compiling a permanent voters' list, charges no fee for voting, allows registration at the polling place on election day, and organizes hundreds of polls in each constituency. Given the barriers to accessibility, it is not surprising that so relatively few Canadians participate in leadership elections.

One Canadian party at the provincial level has come close to replicating the US primary process for selection of its leaders – the Alberta Conservative Party (Stewart 1997). It allows same-day registration, organizes multiple polling booths in each constituency, and facilitates advance voting. Although it does charge a five-dollar voting fee, this leadership selection process is by far the most accessible of those used in the country, which is reflected in participation rates of as much as ten times greater than those realized in other parties.

The situation is similar for candidate nomination contests. All the parties hold nomination meetings at a single location in each constituency, which their dues-paying members need to attend in order to be eligible to vote. Meetings do not occur at a standard date in all constituencies: in fact, the dates vary dramatically. For the October 2008 election, some nomination meetings took place as early as 2006, whereas others were held only weeks before the election. Although every election includes a few examples of highly publicized nomination contests attracting a few thousand members, these are the rare exceptions. The vast majority of candidate selection contests draw a couple of hundred or fewer voters.

Local voters are not always given the opportunity to select their candidate. In recent elections, the national leadership of the major parties has increasingly involved itself in the "local" candidate selection process and in a growing number of cases has dictated the selection of a particular candidate without allowing local party members to vote on the subject (Cross 2006).

These restrictive rules for party candidate and leadership selection are permitted because these contests are largely unregulated by the state. Rules governing general elections, which would never allow these kinds of obstacles to be imposed on voters, do not apply as the state essentially views these elections as internal party affairs. This approach is hard to justify, considering the importance of these events.

Low participation rates in some nomination contests probably reflect a party's poor competitive position in the constituency. Would-be candidates are unlikely to expend the resources and energy necessary to recruit large numbers of members to win a nomination in a constituency where their party has little chance of electing an MP. Similarly, voters, with competing demands on their time, are probably less interested and thus less inclined to participate in nomination contests in these "no hope" constituencies. This constitutes a larger problem concerning the relationship between participation and the electoral system. Much has been written on the connection between voter turnout and the relative proportionality of an electoral system, but little attention has been paid to its relationship with participation in party affairs.

Party constituency associations with no hope of electing an MP have fairly meaningless nomination contests (quite often, as Sayers 1998 points out, the party scrambles to find a sacrificial candidate). Furthermore, partisans have little incentive to actively participate in election campaigns. Our parties are most visible during a campaign, and opportunities for participation are most obvious. Vibrant campaigns are dependent on volunteers to knock on doors, watch the polls on election days, conduct phone banks, erect yard signs, and engage in the many other activities that are part of local campaigns (Carty and Eagles 2005). However, in the zero-sum game that is the single-member plurality electoral system, partisans have little incentive to work hard for their favoured party if it stands no chance of receiving the most votes in their constituency. Improving their vote total by 10 percent or their relative standing from fourth to second is of no real consequence. The campaign finance regime offers modest incentive for parties to maximize their vote totals, but whether this works to motivate local party supporters is not at all apparent.

Reforms

The menu of possible reforms of Canada's parties is extensive, but I focus here on four proposals that would encourage more Canadians to participate in parties. Each of these measures would better connect our parties to civil society and strengthen their capacity to achieve enduring accommodations in public decision making.

All of these reforms reflect the view of parties as the "public utilities" of our politics (van Biezen 2004). It is neither surprising nor contradictory that, though Canadians in large numbers express negative feelings toward their parties, they overwhelmingly believe that these same institutions are essential to a well-functioning democracy (Cross 2004, 4). They recognize that a large, complex, and diverse society such as twenty-first-century Canada requires political parties, but they simply do not think the parties are doing an adequate job of reflecting them and their interests in their decision-making processes. Canadian parties are largely wards of the state, more dependent than ever on taxpayer subsidies to support their activities, and they reside in a privileged world in which they receive favoured treatment in our electoral and parliamentary regimes. In turn, citizens have every right to demand that their conduct is consistent with prevailing democratic values and norms.

POLICY FOUNDATIONS

One of the principal reasons that so few Canadians participate in political parties is that they do not believe this to be an effective method of influencing public policy. In many ways, this is a rational assessment. As discussed above, Canada's major parties typically spend little time on policy study and development, preferring instead to focus on other aspects of electoral preparation. The cost of this neglect extends beyond low levels of voter interest in party activism to a party politics that is often devoid of serious discussion of policy alternatives. The creation of party-operated policy foundations would go a considerable way toward addressing this situation.

Many European parties organize foundations that are charged with ongoing study of public policy and development, as well as the consideration of policy alternatives. When well operated, they can provide many benefits. These include encouraging citizens interested in public policy to view parties as vehicles for public engagement, preparing detailed policy analyses for the parliamentary parties, assisting parties in the transition from opposition to government, involving – at an arm's length from a party's electoral activities – policy experts who might otherwise abstain from partisan activity, and affording an opportunity for policy discussion in a less partisan-charged environment that encourages consideration of the kinds of compromises and accommodations required in Canada.

Policy consideration that is left to think-tanks, advocacy groups, and academics working in isolation is often devoid of the political realities demanded by the practice of brokerage politics. If party policy foundations are run separately from the parliamentary party, they can bring together the serious ongoing consideration of public policy with the realities of politics and governing, and do so one step removed from the cut-and-thrust of daily partisan machinations such as parliamentary question period. These foundations can also ensure the representation of all stakeholders in policy discussions, something essential to successful brokerage practice and not often achieved in the parliamentary parties, which often lack balance on many dimensions including region, gender, and ethnicity (see Docherty, Chapter 4 this volume). Parties might well be required to direct a percentage of their public receipts toward the operation of such foundations.

MORE DIVERSE RECRUITMENT

There is no denying that our parties do not reflect the face of a modern, diverse civil society. In their membership, their candidates for public office, and their elected representatives, they continue to be dominated by older white men. This both alienates Canadians who do not see themselves reflected in this group and artificially limits the range and scope of policy discourse. Parties can do a much better job of reaching out to traditionally under-represented groups, such as women and visible minorities, and encouraging them to participate both at the constituency level and the highest levels of internal party affairs. There is compelling evidence that, at the local level, parties are to a significant extent closed shops, with the traditional method of recruitment being invitation by friends and family (Young and Cross 2002). As a result, they inevitably attract members who share the socio-economic and demographic traits of their existing activist base. In order to break out of this pattern, parties need to build stronger roots in ethnic communities – particularly those representing countries sending large numbers of new Canadians to our cities.

Similarly, parties need to do more to encourage women and young Canadians to become involved in their activities and to seek public office. Experience in Canada and abroad confirms that active candidate recruitment among under-represented communities can make a significant difference in increasing the numbers from these groups who seek party and public office. To put it simply, those encouraged to do so by party leaders and supported with the necessary resources are more likely to engage than are those left to their own devices. A portion of the public financing that parties receive might well be tied to the number of women and visible minorities they both nominate and elect to office. Women and visible minorities are under-represented in our parliament because they are not nominated in sufficient numbers in ridings that parties are likely to win. Similar incentives can be implemented to encourage the inclusion of these under-represented groups on local party executives, which often serve as a pathway to general election candidacy.

Lacking inclusive representation within parties, Canadians who do not see themselves reflected in those decision-making bodies that are dominated by party personnel (such as cabinet, caucus, parliament, and first ministers' meetings) are likely to reject any accommodations reached as illegitimate and unresponsive to their concerns.

More Accessible and Transparent Personnel Recruitment

The selection of party leaders and candidates for public office should be conducted in a manner fully consistent with the democratic norms that dictate the operation of general elections as these intraparty contests are no less consequential. In the case of leadership selection, at a minimum, the party competitions narrow the field of potential prime ministers to just two or three Canadians and not infrequently result in the immediate selection of a prime minister. Candidate selection is no less significant. With rare exceptions, party nominations are the exclusive path to elected office at the federal and provincial levels. The regionalization of our party system means that, in many constituencies, the choice of an MP is effectively made at the nomination stage. Prime examples of this are federal Conservative Party nominations in Alberta, where victory in the general election is all but ensured.

There is no compelling reason that participation in these contests should be more restrictive and burdensome than is general election voting. Requirements of travel to a single voting location in each constituency, limited voting times, and payment of a membership fee, along with early registration cut-off dates and a lack of systematic scheduling, make these events opaque and inaccessible to the average voter. The evidence cited above from the United States presidential primaries and the experience of the Alberta Conservative Party with an open, accessible leadership selection process provide compelling proof that the rules governing these proceedings do influence participation rates. A recent democratic reform initiative in New Brunswick recommended steps to ensure transparency and accessibility in these intraparty contests (New Brunswick Commission on Legislative Democracy 2004). Many of these recommendations, such as a prohibition on unilateral candidate appointments by party leaders, standardized timing for nomination elections, and requirements of adequate publicity and minimal cut-off deadlines, would greatly improve the situation. Additionally, charging a party membership fee to vote amounts to little more than a poll tax, something that would be widely deemed unfathomable in a general election and that is no more justifiable in a leadership or nomination vote. These are not private party events: rather, they are key components of our electoral process. If the parties are unable or unwilling to reform their behaviour, Elections Canada should be mandated to oversee them and ensure that these contests are conducted in a manner fully consistent with the democratic expectations of Canadians.

PROPORTIONAL REPRESENTATION

Our electoral system dictates that parties focus their energy and resources on a relatively small number of geographic constituencies, largely ignoring the remainder. It also makes electoral effort by activists in most local party associations essentially inconsequential. In most electoral districts, only one or two parties have a realistic chance of winning a plurality of the vote and thus of reaping any electoral reward for their labours. Two sets of behaviour rationally flow from this. First, the national parties provide little in the way of resources to all but a few dozen targeted constituencies and, in terms of attracting volunteers and conducting a lively election campaign, have only passing interest in how many of the others are faring. Second, local volunteers know that little is to be gained by working hard for a party whose candidate has no chance of winning the constituency and thus are discouraged from participation. In many parts of the country, the result is both a dampening of party activism and a lack of national campaign presence at the grassroots level.

A change to a more proportional electoral system would have many implications, but two are most relevant here. Parties would have an incentive to compete aggressively throughout the country. They could not tailor their messages exclusively to, and focus their resources almost entirely on, a small number of constituencies but would have their number of elected representatives determined by all voters from all parts of Canada. This would encourage parties to take a pan-Canadian approach to campaigning and to work toward having vital campaign organizations in each electoral district. Local partisans would see a real consequence to their efforts in every constituency. Whether their local candidate is assured of victory or has no chance of finishing first, incremental increases in vote share would result in improved parliamentary representation for their party. Electoral system reform is a complicated subject (see Courtney, Chapter 6 this volume), but debates about its relative merits need to consider the stifling effects of the current system on local party activism and the parties' approach to nationwide campaigning.

Political Parties and a Democratic Canada

There is little doubt that political parties are the public utilities of our democracy. They nominate our candidates for parliament and the prime ministership, they organize our legislatures and governments, and they dominate our public policy agenda. We provide them with many resources including significant amounts of public dollars to support their election activities, their parliamentary work, and the day-to-day operations of their central offices. Parties have a privileged status, both in election campaigns and in parliament, assuring them of primacy of place in both institutions. In return, we expect them to facilitate the democratic aspirations of Canadians.

In doing so, we ask a lot of our political parties. As R. Kenneth Carty (2001) has chronicled, parties played a key role in forging the Canadian federation and have periodically adjusted their organizations and operations to reflect the needs of an ever-changing society. Canadian society continues to evolve, and the parties now face the challenge of meeting the democratic needs and demands of a twenty-first-century Canada.

Our national community is more diverse today than ever before, a trend that is likely to intensify in coming years. At the same time, Canadians are less deferential than ever (Nevitte 1996) and are increasingly skeptical of the elite-dominated brokerage practices that have long characterized their party politics. Parties face two challenges, each difficult in its own right, that must be met simultaneously. These are, first, the facilitation of inclusive opportunities for Canadians to participate meaningfully in public decision making and, second, the ongoing need to play a nation-building role by uniting regional and other interests that potentially divide Canadians, into a single national concern. Canada's parties have traditionally favoured the second of these, often at the expense of the first. For much of our history, this was probably a reasonable calculation, as nation building was of paramount concern and demands for citizen participation were not as strong as they currently are. Many have suggested that the two cannot fit easily together. S.J.R. Noel (1971) has warned that attempts to infuse Canadian politics with a Jacksonian-style populism would place great tension on the state as it would jeopardize the accommodative capacities necessary to the maintenance of the federation. Nonetheless, it is equally true that accommodations seen to be reached in a nontransparent and non-inclusive manner, and that are not reflective of the views of regular Canadians, are increasingly unsustainable.

To many, the demise of the elite-negotiated constitutional agreements of the 1980s and 1990s signalled an end to the willingness of Canadians to blindly follow elite-driven deals, even on the greatest of national questions. Canadians want to participate in public decision making, and parties provide the greatest opportunity for this to occur in a manner that preserves space for accommodation. As Mildred Schwartz (1967, 127) observed, political parties are uniquely situated to find accommodations and to foster a national consensus. Unlike single-issue advocacy groups, our parties by definition concern themselves with all aspects of public policy. To demand that they do so in a way that is responsive to inclusive public participation is necessary to securing their place and with it their brokerage traditions. No other institutions are equipped to fill this role.

The reforms suggested in this chapter will encourage Canadians to see parties as institutions of meaningful democratic engagement. Policy foundations will provide a venue within parties for Canadians to engage in debate on issues of the day and to forge new solutions for managing them. More inclusive parties will ensure that all of the interests integral to the Canadian community are represented and that all Canadians see themselves reflected in these processes. Democratically organized personnel recruitment contests will increase the number of Canadians participating in party-run activities and enhance the legitimacy of these events. A more proportional electoral system will prompt parties to respond to the interests of all Canadians and encourage partisans in all communities to engage in campaign activity on behalf of their favoured parties.

Only if the parties are infused with a more inclusive and participatory spirit will they be seen as responsive to the needs of a modern, diverse Canada. This participation serves the brokerage function in two important ways. First, it ensures that all parts of the Canadian mosaic are considered in fashioning a national interest; and second, it brings needed legitimacy to the process, which will encourage Canadians to accept any emerging accommodations that result from transparent, participatory, and inclusive decision making. Increased citizen involvement should not be seen as a threat to the brokerage practice of party politics but rather as a necessary ingredient to ensure its relevance to modern Canada.

Works Cited

Archer, Keith, and Alan Whitehorn. 1997. *Political activists: The NDP in convention.* Toronto: Oxford University Press.

Arscott, Jane, and Linda Trimble, eds. 1997. *In the presence of women: Representation in Canadian governments.* Toronto: Harcourt Brace.

Axworthy, Thomas S. 2009. A democratic manifesto for the Liberal Party. http://www.liberalrenaissance.ca/.

Bashevkin, Sylvia. 1993. *Toeing the line: Women and party politics in English Canada*, 2nd ed. Toronto: Oxford University Press.

Black, Jerome, and Bruce Hicks. 2006. Visible minority candidates in the 2004 federal election. *Canadian Parliamentary Review* 29(2): 15-20.

Cairns, Alan. 1968. The electoral system and the party system in Canada: 1921-1965. *Canadian Journal of Political Science* 1(1): 55-80.

Carty, R. Kenneth. 2001. Three Canadian party systems: An interpretation of the development of national politics. In *Party politics in Canada,* 8th ed., ed. Hugh Thorburn, 16-32. Scarborough, ON: Prentice Hall.

Carty, R. Kenneth, William Cross, and Lisa Young. 2000. *Rebuilding Canadian party politics.* Vancouver: UBC Press.

Carty, R. Kenneth, and Munroe Eagles. 2005. *Politics is local: National politics at the grassroots.* Toronto: Oxford University Press.

Carty, R. Kenneth, and Lynda Erickson. 1991. Candidate nomination in Canada's national political parties. In *Canadian political parties: Leaders, candidates and organization,* ed. Herman Bakvis, 97-190. Toronto: Dundurn Press.

Clarkson, Stephen. 1979. Democracy in the Liberal Party: The experiment with citizen participation under Pierre Trudeau. In *Party politics in Canada,* 4th ed., ed. Hugh G. Thorburn, 154-160. Scarborough, ON: Prentice Hall.

Cross, William. 2004. *Political parties.* Canadian Democratic Audit. Vancouver: UBC Press.

–. 2006. Candidate nomination in Canadian political parties. In *The Canadian general election of 2006,* ed. Jon Pammett and Christopher Dornan, 171-95. Toronto: Dundurn Press.

–. 2007. Policy study and development in Canada's political parties. In *Policy analysis in Canada: The state of the art,* ed. Laurent Dobuzinskis, Michael Howlett, and David Laycock, 425-42. Toronto: University of Toronto Press.

–. 2008. Democratic norms and party candidate selection: Taking contextual factors into account. *Party Politics* 14(5): 596-619.

Cross, William, and John Crysler. 2009. Grassroots participation in party leadership selection: Examining the British and Canadian cases. In *Activating the citizen: Dilemmas of participation in Europe and Canada,* ed. Joan DeBardeleben and Jon Pammett, 173-94. Houndmills, UK: Palgrave Macmillan.

Cross, William, and Lisa Young. 2004. The contours of political party membership in Canada. *Party Politics* 10(4): 427-44.

–. 2008. Factors influencing the decision of the young politically engaged to join a political party. *Party Politics* 14(3): 345-69.

Dalton, Russell J., and Martin P. Wattenberg, eds. 2000. *Parties without partisans: Political change in advanced industrial democracies.* New York: Oxford University Press.

Docherty, David. 2005. *Legislatures*. Canadian Democratic Audit. Vancouver: UBC Press.

Howe, Paul, and David Northrup. 2000. Strengthening Canadian democracy: The views of Canadians. *Policy Matters* 1(5).

Nevitte, Neil. 1996. *The decline of deference: Canadian value change in cross national perspective*. Peterborough, ON: Broadview Press.

New Brunswick Commission on Legislative Democracy. 2004. *Final report and recommendations*. Fredericton: New Brunswick Commission on Legislative Democracy.

Noel, S.J.R. 1971. Political parties and elite accommodation: Interpretations of Canadian federalism. In *Canadian federalism: Myth or reality?* 3rd ed., ed. J. Peter Meekison, 64-83. Toronto: Methuen.

O'Neill, Brenda. 2001. Generational patterns in the political opinions and behaviour of Canadians. *Policy Matters* 2(5).

Pew Center on the States. 2008. *2008 primary in review*. Washington, DC: Pew Center on the States.

Pitkin, Hannah. 1969. *The concept of representation*. Berkeley: University of California Press.

Sayers, Anthony. 1998. *Parties, candidates and constituency campaigns in Canadian elections*. Vancouver: UBC Press.

Schwartz, Mildred. 1967. *Public opinion and Canadian identity*. Scarborough, ON: Fitzhenry and Whiteside.

Statistics Canada. 2008. *Canada's ethnocultural mosaic*. Ottawa: Ministry of Industry.

Stewart, David. 1997. The changing electorate: An examination of participants in the 1992 Alberta Conservative leadership contest. *Canadian Journal of Political Science* 30(1): 107-28.

Stewart, David, and R. Kenneth Carty. 2002. Leadership politics as party building: The Conservatives in 1998. In *Political parties, representation and electoral democracy in Canada,* ed. William Cross, 55-67. Toronto: Oxford University Press.

Tossutti, Livianna, and T.P. Najem. 2002. Minorities and elections in Canada's fourth party system. *Canadian Ethnic Studies* 34(1): 85-112.

Van Biezen, Ingrid. 2004. Political parties as public utilities. *Party Politics* 10(6): 701-22.

White, Graham. 2005. *Cabinets and first ministers*. Canadian Democratic Audit. Vancouver: UBC Press.

Young, Lisa, and William Cross. 2002. Incentives to membership in Canadian political parties. *Political Research Quarterly* 55(3): 547-70.

–. 2003. Women's involvement in Canadian political parties. In *Women and electoral politics in Canada,* ed. Manon Tremblay and Linda Trimble, 92-109. Toronto: Oxford University Press.

8

ADVOCACY GROUPS

Lisa Young and Joanna Everitt

Government policies affect the everyday lives of Canadians in a variety of ways. Governments determine what children will learn in school, whether citizens can have access to life-saving medical treatments, and what kind of toxic substances industries can release into the environment, to name a few. The pervasiveness of government makes it inevitable that most Canadians will want to influence government decisions at some time in their lives. Many of us are drawn into political activity in an effort to encourage a government to provide a service such as a medical treatment, to keep a school open, or to help students afford post-secondary education. This is often driven by self-interest. In other instances, the desire to affect government decisions can be grounded in values or a conception of the public interest. Much activism is motivated by an aspiration to change government policies to concord with our personal beliefs, ranging from banning abortion to reducing carbon emissions. Indeed, a great many Canadians have been prompted to political action simply by a sense of outrage over government actions or inactions.

When a Canadian wants to encourage a government to do something – change a policy, repeal a law, or just leave well enough alone – what can he or she do? A citizen can certainly act as an individual, by contacting his or her elected representative, trying to get media attention, and even participating in government consultation processes. But lone voices are often lost in conversations about public policy, so many of us try to band together with others who share our concern. Traditionally, individuals have worked to get political parties elected as a way to influence the direction of government policy. However, the parties' need to accommodate diverse interests means that individuals may often support one aspect of their platform, but not others. As a result, a growing number of Canadians are turning to advocacy groups to voice their concerns. Groups may be heard when individuals are not, and they allow individuals to pool their resources to make their case more forcefully. It is not surprising that various kinds of advocacy groups have become the predominant way in which citizens interact with governments to try to influence public policy.

Because they guarantee freedom of expression and association, democratic political systems create the necessary preconditions for advocacy groups to emerge. Where governments are open to – and may even desire – citizen input into the policy process, there are strong incentives for individuals to form organizations to advance their views or protect their interests. Advocacy groups exist in all the democratic political systems where the preconditions are in place, and though their extent and character of mobilization may vary from country to country, they have become an integral part of the political process in modern democracies, Canada included.

Some question whether advocacy groups are good for democracy. To assess this, we examine them using the democratic benchmarks of participation, responsiveness, and inclusiveness that form the framework for the Canadian Democratic Audit. We conclude that, though not all groups meet these benchmarks in their internal operations or have the same access to government decision makers, in general they play an important role in Canadian democracy.

Defining Advocacy Groups

It is not self-evident what kinds of organizations are included in the category of "advocacy groups." We deliberately avoid the term "interest group," even though many of the bodies we are including would classify themselves in that way. The term "interest group" assumes that an organization is lobbying government to take an action that benefits its members, financially or otherwise. Although this is frequently the case, the label of "interest group" is less suited to associations whose lobbying efforts are motivated by beliefs, such as supporting same-sex marriage or taking action to save an endangered species. We prefer the term "advocacy group" as it can encompass groups acting for the best interests of their own members as well as those promoting their opinions on an issue in which they have no direct interest.

To make our enquiry as comprehensive as possible, we have opted for a broad and relatively simple definition for advocacy groups: any organization that seeks to influence government policy but not to govern. By saying that advocacy groups do not aspire to govern, we can distinguish between them and political parties, which seek to influence government policy by governing, or at least by trying to elect candidates to legislatures. This definition would include an organization formed by two or three individuals who live on the same street and are pressuring their municipal government to install a stop sign, as well as a group such as the Council of Canadians, which claims thousands of members and lobbies government on issues ranging from the environment to national sovereignty. The definition also includes industry associations and business lobby groups.

It is important to distinguish between advocacy groups motivated by self-interest and those acting in support of their view of the public good. Take the Canadian Pharmaceutical Association or the Canadian Bankers' Association, on the one hand, and Greenpeace and the Canadian Taxpayers' Federation, on the other. The first two represent industries that lobby government to further their members' pecuniary interests. The latter two are working toward a policy objective, such as a preference to breathe clean air or to pay lower taxes. These policies may well serve their supporters' personal interests but nonetheless represent their conception of the public good. Perhaps the clearest way to distinguish between these two types of groups is to look to the kinds of benefits they seek. The pharmaceutical and bankers' associations work to achieve *selective* benefits, which apply only to their members. Greenpeace and the Canadian Taxpayers' Federation are pursuing *collective* benefits, which are shared by all even if they are not necessarily supported by all.

This distinction is important from the perspective of democracy. Although both kinds of groups are legitimate political actors, they desire very different objectives. If we were to discover that only groups seeking selective benefits are able to find a voice within Canadian democracy, arguing that advocacy groups further a democratic discussion of the common interest would be difficult.

Perspectives on Advocacy Groups

Advocacy groups have become significant players in modern democracies. Citizens tend to think of them as effective vehicles for influencing public policy, and they often enjoy greater public support than political parties. Nonetheless, their role in democratic systems tends to be controversial. Many observers note the potential for groups to enhance the quality of democratic decision making, but others see them as possibly corrosive to public life.

Keeping in mind the Democratic Audit's benchmarks of participation, responsiveness, and inclusiveness, we have identified various functions of advocacy groups that could contribute to the quality of democracy. First, using the criterion of *participation,* we would argue that such groups have the potential to provide a route via which citizens can participate. As other chapters in this book demonstrate, Canadians' participation in traditional political activities such as voting and joining political parties is declining (see Cross 2004, Chapter 7 this volume; Gidengil et al. 2004; Gidengil et al., Chapter 5 this volume). For Canadians and citizens of other industrialized democracies, participation in democratic life is increasingly channelled through advocacy groups, either in addition to or in place of other forms of political activity. Advocacy groups are able to mobilize citizens into periodic participation in the democratic system. To the extent that this is the case, groups contribute to the life of democracy by creating op-portunities for involvement.

Second, in terms of *responsiveness,* advocacy groups can facilitate the development of better public policy by providing governments with relevant information. Jane Mansbridge (1992, 53) contends that groups contribute to deliberative processes in democracy by providing "infor-mation and insight that changes the preferences of the public and their elected representatives. They also provide the institutions through which another set of representatives, the interest group elites, deliber-ates and decides upon the best interests of their constituents and of the polity as a whole."

Advocacy groups can also make government more responsive to citizens by communicating the various views of those who are affected by a policy. When governments are aware of these perceptions, they are better able to mediate among the competing interests. Advocacy groups serve as a vehicle to articulate these stances to government.

Finally, advocacy groups can increase *inclusion* by giving voice to citizen interests, particularly those not represented in mainstream institutions. Although periodic elections are essential to democracy, they are an inadequate mechanism for citizens to express all their views. When a citizen has a strong interest in a public policy area, simply voting or joining a political party might not satisfy her desire to engage in the policy debate. Joining an advocacy group allows that citizen to voice her opinions on issues that are important to her.

In the contemporary era, we often look to advocacy groups to provide a voice for both minority opinion and minority groups defined by their ascriptive characteristics.

The chapters in this book examining legislatures, executives, and political parties document some of the representational failures of these institutions (see Docherty 2005, Chapter 4 this volume; White 2005, Chapter 3 this volume; Cross 2004, Chapter 7 this volume). Ad-vocacy groups may compensate for some of these failures, particu-larly with regard to citizens who are subject to discrimination. Women, Aboriginals, people with disabilities, and ethnic and sexual minorities are under-represented in Canadian legislatures; the presence of groups that speak on their behalf and represent their interests in the policy process may compensate somewhat. This should not be seen as a substitute for achieving proportionate representation for these people but rather as a temporary mechanism to compensate for representational failures elsewhere in the system.

When they are internally democratic, advocacy groups can support the development and maintenance of a culture of democracy and a rich civil society. Groups must often wrestle with the more complex problems of democracy: Under what conditions must majority rule be tempered? How can the interests of different demographic groups, such as anglophones and francophones, or women and men, be accommodated within one organization? How are differing views within the group solicited and debated, and how are group positions reached? Under what conditions is a majority inadequate and a consensus required? By exposing citizens to these kinds of issues, group participation can contribute to the development of a culture that supports a flourishing democracy.

Although advocacy groups have the potential to add to the quality of democracy, they may also detract from it. In fact, "interest group," "special interest," and "pressure group" have all become pejorative terms. At the heart of this perspective is the assertion that organizations pursuing the interests of relatively limited segments of society will achieve their objectives at the expense of that society's collective good. The most elegant statements of this view stem from rational choice theorist Mancur Olson (1965), who argued that the logic of collective action means that groups with specific economic interests will defeat those representing the general public. The eventual result of this is inefficient governmental regulation, subsidies, and oligarchic economic organization.

Some critics maintain that the most consistent and effective groups are those that represent elite portions of society. As a consequence, interest mobilization is likely to defend the concerns of the affluent and powerful against those of the common citizen. We must carefully examine which sections of society are mobilized by groups to determine whether elites are, in fact, the primary beneficiaries of group action, and whether some interests are consistently "organized out" of the picture.

A second critique holds that women, minorities, and beneficiaries of government programs are "special" interests that exert undue influence over policy outcomes, again taking away from the common good as determined through democratic institutions. This stance conflicts directly with the argument that advocacy groups are particularly important in compensating for the representational failures of other democratic institutions.

A third critique maintains that group participation brings out the basest instinct of citizens: to pursue their own self-interest over the common good and to do so in a rigid and uncompromising manner. Critics assert that a single-issue focus makes advocacy groups lose sight of the bigger picture, rendering them unwilling to compromise on the issues they consider to be important, even when such compromise would be in the public interest. Group leaders have an incentive to exaggerate their claims, prolong conflicts, and engage in publicity stunts in an effort to raise money. These tactics contribute little to discussions of public policy and may make it more difficult for governments to find compromises among competing interests.

With this discussion of the potential and the pitfalls of advocacy groups in mind, we examine their participation in Canadian democracy, asking the following questions:

- ♣ Who participates in these groups? What form does this take?
- ♣ How well do groups represent their members and the constituencies for whom they claim to speak?
- ♣ Which interests are "organized in" and which are not?
- ♣ Who is heard? Do some groups typically experience more difficulty than others in gaining access to decision makers? Do some consistently win, whereas others lose?
- ♣ What tactics do groups employ? Are these harmful to democratic debate in any way?

Taken as a whole, the answers to these questions allow us to gauge the extent to which advocacy groups contribute to the quality of democracy in Canada.

Participation

Mobilizing citizens to participate in the political system is one of the most important contributions advocacy groups can make to democracy. Citizen participation requires organization, and groups are one of the most visible means through which citizens become involved. This participation may reinforce citizens' commitment to democratic values by exposing them to democratic practices within the group and enhancing their understanding of the broader political system. That said, groups may activate "too much" participation, or it may take a negative form. Excessive involvement, in this view, can overload the system with excessive demands, rendering it dysfunctional (see Huntington 1975). Likewise, participation that questions the legitimacy of the political system and/or takes on violent forms *may* prove destructive to democracy. Examples of this range from violent anti-globalization protesters to the extreme fringes of the American tea party movement that has emerged since 2009.

Our consideration of participation must take into account three different aspects: extent, equality, and quality. If we accept that democracy is strengthened by widespread citizen involvement, it follows that the greater the number of citizens who partake in advocacy group activism, the better democracy is served. To study the *extent* of group participation, we analyze data from surveys of the Canadian public to estimate how many Canadians are active in advocacy groups. To put this into perspective, we compare this to the number of Canadians active in political parties. Measuring rates of citizens' membership and participation in advocacy groups using survey data is challenging, because questions are not asked consistently over time or across political systems. It is important to keep these limitations in mind when interpreting these data.

Table 8.1

Canadians' involvement in advocacy group organizations (%)

Organization	1981	1990	2000	2008
Women's groups	n/a	7.0	10.0	10.7
Environmental groups	5.0	8.0	8.0	15.0
Labour unions	11.0	12.0	13.0	15.8
Professional organizations	12.0	16.0	16.0	26.6
Voluntary groups: community service/social welfare/health*	13.0	17.0	24.0	44.2

* The 2008 Canadian Election Study question referred only to community service groups (see Gidengil et al. 2009).
Sources: European Values Study Group and World Values Survey Association (1981-2004); Gidengil et al. (2009).

When asked in the 2008 Canadian Election Study (Gidengil et al. 2009) "Do you currently volunteer for a community group or a non-profit organization?" 37.7 percent of respondents said yes. This is a much more encompassing measure than has been used in past election studies, where respondents were asked "Have you ever been a member of an interest group that worked for change on a particular social or political issue?" Only 11.0 percent of Canadians responded yes to this narrower definition in previous years. When asked whether they had ever been a member of a federal political party, only 12.4 percent of Canadians answered yes. This has dropped from the almost 19.0 percent who indicated they were party members in 2000.

Furthermore, there is evidence that this rate of group participation has been growing over the past several decades. Since the early 1980s, more Canadians have become involved in virtually all forms of advocacy organizations, whether they be women's associations, environmental groups, or community bodies (see Table 8.1). This change reflects evolving conceptions regarding the relative merits of interest groups versus political parties. A study comparing young Canadians involved in campus advocacy groups to those who belonged to parties found that the former tended to have quite negative evaluations of parties as democratic entities, perceiving them as ineffective vehicles for achieving political change and unresponsive to the views of their members (Young and Cross 2007).

Lisa Young and Joanna Everitt

Table 8.2

Cross-national involvement in various advocacy group organizations (%)

	1981	1990	2000
Canada	24.4	34.1	39.2
Britain	29.8	29.2	12.4
France	13.0	12.8	10.6
West Germany	25.1	30.7	16.5
United States	26.5	32.6	54.3

Note: These figures were derived by adding the rates of reported participation in the five categories of organization listed in Table 8.1.
Source: European Values Study Group and World Values Survey Association (1981-2004).

The participation rates, as laid out in Table 8.1, are fairly high in comparative terms. Using past data from the World Values Survey to compare Canada to four other democracies, we find that, over the last couple of decades, Canadian rates of participation are second only to those of the United States and substantially higher than those of several European countries (see Table 8.2).

Some critics worry that advocacy group activity furthers a "mobilization of bias" by providing another route through which societal elites find voice for their concerns, whereas others are left without representation. To measure the *equality* of participation in Canadian advocacy groups, it is useful to compare the demographic breakdown of the population involved in group activity to that of the population not involved. As can be seen in Table 8.3, groups that have traditionally been excluded from political decision making are more actively involved in advocacy organizations than they are in political parties (see also Cross 2004). Women and men, and the employed and the unemployed, participate equally in these groups, and there are few age differences in involvement levels except within the youngest cohort, born after 1971. Those with the lowest levels of income participate slightly less than those in the middle- to upper-income brackets, yet they still take part substantially more in groups than they do in political parties. Only in terms of education do stark and significant differences appear. Individuals with a university education are far more likely to be involved

Table 8.3

Participation in advocacy organizations and political parties by group (%)

Grouping		Advocacy group members	Party members
Gender	Women	37.9	10.9
	Men	37.2	13.8
	Difference	0.7	−2.9*
Employment	Unemployed	32.5	14.3
	Employed	36.9	9.6
	Difference	−4.4	4.7
Education	High school	31.3	9.3
	University	51.2	16.7
	Difference	−19.9*	−7.4*
Income	Under $30,000	31.8	12.7
	$30,000-$60,000	38.7	10.3
	Over $60,000	38.8	12.6
Age cohort	Post-1971	25.8	5.1
	1961-70	41.1	8.0
	1946-60	41.2	15.9
	Pre-1945	45.1	21.2

* $p < .01$.
Source: The 2008 Canadian Election Study (Gidengil et al. 2009).

in community groups or non-profit organizations than are those without post-secondary experience.

Quality of participation is also a key measure. Do group members become active participants in the political process by attending the group's meetings, participating in its internal decision making, and being involved in its advocacy activities?

Examining the internal organization of a wide range of Canadian advocacy groups operating at the national level, we find only modest support for the idea that advocacy groups present significant participatory opportunities for their members. Many Canadian advocacy groups have opted not to have members at all. Organizations such as Greenpeace Canada, the Canadian Taxpayers' Federation, and Environment

Voters welcome "supporters," who give them money, but they do not have "members" as such. The distinction between supporters and members is crucial: supporters have no direct input into the group's decision-making processes, whereas members are entitled, at a minimum, to vote in elections for the board of directors. Staff-led bodies tend to be highly professionalized, relying on paid employees to undertake both advocacy work and fundraising. Supporters participate mainly by making financial contributions. It is not surprising that many staff-led groups avoid enrolling members. Membership organizations can be vulnerable to takeover by opponents, can be pushed in directions that are strategically disastrous, and are costly and time consuming to maintain. Nonetheless, the proliferation of memberless organizations limits the potential for citizens to engage in meaningful political participation through direct membership.

One organization that has achieved an admirable balance between group leaders' imperative for autonomy and the desire to allow members to participate actively is the Council of Canadians, which gives its members the right to vote for the executive and on policy-related resolutions at an annual general meeting. In reality, however, since the membership is spread across the country and the yearly meeting is held in one location (which rotates around the country annually), individual members have a limited opportunity to direct the national organization's policy. The council's structure nonetheless provides local chapters with considerable autonomy to pursue the issues they think are important as long as these issues fall within the national group's general mandate. Following what is essentially a franchise model, the national organization distributes materials to help chapters form and operate, and to engage in effective advocacy. It also provides occasional funding for chapters' advocacy work. In this way, members are actively engaged, but the national organization maintains strategic autonomy.

One argument in support of advocacy groups as the mobilizers of citizen participation holds that such involvement instills support for democracy and democratic values (Putnam 1993). Data from the 2008 Canada Election Study (Gidengil et al. 2009) provide some support for

Table 8.4

Participation rates: Advocacy groups, non-members, and political parties (%)

Type of participation	Advocacy group members	Non-members	Party members
Voted in 2000 election	92.7	83.9	96.7
Discussed politics often	68.5	50.5	73.2
Contacted a politician or government official	47.7	24.9	66.1
Persuaded others to vote for a party or candidate	38.6	30.9	60.0
Showed support for a particular party or candidate	24.0	14.7	41.5
Donated money to a federal party	26.7	13.9	68.0

Source: The 2008 Canadian Election Study (Gidengil et al. 2009).

this contention. Advocacy group members are as likely (57.4 percent) to believe that others can be trusted as are members of political parties (57.6 percent). The level of trust among those who belong to neither an advocacy group nor a political party is roughly fifteen percentage points lower (42.6 percent). Similarly, advocacy group members demonstrate more interest in politics than do non-members: on a scale of 0 to 10, where 0 means not very interested and 10 means very interested, the former score an average of 6.4, whereas the latter score 5.7. Political party members score 7.6. Of course, we must be careful in attributing a causal relationship here, as it is also possible that interest in politics drives individuals to join a party or group.

As can be seen in Table 8.4, similar patterns hold in terms of other forms of participation. Although members of political parties demonstrate the highest levels of political participation, advocacy group members are not far behind. They vote at almost the same rate, and they discuss politics almost as often. Their contact with politicians or government officials, their involvement in election campaigns, and their propensity to donate money to parties or candidates are less than those of party members, but they are more likely to participate in these activities than are non-members. In all cases, advocacy group members are more similar to members of political parties in terms of their political engagement than they are to non-members.

Lisa Young and Joanna Everitt

Responsiveness

Ideally, advocacy groups should be responsive to their members. Groups enhance democratic citizenship only when they conduct their internal affairs in accordance with the basic principles of democracy. In this respect, we can compare groups' performance to the democratic ideals of equal participation of members, opportunity for members to influence decisions, and representative internal structures, such as elections of officers.

This presupposes that a group does in fact have members, an assumption that frequently does not hold true. At the national, and even provincial, level, many advocacy groups are umbrella-type structures. Although they are effective for pursuing policy objectives, these structures pose difficulties for achieving relationships of accountability. For example, the Canadian Federation of Students (CFS) is an umbrella organization encompassing over eighty university and college student associations. It claims to represent over half a million post-secondary students, but its relationship with them is indirect: students elect leaders at their institutions, who then select the leadership and direct the affairs of the CFS. The federation is not unique in this: other major national bodies such as the Assembly of First Nations and the National Action Committee on the Status of Women (NAC) share the same basic form.

The other major set of organizations that offer few participatory opportunities to their members are the large staff-led groups discussed above. In these, group leaders often use surveys of either the entire membership (or donor base) or a random sample of the membership as a basis for determining policy stands. For instance, the Canadian Automobile Association surveys a random sample of its over 5 million members, seeking their opinions on issues of interest to the car-driving public. It then uses this survey as a basis for its core policy document, which is distributed to provincial and federal politicians as well as public servants (Canadian Automobile Association 2003). Although this provides at least some legitimacy for the association's claims to represent the auto-driving public, surveys solicit members' opinions only on the issues that the leadership deems important.

In situations where there is no formal membership, responsiveness requires that group leaders consult with Canadians who are supportive of their cause. In the absence of explicit relationships of accountability, the only mechanism making the leaders responsive to supporters is money. If a group relies on supporters for a significant portion of its funds, its financial survival depends upon maintaining the contribution of donors. This is not a trivial mechanism of accountability: if an organization strays too far from the issues its supporters care about, or if it adopts tactics they disapprove of, it stands to lose its livelihood. Even so, many of these supporters are responding to direct mail appeals from the organization and may well be swayed by the content of the appeal. Direct-mail fundraisers emphasize the importance of clear, simple messages and craft letters to invoke their readers' emotional responses of fear, anger, or sympathy.

The third, and most difficult, level of responsiveness involves accountability to the constituency a group purports to represent. When advocacy groups make claims to speak for collectivities such as drivers, women, non-smokers, or the disabled, the veracity of this claim becomes questionable. The larger and the more diverse the collectivity, the more problematic the claim becomes.

Our review of case studies of interest group decision-making practices indicates that group leaders and staffs often enjoy considerable autonomy in setting their organization's priorities and policy stances. In many instances, the leaders use their judgment and knowledge of their constituency to determine the group's actions. For example, a study of advocacy in the disability field found that "consumer groups attempt to achieve the democratic principles of representativeness by focusing on a broad range of activities that are important to all or most persons with disabilities, rather than by formally recruiting a broad range of people to participate. This strategy ... assumes that differences among people with disabilities are not as great as differences between access to activities by persons with disabilities and by able-bodied persons" (Boyce et al. 2001, 150-51).

Such approaches are fraught with potential difficulties. A vivid illustration of this is offered by Francesca Scala, Éric Montpetit, and

Isabelle Fortier (2005) in their account of NAC's interventions into policy consultations over assisted reproductive technologies (ARTs). When NAC first intervened in the public debate over ARTs, it was to make a presentation in 1990 to a royal commission studying the issue. In preparing this presentation, NAC did not consult with its member groups in formulating its stance: rather, its "policy agenda was determined by the views of expert members on the policy committee" (ibid., 591). NAC's opposition toward ARTs drew a great deal of criticism from individuals and women's groups. In particular, lesbians and infertile women who stood to benefit from these technologies rejected NAC's stance and threw into question its legitimacy as a representative organization of Canadian women. Subsequently, commissioners questioned the legitimacy of NAC's claim to represent "women" (ibid., 593). This example illustrates the potential difficulties groups create when they purport to speak for a collectivity but do so based on research and analysis rather than extensive consultations with their members and constituents.

It is difficult to draw broad-based conclusions about advocacy groups' responsiveness to their constituencies, as there is tremendous variation in their internal organization. Certainly, associations with substantial membership bases and methods for consulting members are better positioned to make claims that are representative of their constituencies. In addition, efforts to consult widely within constituencies can certainly produce more representative policy stances. The onus is on decision makers to weigh the claims of advocacy groups based in part on their capacity to speak for their constituency. This creates an incentive for group leaders to remain responsive, both to members and broader constituencies.

Inclusion

INCLUSIVENESS OF GROUPS

As noted above, advocacy group membership appears to be somewhat more socially inclusive than various other forms of political participation, most notably, membership in political parties. That said, group members tend to be better educated, more affluent, and older than non-members. These patterns suggest that income, education, and social status provide individuals with the resources, skills, and confidence that make involvement possible. Here, we transfer our focus to the other side of the equation: how do groups encourage or discourage inclusiveness among their membership?

The definition of inclusiveness shifts, depending on the particular context of the group. National bodies struggle with inclusiveness along the lines of language and region, as well as ethnicity and gender. Even those that are organized according to a shared characteristic must confront this issue: for instance, women's organizations must take into account ethnicity, language, region, sexual orientation, and physical ability. Associations representing socially excluded groups, such as women or the disabled, face some of the greatest pressure to be internally inclusive, largely as a result of the ideologies of inclusion that they espouse.

Canadian groups vary considerably in terms of their efforts to be inclusive of social diversity. Many are largely unconcerned with the issue. For instance, the Canadian Council of Chief Executives (formerly the Business Council on National Issues) restricts its membership to the CEOs of the top 150 corporations in the country. A quick glance at its membership reveals that very few of its members have an ethnic origin other than British or French, and even fewer are women. These patterns reflect the barriers to inclusiveness that are embedded in the culture of corporate life in Canada.

Other groups structure themselves to achieve inclusiveness along regional and/or linguistic lines. This is not surprising in the Canadian context, where regional and linguistic cleavages are highly salient and are reinforced by the institutions of federalism. Many national associations are made up of provincial units. In these cases, regional representation is embedded in the group's fundamental organization, with the national board made up of provincial representatives. Other groups use informal measures to ensure regional representation. For instance, when electing its board of directors, the Council of Canadians employs a nominating committee that has the task of "recognizing the importance of reflecting Canadian diversity, regional membership and activity" (Council of Canadians 2003).

More traditional advocacy groups such as the Canadian Chamber of Commerce or the Consumers' Association of Canada devote little attention to questions of inclusiveness in terms of gender, ethnicity, or other ascriptive characteristics. This does not necessarily mean that they are not internally inclusive but rather that these dimensions of inclusiveness are not highly politicized and regularized within the organization. In contrast to this, advocacy groups emerging out of progressive social movements have tended to focus considerable attention on questions of inclusiveness and, in some cases, have changed their organizational structures to institutionalize these concerns.

Even when associations are genuinely committed to becoming inclusive, they may confront significant obstacles. Financial barriers stand in the way of regional inclusiveness, as travel costs prevent representatives of far-flung regions from attending executive meetings. Linguistic inclusiveness is also costly, particularly when it comes to providing simultaneous interpretation at meetings. In the absence of government funding, most national organizations cannot afford these expenditures. Achieving inclusiveness along lines of gender, ethnicity, sexual orientation, and ability may be even more challenging. These aspects of identity, like language and to a lesser degree region, are sources of profound social and political difference. Accommodating diversity requires more than guaranteeing seats on an executive. It demands a rethinking of an organization's ways of approaching issues and making decisions. It forces dedicated, long-time activists to create space for people with whom they may not be comfortable and who may bring to the table concerns that crowd out traditional issues. Many progressive Canadian advocacy groups have struggled with these matters.

INCLUSIVENESS OF ADVOCACY GROUP SYSTEM

Which interests and identities tend to find representation by advocacy groups in Canada? Is the Canadian advocacy group system inclusive of a variety of these, or does it tend to overrepresent certain kinds at the expense of others? There is a clear potential for some interests to be "organized in" to political decision making, whereas others remain unorganized and therefore unheard.

The most influential theoretical perspective on this question is offered by Mancur Olson (1965), who first articulated the "free rider problem." Olson argues that people have no incentive to participate in political action if they can benefit from its outcome without joining in the mobilization. Free riders are individuals who enjoy benefits without participating in the campaign itself. For example, imagine that a university students' association is holding a rally in hopes of convincing the government to increase university funding in order to make tuition fees lower. A "rational" student might calculate that the cost of attending the rally (such as hours of study lost) is greater than the marginal difference made by her participation in the rally. Any benefits that accrued from the rally in the form of lower tuition would not be limited to those who attended it, so her best interest would lie in being a free rider on the efforts of the other, less calculating, students.

Two propositions follow from Olson's rational choice analysis of group mobilization. First, groups are more likely to pursue selective benefits that accrue only to their members, such as profits for business or monetary rewards, and less likely to seek collective benefits that accrue to everyone, such as clean air or justice. Second, people have greater incentive to focus on narrow interests, such as a tax break for a certain group, than on diffuse interests such as lower costs for a relatively minor consumer good.

Evidence shows that many Canadian advocacy groups pursue selective benefits. A 1995 survey of associations in Canada found that, excluding leisure groups such as sports clubs, only 16 percent of them could be classified as "public interest" groups. More common were industry and trade associations (32 percent), groups focused on the welfare and protection of individuals (28 percent), and unions (24 percent) (Amarata, Landry, and Lamari 1999, 483). A list of advocacy organizations maintained by an Ottawa newspaper shows that little has changed since the survey was done. Industry associations and labour unions continue to outnumber public interest groups by a significant margin (see Hill-watch 2006).

Businesses are well represented within the Canadian advocacy group system. In addition to several major national lobby groups for business such as the Canadian Council of Chief Executives, the Canadian Chamber of Commerce, and the Canadian Federation of Independent Business, hundreds of trade associations operate in Canada, representing the interests of an industry or a subsection within it (Clancy 2008). Pursuing even more selective benefits are the many medium-sized and large corporations that employ government relations specialists to represent their interests.

But many groups pursue the public interest as they perceive it, in the form of collective goods. Thousands of environmental groups seek to improve the quality of the air we all breathe and the water we all drink (McKenzie 2008); their members would not derive any greater benefit from such improvements than would any other member of society, although they might get greater satisfaction from the change. In addition to environmental groups, numerous others advocate for their vision of the public interest on a wide range of issues (see Smith 2008). These include everything from peace organizations, animal rights groups, and children's advocates to Christian right and pro-life organizations wishing to see their values reflected in public policy.

The second expectation of the rational choice approach is that mobilizing on narrow interests is easier than doing so for diffuse issues (those that affect a large number of people in a relatively minor way). Telephone service, which is a common but fairly inexpensive good, is often cited as an example of a diffuse interest. Almost every Canadian household has a telephone, so there is a universal interest in relatively low-cost phone service. The interest is diffuse because it is universal but also because few individuals are so concerned about the cost of their phone service that they would become active on the issue. Under these circumstances, is it possible for mobilization to occur to represent this interest? In the Canadian experience, the answer to this is a tentative yes. Consumers' organizations have managed to represent the interests of consumers on these kinds of diffuse issues. They have proved most effective, however, when their activities receive government funding (see Schultz 2002).

Some accounts suggest that lack of resources is the greatest constraint to the formation of groups. Resources – which include time, money, status, skills, and confidence – are required in order to form associations and take public stands. Segments of society that lack several of these are less likely to mobilize than those that do have access. Compounding this, many of these sets of resources tend to reinforce one another: affluent people are more likely to have the formal education that hones their skills in presenting their case in public and that gives them both the social status and the confidence to pursue their interests in the public arena.

To determine the extent to which lack of resources affects the ability of groups to form, consider the mobilization of people living in poverty, as they are potentially one of the most difficult groups to organize. By definition, they lack an essential element for group formation: money. In many instances, poverty correlates with a lack of education, which means that the skills and confidence needed to engage with government may also be less available to these citizens than to others (see Gidengil et al., Chapter 5 this volume). The experience of poverty can erode individuals' sense of self-confidence, with the same result. Given all these factors, people living in poverty are a crucial test case for the proposition that a lack of resources impairs the ability to mobilize.

Canada has a number of anti-poverty associations at the local, provincial, and national levels. Some consist of people living in poverty, whereas others, such as associations of food banks, work on their behalf. In fact, most anti-poverty organizations consist of middle-class professionals who strive to alleviate poverty. A notable exception to this is Canada Without Poverty, formerly the National Antipoverty Organization (NAPO), founded in 1971. Approximately a fifth of NAPO's members and most of its executives and staff have had experiences of poverty (Haddow 1990, 230). More radical organizations exist at the local level, in some instances mobilizing people in poverty (Greene 2008), but even here, it is not clear to what extent they were the key agents of the groups' formation. Using anti-poverty organizations as a critical case study, one finds it difficult to refute the idea that inequitable access to resources is mirrored in the Canadian interest group system.

ROLE OF THE STATE

The federal government has played a significant role in overcoming the obstacles to group mobilization posed by both the free rider problem and the unequal distribution of resources within society. Since 1970, Ottawa has supported the formation and operations of various disadvantaged groups. By the 1980s, it was funding thirty-five hundred organizations, mainly official language minority, multicultural, and women's groups, but also consumers' organizations, anti-poverty associations, and others (Pal 1993, 246; Pross 1992, 300). As a result, the Canadian interest group system has been more inclusive than would otherwise have been the case.

This funding has increased the extent and the diversity of the advocacy group system. But it has also given government a significant role in determining which marginalized interests will be able to mobilize and which will not. For example, the women's movement, which began to appear in the early 1970s, received much more government funding than did the gay liberation movement that was emerging at much the same time and was therefore able to mobilize more extensively at the national level. Government funding can also affect the tactics a group employs. For example, though associations representing gays and lesbians have not received core funding from government, they have been able to access some funds under the Court Challenges Program, which subsidized the cost of challenging the legality of laws under the Canadian Charter of Rights and Freedoms. This has encouraged gay rights groups to use litigation as a strategy for political change (Smith 1999, 89).

Reliance on government subsidies leaves groups vulnerable to funding cuts. Those who depend on the government for core funding tend not to have developed extensive donor bases or to have solicited other sources of financing. When the government subsidy is withdrawn, they can be thrown into crisis. Since 1990, Ottawa has reduced its funding of advocacy groups, devastating many of them. For instance, loss of funding reduced the National Action Committee on the Status of Women from a prominent and influential national organization to a peripheral one on the brink of bankruptcy. In 2006, the federal government eliminated many of the remaining programs that funded advocacy groups, resulting in the closure of several organizations and leaving others, such as the former NAPO, searching for alternative sources of financial support.

Ideally, groups would be funded entirely by their supporters so that the finances of each one would reflect its public support. Groups that rely on individual donors for funding have an incentive to respond to their opinions and are insulated from the detrimental effects of sharp declines in government subsidies. But to leave funding entirely in the hands of the market assumes that wealth is equally distributed. We know this is not the case, so we look to government to even out inequities between various segments of society. Government also has a part to play in mitigating the effect of the free rider problem. Ottawa has largely abdicated its role in correcting for these biases, and as a result, diffuse interests and marginalized segments of society have been less represented in the political sphere during the past two decades than they were from 1970 to 1990.

Reinstating some public funding for advocacy groups would be beneficial to democracy if it were designed to correct for inequities in resources and the dilemmas posed by the free rider problem. An arm's-length government agency with an explicit mandate to provide core multi-year funding to groups representing marginalized sectors of society and diffuse interests would go a long way toward depoliticizing the process of financing these groups.

Governments should also make funding available to groups to participate in hearings, consultations, and regulatory processes. This involves not only covering travel expenses associated with participating but also subsidizing costs entailed in consulting with group members to develop a policy stance, preparing a submission, and if necessary, hiring legal counsel for regulatory hearings. A distinction must be made between corporations or industry associations and citizens' groups. For the former, expenses associated with lobbying government are the costs of doing business. For the latter, there is no expectation of monetary gain, and financial obstacles may be prohibitive. In these instances, governments that want genuine consultations with interested parties must remove financial obstacles.

The most significant way in which government affects the resources available to all advocacy groups is through the taxation system. Most non-business advocacy groups receive no benefits via the income tax system, although they themselves are exempt from paying income tax. Supporters of the group cannot claim a credit on their income tax when they make a financial contribution to it. The only exception to this comes when a group enjoys charitable tax status. However, such status significantly curtails the group's ability to engage in advocacy activities.

In contrast to this, when a business engages in lobbying the government, it can list the expenditure incurred in the process (including hiring a lobbyist or paying membership fees in an industry association) as business expenses, which are tax deductible. This creates a clear imbalance between businesses and other groups lobbying government and, as one observer noted, has "the peculiar effect of encouraging the lobbying of government by commercial and private interests, and hindering lobbying by non-commercial entities that are often pursuing a broader public interest" (Bridge 2000, 16).

In Canada, the only groups (aside from registered political parties) that can offer tax receipts to their contributors are registered charities. Charities also enjoy a number of other tax benefits, including exemption from federal income tax and the GST. Ottawa's regulations surrounding charitable status specify that a group cannot devote more than 10 to 20 percent (depending on its size) of its available resources to political activities (Canada Revenue Agency 2003).

The federal government could support advocacy groups by extending the charitable tax credit to registered advocacy organizations. The other intermediary associations in Canadian politics - political parties - benefit from a tax credit that is more generous than the one offered to those who contribute to charitable organizations. The political contribution tax credit recognizes the significant role that parties play in

Canadian democracy; why should advocacy groups not receive similar acknowledgment? By creating an incentive for contributors, the tax credit would make groups' fundraising efforts more successful, thereby strengthening their internal capacity and reducing their reliance on direct support from government. Such a system would enable citizens to choose which groups should receive the benefit of their tax dollars, rather than giving the state a monopoly on this decision. Government would continue to play a role in remedying inequities stemming from uneven distribution of resources and in overcoming the free rider problem, but this could be lessened by giving groups an important fundraising tool.

Advocacy Groups and "Compensatory Representation"

One additional dimension of inclusiveness is the extent to which advocacy organizations compensate for some of the representational failures of the broader political system. Although groups such as women, visible minorities, gays and lesbians, and the disabled are not present in the formal political arena in proportions equal to their presence in the electorate, they have frequently found voice through advocacy associations. Employing a combination of protest, lobbying, and litigation tactics, they have transformed both the advocacy group system in Canada and the lives of many citizens. Shifts in the political climate and reductions in government funding for many of these organizations, however, have had the effect of making their voices less prominent on the national political stage in recent years.

Conclusion

The term "advocacy group" encompasses a tremendously large range of activities and actors. From cigar-chomping business lobbyists to Birkenstock-clad environmental protesters, these groups share a common objective of trying to achieve political change. The existence of such a large number and wide variety of groups demonstrates a fundamental strength of Canadian democracy: freedoms of assembly and speech allow advocacy groups to thrive. In turn, these bodies contribute to Canadian democracy by providing a channel through which citizens can voice their preferences, articulating competing points of view and challenging governments to be responsive to them. Although this chapter has shown groups to be imperfect in their ability to channel citizen participation, encourage responsiveness, and foster inclusion, they nonetheless make positive contributions to Canadian democracy. The proliferation of interest groups in the 1970s and beyond broadened political discourse, chipped away at parties' ability to constrain the broad contours of public debate, and allowed previously marginalized groups to make claims in the political arena.

Any evaluation of advocacy groups as democratic actors must take into account their location and role within the political system. They are voluntary associations, not formal institutions. Thus, it follows that they cannot be held to the same exacting standards as are the institutions designed to structure Canadian democracy. Even political parties, which are also private organizations of a kind, can be held to considerably higher standards because they are state funded and play a significant role in structuring formal electoral competition and democratic representation. Advocacy groups exist primarily to promote a cause. Just as the Canadian judicial system assumes that justice is best served when all parties to a legal dispute are represented in court by counsel, our democratic system is arguably best served when all relevant points of view can advocate for their cause within the formal political arena. Some of these claims will be self-interested or even corrosive to public life, but they nonetheless enrich the quality of democracy by increasing the inclusiveness of the political arena. It falls to other actors within the political system to temper these claims, weigh them against counterclaims and interests, and make decisions in the public interest.

That said, considerable scope remains for advocacy groups to reform their practices to become more vibrant democratic actors. We believe that advocacy groups could do more to engage citizens in active participation and that governments could do more to support a diverse advocacy group system. Even though we document the ability of business interests to dominate in many policy domains, we note with considerable satisfaction that the proliferation of citizens' groups over the past thirty years has introduced something of a counterbalance.

These concerns aside, advocacy groups remain one of the healthier elements of Canadian democracy. They are better adapted to Canadians' changing political values than are more traditional hierarchical organizations such as political parties. They are able to act as dynamic and effective players in the policy process, and citizens are coming to recognize this ability. In an era in which citizens' evaluations of democracy are not positive, and many citizens believe they cannot affect government policy, it is essential to strengthen the organizations that citizens do see as an effective means for political engagement: advocacy groups.

Works Cited

Amarata, Nabil, Réjean Landry, and Moktar Lamari. 1999. Les determinants de l'effort de lobbying des associations au Canada. *Revue Canadienne de science politique* 32(3): 471-98.

Boyce, William, Mary Ann McColl, Mary Tremblay, Jerome Beckenbach, Anne Crichton, Steven Andrews, Nancy Gerein, and April D'Aubin. 2001. *A seat at the table: Persons with disabilities and policy making.* Montreal and Kingston: McGill-Queen's University Press.

Bridge, Richard. 2000. *The law of advocacy by charitable organizations: The case for change.* Vancouver: Institute for Media, Policy and Civil Society.

Canada Revenue Agency. 2003. *Policy Statement: Political Activities.* http://www.cra-arc.gc.ca/.

Canadian Automobile Association. 2003. *Statement of policy 2002-2003.*

Clancy, Peter. 2008. Business interests and civil society in Canada. In *Group politics and social movements in Canada,* ed. Miriam Smith, 35-60. Peterborough, ON: Broadview Press.

Council of Canadians. 2003. Annual general meeting, October 2003. Unpublished document.

Cross, William. 2004. *Political parties.* Canadian Democratic Audit. Vancouver: UBC Press.

Docherty, David. 2005. *Legislatures*. Canadian Democratic Audit. Vancouver: UBC Press.

European Values Study Group and World Values Survey Association. 1981-2004. European and World Values Surveys four-wave integrated data file, v. 20060423, 2006. File Producers: ASEP/JDS, Madrid, and Tilburg University, Tilburg, Netherlands. File Distributors: ASEP/JDS and GESIS, Cologne, Germany.

Gidengil, Elisabeth, André Blais, Neil Nevitte, and Richard Nadeau. 2004. *Citizens*. Canadian Democratic Audit. Vancouver: UBC Press.

Gidengil, Elisabeth, Joanna Everitt, Patrick Fournier, and Neil Nevitte. 2009. *Canadian election study, 2008*. Toronto: Institute for Social Research, York University.

Greene, Jonathan. 2008. Boardrooms and barricades: Anti-poverty organizing in Canada. In *Group politics and social movements in Canada,* ed. Miriam Smith, 107-28. Peterborough, ON: Broadview Press.

Haddow, Rodney. 1990. The poverty policy community in Canada's liberal welfare state. In *Policy communities and public policy in Canada,* ed. William D. Coleman and Grace Skogstad, 212-37. Toronto: Copp Clark Pitman.

Hillwatch. 2006. Issues and associations directory. Hillwatch.com. http://www.hillwatch.com/.

Huntington, Samuel P. 1975. The United States. In *The crisis of democracy: Report on the governability of democracies to the trilateral commission,* ed. M. Crozier, S. Huntington, and S. Watunuki, 98-115. New York: New York University Press.

Mansbridge, Jane. 1992. A deliberative theory of interest representation. In *The politics of interests: Interest groups transformed,* ed. Mark P. Petracca, 32-57. Boulder: Westview Press.

McKenzie, Judith. 2008. The environmental movement in Canada: Retreat or resurgence? In *Group politics and social movements in Canada,* ed. Miriam Smith, 279-306. Peterborough, ON: Broadview Press.

Olson, Mancur. 1965. *The logic of collective action*. New York: Schocken.

Pal, Leslie A. 1993. *Interests of state: The politics of language, multiculturalism and feminism in Canada*. Montreal and Kingston: McGill-Queen's University Press.

Pross, A. Paul. 1992. *Group politics and public policy,* 2nd ed. Toronto: Oxford University Press.

Putnam, R.D. 1993. *Making democracy work: Civic traditions in modern Italy*. Princeton: Princeton University Press.

Scala, Francesca, Éric Montpetit, and Isabelle Fortier. 2005. The NAC's organizational practices and the politics of assisted reproductive technologies in Canada. *Canadian Journal of Political Science* 38(3) (September): 581-604.

Schultz, Richard J. 2002. *The Consumers' Association of Canada and the federal telecommunications regulatory system, 1973-1992*. Vancouver: SFU-UBC Centre for the Study of Government and Business.

Smith, Miriam. 1999. *Lesbian and gay rights in Canada: Social movements and equality-seeking, 1971-1995*. Toronto: University of Toronto Press.

–, ed. 2008. *Group politics and social movements in Canada*. Peterborough: Broadview Press.

White, Graham. 2005. *Cabinets and first ministers*. Canadian Democratic Audit. Vancouver: UBC Press.

Young, Lisa, and William Cross. 2007. A group apart: Young party members in Canada. Canadian Policy Research Networks. http://www.cprn.org/.

COMMUNICATION TECHNOLOGY

Darin Barney

9

A common complaint of those who study emerging media is that the dynamic nature of these technologies and the practices they mediate makes committing observations and analysis to print a risky business. Digital technologies, and what people do with them, change so rapidly that claims about the current state of things have a very short shelf life. Politicians these days worry that video evidence of past indiscretions surfacing on YouTube might thwart their campaigns for elected office; scholars of emerging media worry that even *mentioning* YouTube will date their work such that no one will take it seriously a year from now when the platform has gone the way of Napster, replaced by some other "revolutionary" new application. Emerging media are not just emerging; they are also *emergent:* ever unfinished, characteristically unstable, and always in process. This suggests that all claims regarding these media are provisional at best and invite refutation by technological change and the unpredictable choices made by the people who take up with it.

The Democratic Audit volume *Communication Technology* was published in 2005 (Barney). It began by referring to the 2000 Canadian general election, heralded at the time as the country's first "Internet election," and pointed out that, despite the affordances of digital networks, that election featured the lowest voter turnout in Canadian history (to that point). Much has happened in the world of emerging media since that time. We have seen the proliferation of so-called Web 2.0 and social-networking applications that enable an unprecedented variety of user-driven multimedia content production, sharing, networking, and collaboration. This has been paralleled by the availability of an ever broader array of powerful portable devices for generating, distributing, and consuming information in various forms. By 2009, blogs, wikis, instant messaging, video sharing, podcasting, geo tagging, RSS feeds, and social networking made their way into the daily media experience of vast numbers of Canadian citizens and have been heavily integrated into the operations of Canada's political parties and social movements. It is as if the technical features of the early Internet, upon which brash promises of democratization and widespread political engagement had originally been built, have multiplied exponentially. Canadians have more convenient access to more, better, and more diverse political information, as well as more opportunities for interactive participatory communication than ever before. And yet, we can say the same thing about the 2008 Canadian general election as we did about that of 2000: it featured the lowest voter turnout in Canadian history to date.

Voter turnout is a complex and ambiguous indicator of politicization. Refusing to vote can be a political act signalling either satisfaction or refusal, and citizens might be engaged in a variety of political activities beyond the conventional scope of partisan electoral competition. Emerging technologies might be playing an enabling and sustaining role in relation to these other sorts of engagements, and these may have a bearing on the degree to which citizens experience political life as responsive, inclusive, and participatory. This is certainly the case when it comes to the diverse array of social movements, community organizations, alternative media providers, and citizen-journalists who continue to use new technologies to tremendous effect in organizing and executing their political activities. Nevertheless, historically low levels on this most basic measure of political engagement at least suggest the possibility of relatively widespread depoliticization on the part of a large number of Canadians whose daily lives are otherwise highly mediated by these same technologies. There are many possible reasons for why record numbers of Canadians are abstaining from voting (see Gidengil et al., Chapter 5 this volume), and this abstention potentially carries a variety of possible meanings. At a minimum, however, it suggests that the relationship between emerging technologies and a reinvigorated democratic politics is not as straightforward as we might like to believe. This was the premise of *Communication Technology,* and it still holds today, despite the significant technological developments that have occurred in the intervening years.

The Canadian Democratic Audit asks whether emerging media technologies are contributing to a more participatory, inclusive, and responsive democracy in Canada. Answering this question is difficult not only because the relationship between these technologies and political institutions and practices in Canada is constantly shifting but also because the sites at which we might locate politically significant implications of these technologies are multiple and proliferating. A wide variety of novel media technologies are put to a broad range of uses by a diverse array of mainstream and marginal political actors and institutions, including political parties, social movements and activists, agencies of government, and professional and amateur journalists. Already the phrase "democracy and emerging media" refers to a multiplicity of technologies, a multiplicity of uses, applications, and practices, and a multiplicity of actors. Due to their continually escalating importance as the basic infrastructure of everyday social, political, cultural, and economic life for most Canadians, emerging media technologies are also themselves the site of considerable political stakes, judgments, and contests between actors that are differently situated and have diverse, often competing, interests. When we consider that digital and network technologies also comprise the terrain of a range of important democratic political issues in their own right, the complexity of the phrase "democracy and emerging media" increases significantly. Furthermore, even when they are not deployed for directly or explicitly political purposes, the latest media technologies (and the way we think and talk about them) are also an important part of the broader material and cultural context in which the practices and prospects of democratic citizenship are situated.

The complexity of the field demarcated by emerging media technologies is such that the question of whether they contribute to an improved democracy in Canada would seem to defy a straightforward answer. This is apparent even before we recognize that the substance of the normative standard "improved democracy" is *itself* exceedingly complex and deeply contested. What, after all, would an improved democracy in Canada look like or demand? For some, democracy is a critical standard of radical egalitarianism and politicization whose realization demands fundamental restructuring of the economic and institutional basis of political life in Canada. With this view in mind, one could ask whether and how emerging media technologies and practices contribute to the struggle for (or against) a political order in Canada that is fundamentally transformed along strongly democratic lines. The answer to this question would probably be very complex and ambiguous. However, for others, improved democracy means enhanced functioning of extant institutions and structures of political power, along lines that are well within the existing normative self-understanding of Canadian democratic politics. In this latter view, democracy is not so much a radical critical standard that can be brought to bear *against* contemporary political arrangements as it is a principle of legitimacy toward which existing institutions and actors in Canada are already oriented, even if their performance in relation to this principle is not always perfect, or even adequate. From this perspective, one would be inclined to ask the sort of question posed by the Canadian Democratic Audit: do emerging media technologies contribute to making Canadian democracy more, or less, participatory, inclusive, and responsive? Bearing in mind the complexity sketched above, we find that the answer to this question is still unlikely to be unambiguous and universal. Approaching it requires attention to the various ways in which innovative technologies bear on the possibilities of democratic politics: as means, objects, and the setting of political engagement.

Darin Barney

Emerging Media as Political Means

When questions are raised about the political implications of emerging media, the default assumption is typically that the issue primarily concerns the ways in which various political actors or institutions *use* such technologies as *means* of communicating, or producing and distributing information. In this respect, the question is as follows: what are people doing *with* these technologies? Their status as instruments or means of engaging in political activity and accomplishing political goals is certainly central to any evaluation of their democratic implications. In terms of the Canadian Democratic Audit, the operative question is whether, across the vast array of uses to which these technologies are being put, they are mediating enhanced opportunities for political participation and greater degrees of inclusiveness and responsiveness than was characteristic of politics under previous media regimes. Are there ways in which these technologies are being applied that decrease opportunities for participation and undermine inclusiveness and responsiveness?

Communication Technology investigated the use of emerging media technologies by a range of political actors including government, political parties, advocacy groups and social movements, activists, and individual citizens. Little evidence was found to support the notion that mainstream institutional political actors – primarily governments and parties – are consistently using these technologies in ways that significantly expand opportunities for meaningful political participation by a broader, more inclusive range of Canadian citizens. This is a surprising conclusion, given the widespread adoption of these technologies by governments and political parties. However, despite what is generally acknowledged as the potential for emerging technologies to mediate enhanced citizen engagement, the priorities that have guided parties and governments in their deployment of them have tended in other directions.

For several years, the Government of Canada has characterized itself as among the world's most connected to its citizens, an image supported by consistently high scores in international rankings of e-government preparedness. Canada's Government On-Line (GOL) project, inaugurated in 1999, has entailed a comprehensive effort to make government services and information available via the Internet, to the point of establishing electronic service delivery as the primary locus of contact between citizens and government. The government's priorities in these efforts have included realizing efficiencies and cost savings in the delivery of services, effective management of information privacy and infrastructure security concerns, and a "client-centred" effort to make electronic services accessible, convenient, and responsive to users. The Canadian government has also explored, somewhat more tentatively, the potential of emerging media to facilitate expanded, enhanced, and new forms of citizen engagement in the political processes of government, so-called e-democracy. This has included an endeavour to make increasing volumes of government information available on-line, as well as to integrate the utilities of new technologies in processes of public consultation between elections.

In relation to the criteria of participation, responsiveness, and inclusiveness, the outcomes of government's adoption of emerging media technologies have been ambiguous. On the one hand, it could be argued that on-line service delivery has increased government responsiveness and that digital technologies have made it possible to include more, and more diverse, citizens in the decision- and policy-making processes of government than ever before. On the other hand, one might argue that it is remarkable how little has changed, given the formidable affordances of these technologies and their normalization in other sectors of social and political life. The government's imagination of its relationship to citizens, as characterized primarily by transactions between a service provider and its clients, limits rather than opens democratic horizons, especially in a context where digital networks have also enabled the rationalization and privatization of many state agencies.

In a similar respect, the democratic significance of government efforts to make some forms of information available on-line must be measured against the broader trend toward increased commoditization, commercialization, and centralization of control over much government information and the ongoing escalation of state-led deployments of new technologies for purposes of civilian surveillance. In light of this, despite technologies that promise unprecedented access to information, critics have consistently described recent governments as carrying out an equally unprecedented narrowing of the scope of access to information in Canada, as well as a "securitization" of the public sphere, the combined implications of which are anything but salutary for democratic citizenship. And though emerging technologies have been deployed with some regularity in public consultation exercises – see, for example, the government's Consulting With Canadians web portal at www.consultingcanadians.gc.ca – consistent opportunities for citizens to participate meaningfully in transparent processes that are clearly linked to discernible outcomes remain the exception rather than the rule. Even as government takes tentative steps toward adopting the hypercollaborative social-networking platforms of Web 2.0, emerging media will succeed in democratizing policy making only if driven by a serious shift in government's motivation for engaging in consultation in the first place. So long as consultation is understood as a strategically necessary risk to be managed, no technology will be able to independently produce more or better opportunities for meaningful participation. As always, the motivation of the particular agency, institution, or actor in using a given information or communication technology is more important to the possibility of a democratic outcome than the mere fact of the technology's use.

The same can be said of the application of emerging media by political parties. *Communication Technology* found that the parties had made relatively modest use of emerging media for purposes of substantial democratization. Several parties have sought to integrate emerging social media utilities into their on-line communications strategies, including social-networking applications, blogs, content aggregators, and user-generated content sharing. For the most part, the orientation of the parties toward these technologies has been entirely strategic. Efforts to capitalize on their potential to democratize decision and policy making within parties on an ongoing basis have been conspicuously absent. On the other hand, parties have made extensive use of these technologies for internal administration, fundraising, publication of party and campaign information, media and public relations management, and data gathering and analysis pursuant to crafting and executing highly agile and customized electoral campaigns. Indeed, it could be argued that this latter is the single most important impact that novel digital and network technologies have had upon the practice of Canadian political parties. As in most advanced liberal democracies, technologically mediated information gathering, processing, and management are now major elements of partisan electoral campaigns in Canada (Cross 2004). In the 2008 election, this activity reached unprecedented levels of extension and sophistication, as parties utilized powerful database and processing techniques to gather massive volumes of complex geo- and psycho-demographic information on citizens, combined with in-house and commercially available consumer and opinion data, to produce fine-grained profiles aimed at increasingly precise voter targeting and election day vote-mobilization strategies. In the 2008 campaign, it was reported that "the Conservative Party's campaign computers hold the most detailed electoral data on Canadians ever assembled by a political party ... enabling the Tories to run the most micro-targeted campaign the country has ever experienced" (Valpy 2008, A11). In fact, all five main parties were reported to be using a "micro-targeting voter-profile tool, which outlines people's ethnicity, social values, and income level, cross-referenced with their political support" (Jiménez 2008, A6). Perhaps one could argue that such tools simply make parties more closely responsive to the preferences and needs of broader, more inclusive swaths of voters. An equally plausible conclusion would be that we are approaching the moment when partisan electoral competition in Canada becomes purely technological, not just in its preferred instruments but in its basic character.

The promise of emerging media to revitalize democracy through enhanced opportunities for more inclusive participation has been invested with greatest hope not in established institutions and agencies but rather at the level of individual citizens. In the midst of widespread diagnoses of citizen disengagement and disaffection, it is hoped that emerging technologies will mediate a revitalization of political participation in the democratic public sphere. It is certainly the case that individual Canadians have taken up novel technologies with great fervour, as evidenced by steadily escalating rates of Internet use, including especially among those already inclined to look for political information, as well as use of a broad range of related digital and networked devices and applications. Nevertheless, it is far from clear that engagement in politics – whether mainstream partisan competition or alternative non-partisan forms of engagement – accounts for a significant portion of the time most Canadians spend with emerging media technologies. Recent research in the United States reports that "political traffic is a tiny portion of Web usage. Traffic to political Web sites is sparser even than many skeptics have expected" (Hindman 2009, 131). Most statistical accounts confirm that, when it comes to how most Canadians use emerging media most of the time, politics ranks far below other forms of information gathering, socializing, consumerist, entertainment, and communicative activities. In this respect, these technologies would seem to reinforce, rather than reverse, the general depoliticization characteristic of the Canadian population.

The advent of so-called Web 2.0 applications, including social-networking utilities such as Facebook and Twitter, multimedia content-sharing sites such as YouTube and Flickr, aggregation and syndication services, "folksonomic" utilities for the tagging, ranking, and evaluating of on-line information, and, of course, the proliferation of wikis and blogs, have significantly altered the terrain of political communication in Canada. These platforms are all characterized by relatively easy facilitation of production and circulation of high-quality user-generated content, linking between sites and information items, and provision of opportunities for users to collaborate and comment. Comedian Rick Mercer (2008, F3) has observed that "ordinary Canadians don't spend a lot of time reading blogs because ordinary Canadians know that blogs are basically the domain of idiots, mad people and news anchors." Nevertheless, even more than e-mail and the basic web utilities that preceded them, applications associated with Web 2.0 have brought with

them renewed hopes of a highly participatory and inclusive transformation of both politics and the mass media.

Whether these hopes are coming to fruition awaits the sober assessment of careful empirical analysis. It is clear that significant numbers
of people use Web 2.0 applications to engage in politics, whether this
takes the form of media consumption, organization of political action,
or participation in the production and circulation of political information and opinion. Whether this constitutes a significant increase over
the number of people who were already involved in political activity via
other media is not at all clear. It may be that, though emerging media
present powerful and interesting new instruments to politically engaged citizens, the overall quotient and distribution of political involvement is simply reinforced in this setting, rather than significantly
increased. After a thorough empirical study of recent patterns of web
use in the United States, Matthew Hindman (2009) argues that claims
regarding the inherent egalitarianism and inclusivity of web-based
political activity are difficult to sustain, given the persistence of
existing hierarchies in the on-line environment and the materialization
of new ones. Affirming that blogs have become a primary venue to which
citizens turn for political commentary, and that active political blogs
number in at least the hundreds of thousands, Hindman (ibid., 133,
emphasis in original) nevertheless concludes that "a small list of A-list
bloggers actually gets more political blog traffic than *the rest of the
citizenry combined.* Talk about blogs empowering ordinary citizens
rings doubly hollow when the top bloggers are better educated, more
frequently male, and less ethnically diverse than the elite media the
blogs often criticize." It is possible that the Canadian blogosphere is
different, but absent comparably thorough evidence, one would be hard
pressed to come up with reasons for reaching this conclusion. At a
minimum, we should be skeptical of claims that simply assume that
the apparent proliferation of a medium such as the blog equates with
significant democratic gains.

Parties and mass media have had to become more responsive to
currents originating in the changed media environment. Bloggers,

whether as quasi-partisan commentators or independent citizen-journalists, have come to play a prominent role in investigating and scrutinizing the conduct and statements of public officials and candidates for office, and placing this information into wider public circulation. Sometimes, these items spread virally across the blogosphere and related media-sharing networks; sometimes they act as seeds that grow into major stories covered by traditional mass media outlets. In either case, political actors find themselves being held to account for their actions, statements, personal histories, and associations to a much greater degree than before. Early in the 2008 Canadian federal election cycle, major party candidates were forced to withdraw when "embarrassing" revelations about past statements and behaviour surfaced on the web. Partisan bloggers and activists also routinely produce and circulate media content that, though at an arm's length from official party campaigns, nevertheless compels candidates and mainstream media to respond. For example, candidates and mainstream news organizations alike now routinely find themselves in the position of having their claims "fact-checked" by a distributed network of bloggers and citizen-journalists. These same platforms and users also serve important networking and mobilization functions, as reader/contributors in the blogosphere and on social-networking sites such as Facebook can be quickly rallied to act on behalf of, or against, particular positions or actors. Such was the case in the 2008 election, when large numbers of voters were mobilized on-line to support the inclusion of Green Party leader Elizabeth May in the televised leaders' debates. This was an example of the participatory affordances of emerging media being taken up in a manner that prompted a significant official response that might not otherwise have been forthcoming.

Without question, these technologies have given formidable new tools to partisans and activists, and have changed the landscape in which governments, parties, and traditional mass media outlets operate. One way to describe these developments is to say that emerging media have presented individual political actors with an expanded range of participatory opportunities and that these in turn have forced institutional actors to be more responsive. Still, it remains unclear whether the character of political engagement mediated by these technologies is such that we should uncritically accept that their proliferation entails a substantive improvement in the quality of democratic participation. One need not be prejudicially dismissive of the potential diversity of forms of legitimate popular expression to wonder whether repeated opportunities to register opinion, to have one's prior partisan prejudices confirmed, or to click through to grainy video-clips of potential candidates skinny-dipping in their youth constitutes a democratic renaissance. The tools may be far less important than the motivation and imagination of those wielding them. In this light, those looking for pointers to the democratic potential of emerging media would do well to focus their attention upon those highly politicized social movements, advocacy groups, and independent and community media activists who inhabit the oppositional margins of Canadian political culture. These remain largely silenced in the mainstream mass media environment, and they have found in emerging media the means by which they might organize, mobilize, publicize, and intervene toward the end of a more egalitarian and just democratic politics. Here, emerging media appear as inclusive, participatory, and responsive because the actors using them tend to be committed to these norms regardless of the strategic utilities presented by the technologies themselves. However, as significant as these movements and activists are, and as encouraging as their genuinely democratic uses of emerging media may be, the brutal fact is that they remain a tear in a salty sea of highly privatized, strategic, and consumerist technological culture in Canada.

Emerging Media as Political Objects

As important as they are, instrumental questions about new technologies as means of political engagement should not exhaust our inquiry into their democratic status. These technologies are not just political instruments: they are also political objects, which is to say that citizens ought to be able to participate in making political decisions about them.

Darin Barney

All technologies are political in this sense. They are political because their development, application, and regulation are outcomes of decisions made in particular settings by particular actors (the Internet, for example, did not just drop out of the sky). Technologies are also political because their development, application, and regulation in a given context can influence the character of human relationships and the distribution of opportunities, resources, and power. This is especially true of emerging information and communication technologies because of the role they play as crucial infrastructures for a broad and increasing array of economic, social, and political practices. For this reason, we are justified in asking not just what people do *with* these technologies but also what people can do *about* them. The question here is whether the contexts in which decisions about the development, application, and regulation of emerging media technologies have been made have been inclusive, participatory, and responsive enough to qualify as democratic.

Communication policy, regulation, and governance have historically been one of the most democratic areas of public policy in Canada, both in terms of the principles guiding it and the processes by which it is developed and implemented. For nearly a century, the public interest in accessible, diverse, and high-quality media systems occupied a place of prominence in the imagination of Canadian communication policy. And whenever technological changes – the development of telegraphy, telephony, and radio and television broadcasting – have prompted re-evaluation of the policy and regulatory framework surrounding communication media in Canada, the government has solicited broad-based public input from the diverse variety of stakeholders and communities whose interests are bound up in these changes. In the terms adopted by the Canadian Democratic Audit, it could be said that communication policy, regulation, and governance have historically comprised a domain where responsiveness, inclusion, and participation have been highly valued.

Communication Technology explored whether regulation and policy making concerning emerging information and communication technologies has conformed to this historical standard. This policy cycle began in 1993, when the Department of Commun.   banded and Industry Canada took over responsibility for policy   ng the development of emerging media technologies in Canada. It included the establishment and privatization of the Canadian Network for the Advancement of Research, Industry and Education (CANARIE), the activity of the Information Highway Advisory Council (established in 1994, with reports in 1995 and 1996), the National Broadband Task Force (2000), and a number of important hearings and reports by the Canadian Radio-Television and Telecommunications Commission (CRTC), the federal regulator of broadcasting and telecommunication. These latter included 1995's *Competition and Convergence* report (which paved the way for unprecedented media concentration and cross-ownership of telecommunication and broadcasting enterprises in Canada) and the *Report on New Media* in 1999, which exempted on-line activity and enterprises from CRTC regulatory oversight (Canadian Radio-Television and Telecommunications Commission 1995, 1999).

In a departure from the tradition of modestly public and democratic communication policy making in Canada, the media policy cycle surrounding emerging media has been undemocratic in its processes and anti-democratic in its outcomes (Barney 2005). Processes have been characterized by systematic overrepresentation of industry interests, a routine lack of transparency, and a persistent denial of opportunities for meaningful public participation. An exception in the latter case was the CRTC, which is mandated to hold public hearings pursuant to major regulatory changes and to allow public intervention in licensing proceedings. The CRTC stood alone through this period in terms of providing opportunities for the considerable number of citizens mobilized by emerging media issues to participate in the processes by which decisions were being made. However, the CRTC's regulatory decisions – for example, its 1999 resolution to exempt new media enterprises from regulatory oversight – were not clearly responsive to the breadth and diversity of alternatives and interests generated through these public proceedings, opting routinely for measures that primarily reflected the private interests of a fairly narrow cohort of industry stakeholders. These decisions were consistent with government policy through this period, which viewed emerging media primarily through the lens of industrial development and economic competitiveness rather than placing priority on developing them as an infrastructure of Canadian culture, communities, and the democratic public sphere. Media policy scholars Marc Raboy and Genevieve Bonin (2008, 60) observe that, though the CRTC was once understood to be the guarantor of the public interest in communication in Canada, "somewhere along the way, it became an enabling mechanism for Canadian capital accumulation." The same could be said of Canadian communication and media policy more generally. The proliferation of digital information and communication networks in the 1990s might well mark the point "along the way" where the institutional structure for inclusive democratic participation in communication policy making and regulation, oriented toward outcomes that are responsive to the public interest, was decisively undermined.

The situation has not improved considerably in recent years. In 2005, the federal government created a three-member Telecommunications Policy Review Panel charged with recommending sweeping changes to the 1993 Telecommunications Act. Media scholar and activist Leslie Shade (2008, 112) has characterized the process as follows: "Public input into the process was minimal ... Two public forums were held: one in the Yukon Territories [sic] for public interest groups and the other in Gatineau, Quebec, mostly for industry groups. Dominated by industry and government concerns about issues such as competitiveness, productivity and deregulation, the Panel received 200 submissions totaling thousands of pages, but a content analysis revealed that Aboriginal, consumer, women's and community groups represented only 15.5% of the total submissions, versus 60.1% for industry groups." It could be argued that people just are not that interested in these issues. However, critical public policy scholars in Canada routinely report that the administrative and expertise burdens of monitoring and participating effectively in CRTC proceedings typically exceed the capacity of many of the constituencies that would otherwise be inclined to engage in these issues, especially in light of the consistently disappointing returns for doing so. In this case, the panel's 2006 report reflected both its mandate to approach telecom policy review from the perspective of securing the competitiveness of major Canadian firms in global markets and the vision for how to accomplish this that was endorsed by the industrial stakeholders with whom it primarily consulted. Its major recommendation was for less regulation and more reliance on market forces in order to promote accelerated growth and competitiveness of Canada's telecommunications industry. Shade (ibid.) reports that those community and public interest groups that did participate in the panel's consultations were "dismayed" by the report's neglect of the indispensable role of state regulation in securing the conditions of an accessible democratic infrastructure, the role played by community-based groups in supporting this sort of access, and the need for state support of programs aimed at bridging the various digital divides that continue to face many Canadians.

This is not the only example. Between 2004 and 2008, Industry Canada, without public consultation, moved to auction a significant portion of the radio spectrum, a move widely interpreted as a transfer of significant public resources into the private hands of major telecommunication enterprises hoping to use them to deliver a range of lucrative digital services. According to Graham Longford (2008, 99), these auctions "have led to the concentration of spectrum in the hands of a few, deep-pocketed firms, and threaten to place it further beyond the reach of Canada's citizens and communities. These and other developments constitute a regulatory clearing of the spectrum commons, and enclosure and expropriation of the public airwaves for private gain that ignores the interests of consumers and undermines public rights to the airwaves." In 2007, Ottawa introduced long-awaited legislation to enact changes to Canada's copyright regime in response to the proliferation of digital media. Bill C-61 was the result of considerable consultation with industry stakeholders, including major interests in the US entertainment and media sectors, alongside nearly total exclusion of public interest advocates and non-commercial groups with a stake in the legal framework surrounding intellectual property. The planned legislation would have imposed industry-friendly restrictions on the fair use, copying, and circulation of copyrighted materials, in a manner that many

Canadian activists and scholars characterized as even more severe than similar legislation in the United States. The legislation was withdrawn, however, after an unprecedented public protest, mobilized with the aid of a range of social-networking applications, which has yielded an organization known as Fair Copyright Canada, a coalition of activists, critical media scholars, creative workers, and community organizations, with whom the government will now most certainly have to contend whenever it decides to remount its effort to reform the Copyright Act. Again, this is a clear example of a case in which political participation facilitated by emerging media provoked a response that would not have occurred otherwise. That this had to transpire outside the official framework in which the legislation was developed speaks to ongoing deficits of participation, inclusion, and responsiveness in those institutions charged with charting a policy course in relation to emerging technologies.

The role of the CRTC as a venue for democratic public consultation on new technological issues has been mixed through this period. On the one hand, as Richard Schultz (2008) has documented, 2006-07 brought with it an unprecedented degree of ministerial intervention in CRTC decision making, pursuant to enforcing the government's industry-friendly laissez-faire approach to the sector, in a manner that paid little attention to constituencies beyond industry stakeholders. On the other hand, the CRTC nevertheless continues to provide the most significant institutional venue in which Canadian citizens, community groups, and public interest advocates can participate in relatively inclusive processes related to media policy and regulation. In 2007, the CRTC commissioned an expert report, known as the Dunbar-Leblanc report (Dunbar and Leblanc 2007), which reviewed existing regulation and made over a hundred recommendations for reform. Simultaneously, the commission sponsored an unprecedented (for the CRTC) set of public meetings concerning the issue of concentrated media ownership in Canada. The Diversity of Voices hearings were held over several days in Gatineau, Quebec. Fifty-two parties appeared, and the commission received 162 written comments directly, as well as 1,800 comments filed as part of a campaign by the group Canadians for Democratic Media.

In January 2008, the CRTC announced new restrictions on cross-media ownership, the common ownership of television services, including pay and specialty services, and the common ownership of broadcasting distribution undertakings. Although these restrictions fall short of reversing a decade of "blindly approving every mega-merger placed before it" (Raboy and Bonin 2008, 61), they do signal an openness to something other than the promotion of industrial interests and a potential shift in the balance of priorities for the regulator to include greater scope for public interest considerations.

Whether this is an anomaly or the start of a new trend is difficult to say. In 2009, the CRTC reviewed its 1999 new media exemption order, in which Internet content and services were exempted from broadcasting regulation. The consultation process elicited 150 comments, over seventy final submissions, and more than fifty oral submissions. Many of these called upon the CRTC to assert its jurisdiction over emerging media in a manner that leaves open the possibility of regulation in the public interest. Nevertheless, the CRTC decided to continue the exemption of new media enterprises from regulation, an outcome that reflected the priorities of the industry stakeholders, whose voices dominated the proceedings. Also in 2009, the CRTC undertook an investigation into network neutrality and the practice of Internet throttling, or traffic shaping, whereby major Internet service providers (ISPs) manage network traffic in ways that discriminate against certain types of content and practices by reducing the bandwidth available to them, thus slowing transmission and download speeds in order to reserve bandwidth for preferred content and applications. The typically cited example is deceleration of peer-to-peer file-sharing traffic, but critics worry about extensions of throttling whereby major providers might reserve preferred service for content and applications in which they have a business interest while reducing the bandwidth available to competing applications and content (Geist 2008). Such practices violate the long-standing principle of common carriage in telecommunications, whereby private owners of major infrastructure are required to provide equal access and service to all legal users of that infrastructure and to refrain from anti-competitive or abusive discrimination aimed at securing monopolistic advantage. In 2008, the CRTC responded to a complaint filed by the Canadian Association of Internet Providers against Bell Canada, challenging the company's right to manage the network traffic of its wholesale customers. The CRTC ruled in Bell's favour, finding that its practices were not discriminatory (it was doing the same thing to all its wholesale and retail customers) and therefore permissible.

Perhaps anticipating the controversy that would greet this ruling, and acknowledging the complexity of the issue, the CRTC simultaneously announced that it would undertake a comprehensive review of the question of network neutrality, complete with public hearings. In response to this, it received nearly five hundred comments and over thirteen thousand e-mail submissions from individuals, many mobilized by highly motivated activist networks and coalitions of social movements working in this area. At the oral hearing in July 2009, twenty-six presentations were made, and an on-line consultation initiated by the commission elicited fourteen hundred individual comments. The CRTC's decision was mixed. On the one hand, it placed real limits on the practice of traffic shaping: in response to consumer complaints, ISPs can be called upon to fully disclose and justify specific traffic management measures and their impacts on service levels, and are banned from using personal information gleaned from packet inspection for anything other than traffic shaping. On the other hand, critics have been unsatisfied with the tying of compliance to the trigger of consumer complaint and have interpreted these measures as merely setting the conditions whereby major ISPs can continue Internet throttling, as opposed to banning it altogether. Thus, the decision concerning network neutrality could be described as an instance in which the CRTC's mandate to provide for public participation in its regulatory processes, in this case made more inclusive by a highly orchestrated on-line campaign, resulted in an outcome that was responsive to a public interest defined at least somewhat more broadly than that of the telecommunications industry.

Emerging Media as the Setting of Politics

A common refrain in contemporary popular culture is that emerging information and communication technologies influence or change everything. This signals the third way in which these technologies bear on the possibility of a more inclusive, responsive, and participatory democratic politics in Canada. Emerging media are means of engaging in politics, and also (at least potentially) the object of political engagement, but their political significance does not end there. Because these technologies are involved in an expanding array of economic and social practices, they also constitute an important part of the general setting in which democratic citizenship is situated and unfolds. The setting provided by emerging media for citizenship is equal parts material and cultural: we live in the midst of these technologies and also identify with the culture that surrounds them. In approaching emerging media as means of politics, we ask what people do *with* them; in approaching them as objects of politics, we ask what people can do *about* them. In approaching them as the setting of politics, we ask what they do to people as citizens and how this affects the prospects of a more inclusive, participatory, and responsive democratic experience.

Communication Technology investigated the relationship between emerging media technologies and globalization, and the implications of this relationship for the possibilities of an inclusive, participatory, and responsive democratic politics in Canada. The transnationalization of the capitalist economy and the restructuring of national sovereignty to accommodate it have had a reciprocal relationship with emerging media, whereby the latter have been crucial enablers of the various practices of transnational capitalism and have also developed under the conditions established by this economy and the state forms that attend to it. In this volume, I argued that globalization has made the problem of subjecting the development of these technologies, and the activities they mediate, to substantially democratic judgment and governance in the public interest even more difficult to solve, largely by defining communication as a commodity best managed under an industrial, as opposed to political or cultural strategy. I also suggested that the global media system, in which novel technologies play a crucial role, is one in which the private interests of massive transnational media corporations are increasingly shielded from regulation by, and accountability to, state-level institutions and the citizenries they represent. There have been some exceptions, such as the role played by civil society organizations at the 2003 and 2005 World Summit on the Information Society. Nonetheless, despite the mobilization of transnational activist networks and movements devoted to democratic media reform, international forums in which decisions affecting the global deployment and governance of emerging media are made do not embody the norms of representation, participation, and scrutiny that we typically expect from democratic political institutions (Raboy and Landry 2005). Ironically, Canada's subscription to the rising global media order has been supported by a consistent discourse of technological nationalism at the domestic level, whereby the country's future prosperity is staked to a commitment to technological innovation. The necessity of this commitment is so taken for granted that it - along with the various financial, regulatory, and distributional entailments supporting it - is effectively insulated from democratic political contest and judgment.

Communication Technology also examined the relationship between emerging media and the distribution of power in Canada, a relationship that defines the material and cultural setting in which citizenship is situated. If emerging media are involved in a substantial democratization of Canadian political life, we should find evidence of their contribution to social and economic equality in Canada. In this respect, the assessment focused on three issues: the digital divide, the political economy of emerging media and work, and emerging media and the democratic public sphere.

Although the digital divide, conceived in terms of basic connectivity to, and use of, the Internet, has narrowed significantly, important power differentials continue to exist, recognizable only if our understanding of the digital divide includes questions about how people apply this medium (as passive consumers or as active contributors), their capacity to employ these technologies in ways that contribute to, rather than diminish, their autonomy, and their ability to influence (either individually or collectively) the development, design, content, and regulation of the medium and its applications. The creation and popularity of Web 2.0 applications that provide greater degrees of user collaboration in the generation and circulation of content on the Internet have blurred the line between information consumers and information producers, and this has enabled a broader public of users to approach these media as agents rather than simply as an audience. That said, it is far too early to conclude whether the likes of blogs, YouTube, and Facebook have fundamentally altered the distribution of material (not just symbolic) power in Canada such that perennially marginalized and disadvantaged groups now experience Canadian society as somehow more inclusive, egalitarian, and just.

Much has already been said in this chapter about the relationship between emerging media and the consolidation of prevailing distributions of economic power in Canada. However, one of the most important domains in which new technologies affect the setting of citizenship is that of work. *Communication Technology* also considered the role emerging media have played in the explosion of non-standard, contingent, precarious work and employment arrangements characteristic of recent years in Canada. For some people, these are voluntary and are experienced as a source of relative autonomy and empowerment. However, for many, these non-standard arrangements, which are crucially enabled by a variety of networked technologies, are involuntary and experienced as a source of ongoing material insecurity and diminished leisure. In this sense, emerging media have been instrumental to an unequal distribution of the material resources of security and leisure in the Canadian economy, and so may undermine the prospects for citizenship for an increasing number of Canadians who work under these conditions (see Menzies 2005).

Finally, the question of the connection between emerging media technologies and the democratic public sphere as an essential setting for citizenship has been a favourite topic of scholars in media and political studies in recent years. This interest has been fuelled by a sense of the potential for emerging media to facilitate more informed, more intensive, and more interactive political discussions between citizens separated by great distances than were possible under conditions established by broadcast media such as television and the mass press. Although the participatory opportunities afforded by emerging media, especially in relation directly to political affairs, are considerable, *Communication Technology* found evidence suggesting that the opposite may also be true: these media enhance the construction of the public sphere as a site of entertainment, commerce, consumption, and surveillance rather than one of politicization and democratic citizenship. As discussed above, there are many highly politicized public realms and a great deal of citizenship activity mediated by emerging media, particularly in the context of social-networking and collaborative platforms, that make it easier for politically inclined people to organize, mobilize, and publicize. However, these are not necessarily characteristic of the broader relationship between emerging media, the public sphere, and the culture of citizenship more generally. Indeed, critical scholars are beginning to wonder whether the setting provided by these media might require us to rethink the status of the norms of publicity – information, communication, and participation – in light of the fact that these technologies appear to deliver on these goods so copiously, while leaving fundamentally inegalitarian and depoliticized structures of power and advantage not only intact but bolstered and legitimated (see Barney 2008). This prospect invites an unsettling, but perhaps necessary, question: what if emerging media succeed in making Canadian politics more participatory, inclusive, and responsive but, for all that, less democratic?

The hope for a better outcome is not at all technological: it is strictly political. It relies on the choices of influential actors and decision makers, and the distribution of power in the institutional and material settings in which these decisions are reached. To make emerging media technologies more democratic means of political engagement requires not only using them for abstract purposes of increased information and communication but mobilizing them in ways that are concretely tied to the democratic principle of equality as access to power and resources. Obviously, this would entail a fundamental shift in the priorities and practices of partisan and government institutions, whose primary disposition in regard to these technologies remains almost exclusively instrumental and strategic. Imagining the possibility of emerging technologies being used to facilitate a radical equalization of political decision-making power in Canada does not require much in terms of reconfiguring these technologies on a technical level. It would, however, demand a transformation of conventional partisan and governing institutions such that would leave them barely recognizable. They would have to start thinking and acting more like cooperatives or democratic social movements. This is why very few of those who call for democratic "improvements" to existing institutions by means of emerging media technologies can be taken at their word. What they probably have in mind is that we had better be careful to manage the development of these technologies such that existing institutions, despite the inequalities upon which they thrive, might survive the onslaught.

The same basic spirit prevents the Canadian state from creating institutional spaces in which new technologies might be approached by citizens as objects of democratic political judgment. The development and regulation of these technologies, driven by the political priorities of powerful stakeholders in the Canadian economy, are simply too important to be exposed to the alternative political priorities that might arise from genuine engagement with those whose stakes in that economy are considered marginal. To actually democratize new technologies as objects of political judgment would require a shift in the political economy of technology that would potentially place Canadian capitalism in a very unstable position. Thus it is that technology and its development must be kept safe from democracy through highly inegalitarian institutional arrangements and through the reproduction of radically depoliticizing rhetorics of technological nationalism and innovation. Dismantling this cultural setting, whereby technology relates to democracy as some kind of fantasy, rather than as a demanding and radical material condition, is the first step toward the democratic outcomes we purport to want.

Darin Barney

Works Cited

Barney, Darin. 2005. *Communication technology.* Canadian Democratic Audit. Vancouver: UBC Press.

–. 2008. Politics and emerging media: The revenge of publicity. *Global Media Journal – Canadian Edition* 1(1): 89-106. http://www.gmj.uottawa.ca/.

Canadian Radio-Television and Telecommunications Commission. 1995. *Competition and culture on Canada's information highway: Managing the realities of transition.* Ottawa: Public Works and Government Services Canada, 19 May.

–. 1999. *Report on new media.* Ottawa: Canadian Radio-Television and Telecommunications Commission, 17 May.

Cross, William. 2004. *Political parties.* Canadian Democratic Audit. Vancouver: UBC Press.

Dunbar, Laurence, and Christian Leblanc. 2007. Review of the regulatory framework for broadcasting services in Canada. Ottawa: Canadian Radio-Television and Telecommunications Commission. http://www.crtc.gc.ca/.

Geist, Michael. 2008. Network neutrality in Canada. In *For sale to the highest bidder: Telecom policy in Canada,* ed. Marita Moll and Leslie Regan Shade, 73-82. Ottawa: Canadian Center for Policy Alternatives.

Hindman, Matthew. 2009. *The myth of digital democracy.* Princeton: Princeton University Press.

Jiménez, Marina. 2008. Parties get sophisticated in bid for immigrant vote. *Globe and Mail,* 7 October, A6.

Longford, Graham. 2008. Spectrum matters: Clearing and reclaiming the spectrum commons. In *For sale to the highest bidder: Telecom policy in Canada,* ed. Marita Moll and Leslie Regan Shade, 95-107. Ottawa: Canadian Center for Policy Alternatives.

Menzies, Heather. 2005. *No time: Stress and the crisis of modern life.* Vancouver: Douglas and McIntyre.

Mercer, Rick. 2008. Oh, no. I was going to run for office one day – but I have a blog. *Globe and Mail,* 27 September, F3.

Raboy, Marc, and Genevieve Bonin. 2008. From culture to business to culture: Shifting winds at the CRTC. In *For sale to the highest bidder: Telecom policy in Canada,* ed. Marita Moll and Leslie Regan Shade, 61-72. Ottawa: Canadian Center for Policy Alternatives.

Raboy, Marc, and Normand Landry. 2005. *Civil society, communication and global governance: Issues from the World Summit on the Information Society.* New York: Peter Lang.

Schultz, Richard. 2008. Telecommunications policy: What a difference a minister can make. In *How Ottawa spends 2008-2009: A more orderly federalism?* ed. Allan Maslove, 134-62. Montreal and Kingston: McGill-Queen's University

Press.

Shade, Leslie Regan. 2008. Public interest activism in Canadian ICT policy: Blowin' in the policy winds. *Global Media Journal – Canadian Edition* 1(1): 107-21. http://www.gmj.uottawa.ca/.

Valpy, Michael. 2008. What the Tories know about you. *Globe and Mail,* 13 September, A11.

CANADIAN DEMOCRACY: AN ASSESSMENT AND AN AGENDA

10

R. Kenneth Carty

Was it really necessary to do a democratic audit of Canada? After all, most people would readily agree that Canada is one of the world's most successful liberal democracies. But even if it seems worthwhile to hold the country up against a set of absolute standards, we might still pause to ask a second question. Is it realistically possible to audit a phenomenon as notoriously slippery as democracy, especially in a country as diverse and continually changing as Canada? Each of the specialized studies in the Canadian Democratic Audit is based on the premise that the answer to both these questions is a resounding yes. However, though all the auditors point to aspects of Canada's common political life of which Canadians can be justly proud, they do not hesitate to draw attention to political challenges that confront the country and its peoples. This book, which brings together the key observations, conclusions, and recommendations of the individual studies, allows us to stand back and ask where Canadians need to turn their attention as they continue to pursue something as elusive as a democratic common life.

Canada: By Comparison

Canadians may feel a bit smug about their record of building and maintaining a prosperous, healthy society of caring citizens, but the reality is that they have been remarkably successful at it. Year after year, the United Nations issues an annual report with a Human Development Index (HDI) that combines measures of life expectancy, education, and the standard of living to compare how well countries have done in creating livable societies. And for decades now, Canada has found itself near the top of the list of over 140 nations: in 1975, it ranked third; in 1985 and 1995, it came first and second respectively; and in 2006, it was third. These small differences in Canada's position in the rank order are not really significant, for they generally reflect variations in the third decimal place of the UN's statistical index. The important story is that, by this comprehensive measure, modern Canada has for decades surely rated as among the very best places in which anyone could live.

The high score Canada receives on the HDI reflects its success in creating a society whose members share the benefits of a long and good life. Its life expectancy rates are among the highest in the world, and Canadians enjoy one of the most generous standards of living anywhere on the planet. Sensitive to the realities of important differences in the experiences of women and men in many parts of the world, the UN recalculated its assessments in terms of a gender-related development index. On that measure, Canada ranked fourth (again by a matter of decimal points), which suggests that it has done comparatively well in ensuring that both men and women enjoy its advantages.

In an attempt to discover what living in various communities is actually like, Mercer, a large international consulting firm, regularly compares over two hundred of the world's major cities on thirty-nine different criteria that consider both broad socio-political, economic, cultural, and environmental conditions as well as the practical on-the-ground realities of health, education, housing, and transport infrastructure. This information is all summarized in a comprehensive Quality-of-Living Index, and the evidence makes it clear that Canadian cities are places in which people are able to live well. In its 2008 report, Mercer ranked five Canadian cities – Vancouver, Toronto, Ottawa, Montreal, and Calgary in that order – in the top twenty-five in the world; only Germany had as many.

R. Kenneth Carty

Table 10.1

World Bank indicators of governance and institutional quality, 2008

Indicators	Canada	USA	UK	Australia	Sweden	Germany	France
Voice and accountability	96	L	L	L	H	L	L
Political stability	84	L	L	H	H	H	L
Government effectiveness	97	L	L	L	H	L	L
Regulatory quality	95	L	H	H	H	L	L
Rule of law	96	L	L	L	H	L	L
Control of corruption	96	L	L	H	L	L	L

Note: H stands for higher; L stands for lower.
Source: World Bank Group (2009).

In large part, Canadians live well because their political institutions allow them to govern themselves well. Freedom House, an American-based voluntary organization, has been providing a comparative assessment of the state of political rights and civil liberties in almost two hundred countries for the past quarter century. It considers ten indicators of political rights, and fifteen of civil liberties, and has consistently given Canada its highest rating. In parallel examinations of both press and religious freedom, it rates those dimensions of Canadian life equally highly, concluding that Canada is one of the world's genuinely free societies. And Transparency International, an international non-governmental organization devoted to combating corruption, ranked Canada as one of the cleanest countries (tied for eighth out of 180 in 2009) on its widely regarded Corruption Perception Index.

The World Bank sponsors a worldwide governance indicators project that has created a set of measures to assess just how well countries are actually governed. Its findings also provide strong evidence that Canada does remarkably well. Table 10.1 provides a schematic summary of the project's measures of its six key multi-dimensional aspects of a country's governance. The numerical score indicates what percent of the over two hundred countries included in the survey rank lower. Thus, a score of 96 on the "voice and accountability" criterion indicates that 96 percent of the surveyed countries performed more poorly than Canada on that aspect of political life. To put Canada's performance in perspective, the table reports how six other important industrial democratic countries scored on the same indicator in 2008. Of the other countries, none did better on every measure, and two of them (the United States and France) scored lower on every one of the six indicators; only Australia had a higher UN Human Development Index ranking that year.

By contemporary comparative standards, Canada clearly has an extraordinary record of good government and has developed a highly desirable quality of life for its citizens. Any audit of the Canadian political system needs to keep this reality in perspective. At the same time, however, other pieces of comparative evidence suggest that Canadians have not always managed to meet their own high standards and that not all Canadians have shared in the benefits of the system. Amnesty International is a highly respected worldwide organization dedicated to promoting human rights; many Canadians belong to it in an effort to improve conditions in other corners of the world. In a recent annual report, Amnesty International (2006, 84) pointedly noted that "indigenous women and girls continued to suffer a high level of discrimination and violence," and it returned to that theme in a moving 2009 document entitled *No More Stolen Sisters* (Amnesty International 2009).

Even though Canada ranked as high as fourth on the United Nations' gender-related HDI, Canadian women have not found that the doors to political and economic power and opportunity have opened as far or as easily as they might have expected. The 2006 comparative gender empowerment measure developed by the UN put Canada further down the list - in eleventh position. Clearly, the high HDI score does not guarantee that all Canadians have access to the good life. Of the twenty countries with the highest HDI scores, Canada ranked only ninth in terms of income equality, and its unemployment rates are typically higher than those of the United States and Australia. Perhaps this partially accounts for the unusually high level of labour conflict in the country. Joanne Monger (2004) reports that, during the decade from 1993 to 2002, the number of days lost to workplace disputes in Canada was much larger than in most other industrial countries. These conditions all have a political face, and an audit of democratic practice ought to explore which Canadians are not being fully included in the political life of the nation and why the system appears to be comparatively less responsive to their needs.

Canada: A Democratic Malaise?

Paul Martin conducted his 2003 campaign for the leadership of the Liberal Party, and ultimately the prime ministership of the country, on the theme that Canada was suffering from a "democratic deficit." He argued that, for too many, "the existing political process just doesn't appear to be working" and that this could be seen in the "growing dis-interest Canadians express in their democratic institutions and the increasing disengagement of Canadians from the political process" (Martin 2000, n.p., 2002, n.p.). This was not just political rhetoric, for Martin recognized that a growing mountain of evidence revealed a disconnect between citizens and their political institutions.

For some time, public opinion surveys have reported that Canadians say they are generally satisfied with how democracy works in the country. But it is also true that a significant majority now believe that "those elected to parliament soon lose touch with the people" and are of the opinion that "people like me do not have any say over what the government does" (Howe and Northrup 2000, 9). In practice, this increasing political cynicism and alienation left Canadians with sharply declining confidence in political parties – the very institutions that exist to allow them to control and direct their government. One immediate result is that few Canadians now participate in the activities of national political parties. Although the comparative evidence is sketchy and uneven, the best estimates we have indicate that party membership rates are lower in Canada than in virtually any other Western democracy. And the parties have recently demonstrated an "apparent inability to recruit young Canadians," which "raises the spectre of virtually member-less parties in the not too distant future" and "throws into question the viability of parties as democratic institutions" (Cross and Young 2004, 440).

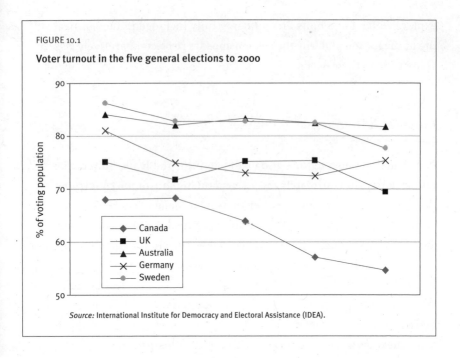

FIGURE 10.1

Voter turnout in the five general elections to 2000

Source: International Institute for Democracy and Electoral Assistance (IDEA).

One of the most obvious and widely lamented characteristics of Canadian politics in the past two decades has been the steadily falling numbers of Canadians who bother to participate in general elections. Voter turnout has declined in every general election since the 1980s, when it was already comparatively low (see Gidengil et al. 2004, 103-4; Courtney, Chapter 6 this volume; Gidengil et al., Chapter 5 this volume). This can be seen in Figure 10.1, which charts the proportion of the voting-age population that participated in each of the last five general elections of the twentieth century held in five parliamentary democracies with comparable standards of government. Two features of the figure stand out. First, Canadian voter turnout was lower than in all the other countries throughout the period. Second, although the proportion of the voting population has fallen in all these countries, the fall has been further, faster, and more consistent in Canada. Some of these discrepancies in voter turnout may reflect institutional differences, for of these five countries, only the United Kingdom uses the same single-member plurality electoral system as does Canada. A quite different system is used in each of the other three, and Australia also has a law requiring everyone to vote. Clear evidence of public concern for this development appeared in the emergence of electoral reform on the political agenda of several of the provinces during the early years of the new century (Carty 2006).

As Canada entered the twenty-first century, voter turnout in national general elections had fallen to about the same level as that in American presidential elections, a figure Canadians once pointed at with some disdain. The drop in participation has a particularly ominous dimension, for, as the Audit study titled *Citizens* reveals, much of this decline is to be found among young people (see Gidengil et al. 2004, 109-12; Gidengil et al., Chapter 5 this volume). If they do not soon find their way back into the system, electoral participation rates may well fall below 50 percent, which would raise serious questions about the very legitimacy of elected governments. Whatever the cause of the collapsing turnout, a phenomenon that is being replicated in provincial election contests all across the country (Stewart and Carty 2005), it is now widely agreed that it is symptomatic of a significant democratic malaise.

Prime Minister Martin's analysis of Canada's democratic deficit (at least while seeking the Liberal leadership) was that the problem was an institutional, not a civic, one. To put it simply, he argued that parliament did not work as it should, because excessive top-down party discipline constrained individual MPs in a way that alienated them from any significant role in the governance of the country. On the one hand, this centralized power and strengthened the hand of the executive; on the other, it weakened electoral accountability as MPs followed their party's instructions and not their constituents' preferences in casting votes in parliament. Citizens could hardly be expected to see this as democratic. Martin's prescription involved a set of proposals to reform the rules and operating norms of the House of Commons. Perhaps his projected changes would increase the general sense of efficacy of some MPs, but one ought to be far less confident that they would make a difference to most Canadians. One of the challenges of the Audit was to get beyond this simple diagnosis to explore how well all our principal institutions do work and whether they are really capable of responding to the democratic needs of a rapidly changing Canadian population.

Canada: Institutional Stability amidst Constant Change

John Courtney's *Elections* (2004, 77) rightly notes that "part of the task of any democratic audit is to assess the appropriateness of political and governmental institutions to a society's cultural and social values." Seen in these terms, Canadian politics has a peculiar and persistent challenge. It must continually find a way to balance old imported (European) institutions against a homegrown New World (North American) society. In an audit designed to measure the ongoing successes and limitations of these institutions, it is important to keep this dynamic tension in sight, for, as Graham White reminds us in *Cabinets and First Ministers* (2005, 13), "Canadian society may have experienced a marked 'decline of deference' in recent years, but its most powerful political institutions continue to reflect the mindset of the nineteenth century."

The central institutional framework of Canadian government was inherited from Britain. The country's founding document, the 1867 British North America Act (now retitled as the Constitution Act, 1867), was an act of the British parliament, which guarantees in its preamble that Canada will have a "Constitution similar in Principle to that of the United Kingdom." As a result, Canada is a monarchy - its Constitution, in one of its few written sections describing the structure of government (section 9), formally vests "the Executive Government and Authority of and over Canada" in the monarch - so at its institutional heart sits a queen who personifies the values of inheritance and English traditional practices. The principal institutions of the state reflect this fundamental bias. They are essentially hierarchical, bureaucratic, and closed: public servants work for the Crown, not the people. Parliament stands between the population and the government. Citizens get to vote for one House of a parliament (traditionally at a time convenient to the sitting prime minister) but not for their government. The government is elected only indirectly: a prime minister, who chooses its members as he likes, is formally appointed by the governor general (acting as the monarch's local representative) on the basis of his apparent ability to command the largest number of seats in the House of Commons. Those seats are organized on the basis of an old, geographically ordered bargain (modified by subsequent political accommodations), not by demographic equality (see Courtney 2004, ch. 3). In this system, no direct or obvious connection exists between the number of votes a party receives and the number of seats it wins. As a result, there is no guarantee that governments will represent a majority of the population; most do not, and governments can even come to office after elections in which their opponents receive more votes (four men became prime minister in this fashion).

That pattern of institutional arrangements evolved to suit the demands of a set of comparatively stable, slow-growing, self-contained political systems. The realities of Canadian development were quite different. The country grew from an initial arrangement of four small communities by adding new provinces (as late as 1949) and territories (as recently as 1999) to become a sprawling continent-wide state that is now the second largest on the planet. Not surprisingly, its social character was also transformed as dramatically.

According to best estimates, about 3.5 million people lived in Canada at the time of Confederation. The current population is about ten times that number, with half the growth coming in the last fifty years. With an electorate growing far more than in other established democracies – six times that of the United Kingdom, four times that of France – this has put enormous continuing pressure on the political parties to find ways to integrate and involve a rapidly changing population. That challenge has been accentuated by the altered character of how and where Canadians live. In 1867, 80 percent lived in rural areas; today, 80 percent live in urban centres. And this urbanization has hardly been even, as a few metropolitan areas continue to attract the largest growth: in 1961, one-quarter of the population lived in the three largest cities (Toronto, Montreal, and Vancouver); now, over one-third does. And Canadians are movers: recent census estimates suggest that about 14 percent of them move in a given year, and as many as 40 percent move over a five-year cycle. Such a constantly shifting population would seem to run counter to the spirit and principles that underlie a political system designed to operate on the fixed geography of federalism and single-member territorial electoral districts.

The make-up of the Canadian population has also dramatically altered in recent decades. Once dominated by European offspring, recent immigration patterns, as described in the introductory chapter of this volume, have produced a far more culturally diverse society populated by individuals who come with very different political traditions. As late as the decade after the Second World War, 80 to 90 percent of all immigrants (the principal source of the continual population growth) came from Europe: by the last decade of the century, 60 percent were coming from Asia. This transformation of the ethnic cast of the country was matched by an increasing secularization. Once, Canada was a nation of churchgoers (70 percent attended weekly in the 1950s), but by the end of the twentieth century, only about one in five Canadians regularly attended weekly services. Both these transformations testified to the growing disconnect between the country's formal constitutional arrangements, which have long singled out particular religious and linguistic groups for special protection, and a society in which increasing numbers could not relate to the divisions that were being privileged and perpetuated.

Tension between an old institutional arrangement and changing social realities that underpin the imperatives of national governance has always been a central part of the political dynamic in Canada. It has been continually recalibrated in a number of ways: new provinces have been created (Alberta and Saskatchewan) or welcomed (Prince Edward Island and Newfoundland); the Constitution has been amended in ways that are both minor (age limits for senators) and major (the Charter of Rights and Freedoms); the party system has been disrupted by new political formations from the West (the Progressives) and Quebec (the Bloc Québécois); Aboriginal peoples have begun to claim a fair place in the wider society; the institutional balance has shifted dramatically as both provincial governments and the courts took on increased roles; and always the political and electoral agenda has responded to democratic pressure.

The Audit: Assessing the Balance, Recommending Adjustment

The Canadian Democratic Audit sought a balanced assessment of Canadian democracy by holding its practices up to three benchmarks – *inclusiveness, participation,* and *responsiveness.* As William Cross notes in his account of the establishment of the Audit team (Chapter 1 this volume), those criteria were chosen to speak to the issues that underlay many Canadians' perception of a democratic deficit. They addressed Canada's particular challenge by allowing the auditors to explore the extent to which the old institutional framework matched the needs of the country's new social realities. Thus, seven of the Audit monographs are explicitly focused on the institutional side of this balance, one looks at the social side by considering the citizens served by the system (Gidengil et al. 2004), and one explores how the two come together in the specific policy area of communication technology (Barney 2005). As an audit, rather than an agenda for a radical overhaul, the project has sought to identify points at which Canadian practice is not inclusive, participatory, or responsive enough for contemporary society and to suggest changes that might help bring the relationship between its institutions and society into a better balance.

Each of the Audit's individual studies provides a careful and comprehensive canvass of the issues of democratic performance related to its subject. In this summary volume, the auditors have briefly highlighted their key findings and pointed to a number of reforms that they believe would strengthen Canadian democracy in the early decades of the twenty-first century. Table 10.2 lists some twenty-one of these, grouping them into four distinct categories: the first focuses on the social side of the society-institution balance; the other three sets suggest institutional changes. These latter range from recommending amendments to existing public policy to altering institutional practice to making major changes in some of the system's fundamental institutional and constitutional arrangements.

The first set of reforms suggests that improving Canadian democracy needs to start not with the structures of government but with the underlying society and the citizens that make it up. Darin Barney contends that democracy cannot thrive in a society marked by significant socioeconomic inequalities and power differentials, and he argues that the new communication technologies that are rapidly invading and pervading our lives may well be accentuating already existing differentials. This leads him to conclude that we need to start by "dismantling this cultural setting" that currently connects technology to democracy. Now, that is a radical recommendation, calling as it does for transformative change of the basic social order. If it is not clear how we are to go about it, or where it might ultimately lead, Barney does remind us that the country's existing political economy does set real bounds on the very nature and character of its fundamental political relationships.

In their review of Canadians' interest, knowledge, and behaviours, Elisabeth Gidengil and her colleagues help us understand some of the issues that stimulated the Audit, and they report that there is powerful evidence that "structural inequalities contribute to some deep democratic divides in Canada's political life" (99). In particular, they highlight the major generational divides that now see large numbers of young people divorced from politics. This growing gap, which is a big part of the story accounting for the collapse in voter turnout during recent decades, leads them to focus on recommendations aimed at engaging young voters. Some of their proposals would help mobilize young people, with the hope of instilling the habit of voting; others are directed to engaging their hands and minds more broadly. But young people are not the only target. The auditors recognize that a healthy democracy requires informed citizens, and they believe that civic literacy in general needs to be encouraged and strengthened. Given the contemporary weakness of the newspaper industry, and Barney's deep pessimism about the capacity of information technologies to help, this challenge

Table 10.2

The auditors' proposed reforms

Recommendation	Study
Social change	
Dismantle the cultural setting	*Communication Technology*
Engage young citizens	*Citizens*
Produce more informed citizens	*Citizens*
Public policy	
Create party policy foundations	*Political Parties*
Voter identification standards	*Elections*
Public financing of political parties* (but see *Political Parties*)	*Citizens*
Reinstate public funding for advocacy groups	*Advocacy Groups*
Institute tax credits for advocacy groups	*Advocacy Groups*
Institutional practice	
Government-parliament relationships	
Create legislative role in Supreme Court appointments	*Federalism*
Strengthen role of parliamentarians	*Legislatures*
Establish minority parliament practices	*Legislatures*
Involve backbenchers in cabinet process	*Cabinets and First Ministers*
Internal (party and group) relationships	
Leadership process to recognize caucus	*Cabinets and First Ministers*
More diverse political recruitment	*Political Parties*
More transparent candidate recruitment	*Political Parties*
More participatory organization	*Advocacy Groups*
Major institutional reform	
Council of the Federation	*Federalism*
Electoral reform (toward proportional representation)* (but see *Elections*)	*Political Parties*
	Citizens
	Cabinets and First Ministers
Fixed election dates	*Legislatures*
	Cabinets and First Ministers
	Citizens
Senate reform* (but see *Legislatures*)	*Federalism*
	Citizens
Virtual Atlantic region	*Federalism*

* Issues on which auditors make conflicting recommendations.

will not be dealt with easily. By identifying the problem, Gidengil et al. remind us that strengthening Canadian democracy is not just a matter of altering institutional forms and practice: it must begin by building on a foundation of informed and engaged citizens.

Canadian Democracy: An Assessment and an Agenda

However, most of the reforms proposed by the Audit do focus on changes to political policy, practice, or structure, with recommendations of each kind. The first of these, which would seem to be easiest to implement, requires only that parliamentarians make a policy decision in their favour. In *Political Parties,* William Cross (2004) recommends the establishment of a system of party foundations of the kind that exist in a number of West European democracies. The proposed foundations would serve two important functions. On the one hand, they would give political parties a much increased policy capacity, better preparing them for the challenges of governing while giving voters a clearer picture of just what they were offering. On the other hand, foundations would provide party members with a forum within which they could effectively participate, engaging their leadership and contributing to internal partisan decision making. As both these external and internal benefits ought to strengthen democracy on all three of the Audit's benchmark dimensions, it is not surprising that this is not a radically new idea. The (Lortie) Royal Commission on Electoral Reform and Party Financing made this same recommendation in its 1991 final report, and the Audit's endorsement of it seems another attempt to promote public debate about its merits.

None of the national political parties has taken up the idea; nor have any parliamentarians promoted it, perhaps a clear sign that party leaders have no appetite for a serious attempt to democratize party policy making. But it is just this continuing elite control of party life that Cross believes is contributing to the erosion of partisan attachment and political involvement in Canada. With some of the lowest levels of membership in the democratic world, Canadian political parties are facing a growing crisis of legitimacy, rooted in their failures of participation and inclusiveness, and their resistance to this, or other significant internal reform, would seem to be central to citizens' perceptions of a democratic deficit.

Courtney's comprehensive review of the development of the electoral system that structures political competition reminds us that reform is a process of continuing evolution as policies and practices change to meet the demands of an evolving society. Inevitably, some of these changes work better than others and so need to be constantly monitored. He points out that one of parliament's recent (2007) changes - the requirement for identifying voters at the polls on election day - has misfired and may well have contributed to the record low participation rate recorded in the 2008 general election. Here is a strong case for reconsidering that measure and making an adjustment that would increase participation and improve the system's capacity to be fully inclusive of all its citizens, not just responsive to active voters.

Three other policy recommendations all involve providing public financial support - either directly or indirectly via tax credits - for political parties and advocacy groups so that they could enhance their capacity as the primary linkages between citizens and the state. Elisabeth Gidengil et al.'s *Citizens* (2004) and Lisa Young and Joanna Everitt's *Advocacy Groups* (2004) both suggest that these would make important contributions to levelling the democratic playing field. Cross (2004) seems less sanguine about the use of public funds for political parties and suggests they be decreased unless they can be redirected to his proposed party foundations. However, recommendations for more public spending on politics are hardly uncontentious, and they have become matters of clear, and active, partisan difference. The Reform Party (in opposition during the 1990s) opposed public financing for political parties, and as the reborn Conservative Party (in government), sought to cut subsidies to the parties in its ill-fated economic plan of November 2008. Though the threat of parliamentary defeat forced the Conservatives to back away from that proposal, there is no evidence that they are reconciled to the principle of public party financing. Recommendations that call for the public support of advocacy groups represent a call for a return to an earlier period in which Liberal Party governments were more willing to provide financial help to these kinds of bodies. Again, governments of the right (first, Brian Mulroney's Progressive Conservatives and then Stephen Harper's new Conservatives) oppose such funding, and both have cut spending programs of that sort. In important ways, these recommendations for policy shifts are now matters of vigorous partisan difference. This turns them into issues for active public debate and opens decisions about change to electoral resolution. At the same time, as the issue of party financing so clearly demonstrates, continuing partisan disagreement seems to ensure that permanent change remains elusive. But that is surely both inevitable and desirable on questions of public policy over which citizens can reasonably disagree.

Recommendations calling for changes in institutional practice seem no more likely to generate consensus than those regarding policy, although their antagonists are not necessarily divided along partisan lines. Four of the auditors' suggestions would seem to pit governments (and perhaps especially their leaders) against elected parliamentarians. The first two of them refer to issues on which some initial, if very tentative, steps have been taken. The name of Prime Minister Harper's first appointee to the Supreme Court of Canada was submitted to MPs and a parliamentary committee subsequently questioned him in public before indicating its approval. However, the prime minister made it clear that the decision was his alone and did not use a similar process for his second appointment, so no significant change has occurred in the role parliamentarians play in Supreme Court appointments. Members of the House of Commons did move to strengthen their position during the waning months of Jean Chrétien's prime ministership by voting to elect committee chairs. However, even that modest gain seems to have been eroded under the Harper government as the prime minister reasserted control over his caucus and the organization of the House. Although this assertion of the centralizing impulses of first minister government in Ottawa indicates that it would be premature to herald an increase in the power of individual parliamentarians, these experiences suggest that the merits of these proposed changes have been recognized so that they are now at least on the active agenda.

David Docherty's account of the November 2008 parliamentary upheaval, in which a coalition of opposition parties (unsuccessfully) conspired to bring down the third consecutive minority government, reveals how unprepared Canadian politicians are to work in a minority parliament. In the absence of a set of conventions governing such situations, their instinct is to play for time and hope that a quick election will return a majority government. However, the continuing fragmentation of the party system, engendered by the political earthquake of 1993 that threw up the Bloc Québécois and fractured the national parties, suggests that minorities have become the expected outcome of a general election. Thus, the challenge is to establish recognizable and widely acceptable rules governing the relationships – creation, operation, and removal – between parliament and government in this context (Russell 2008). Both the Australians and New Zealanders have done this in ways that stabilize their politics, and Canadians ought to do so before further "crises" lead to dysfunctional outcomes such as the prorogation of a parliament within days of its first meeting.

Many Canadians now believe that the country's national government suffers from a collapse of collegial decision making in the cabinet and the centralization of authority in the Prime Minister's Office, a phenomenon Donald Savoie (1999) has called the rise of court government. In an attempt to counter the limits to participation and responsiveness that those patterns imply, White recommends that national governments alter their practices to involve backbench parliamentarians in the cabinet process. The experience of several of the provinces is offered as evidence that doing so could work while not violating some hallowed constitutional principle (see White 2005, Chapter 3 this volume). But, of the four recommendations touching on the relations between government and parliament, this seems the least likely to be embraced by government leaders. In recent years, prime ministers have moved in the opposite direction, shrinking the number of ministers from the unwieldy size (almost forty) to which the cabinet had grown under Brian Mulroney. And despite regular promises to be more inclusive and responsive than their predecessor, no prime ministers (of either party) in recent decades have shown any inclination to share their hard-won power.

Three other Audit proposals for changing institutional practice are aimed at altering the internal dynamics of the political parties. The first is White's recommendation that leadership selection and removal processes ought to become much more sensitive to the members of the parties' parliamentary caucuses. Changes of the sort he proposes might be portrayed as making those critical intraparty decisions less participatory and inclusive, but they would contribute to making leaders more responsive to popularly elected representatives. Although the parties may resist moving in that direction for fear of being branded undemocratic, the Liberals implicitly recognized the political logic of White's suggestion in the aftermath of the November 2008 parliamentary contretemps when the caucus forced Stéphane Dion's resignation and then quickly rallied behind Michael Ignatieff. With that precedent, the door may be open for other parliamentary caucuses to take a more decisive role in the leadership politics of their parties, although this may wait upon a final judgment of Ignatieff's leadership.

Cross' analysis of Canada's political parties concludes that they need to develop more transparent candidate recruitment processes and work to attract a more diverse and representative political class. The major parties would not (publicly) disagree with those propositions, but progress on implementing such changes continues to be slow. Candidate recruitment, in a system of single-member electoral districts, often pits the interests of local party activists against those of the national organization. Individual party members do not like being told they must have a candidate from this or that particular group, a directive that may be necessary if parties are to be successful in diversifying their parliamentary caucuses. Thus, these key personnel issues can easily lead to a clash between the values of (local) participation and responsiveness, on the one hand, and (societal) inclusiveness, on the other. In an attempt to maintain internal harmony in complex organizations peopled by volunteers, the parties often instinctively resort to processes that are more opaque than transparent. The continuing challenge for the parties is to balance these tensions in a way that will maximize the democratic values of the Audit.

Young and Everitt are critical of the way in which many advocacy groups have come to be dominated by their professional staff. They argue that not only does this diminish the capacity of advocacy groups to fully represent the diverse interests of Canadians but that reducing the opportunities for genuine democratic participation weakens the role of these groups in fostering the development of a rich social capital. Quite how national groups can build more inclusive and participatory

organizations, especially if they come to depend on the increased public funding Young and Everitt recommend, is not clear, but they believe
that finding a solution to this challenge must be an important part of
any reform agenda designed to enhance Canadians' ability to play a
meaningful part in the democratic governance of their society.

The final set of recommendations argues that responding to Canada's
democratic challenges requires some significant institutional changes
that transform elements of the country's fundamental constitutional
arrangements. Given the recent decades of constitutional frustration,
one would assume that little progress can realistically be expected on
these items, but all continue to command attention and some real
popular support. Although some of these proposals are not new and do
not offer much hope for immediate adoption, several of the auditors
remain convinced that they ought to be essential elements of any effective democratic reform agenda.

In *Federalism,* Jennifer Smith (2004) advocates the creation of a
Council of the Federation as a mechanism for strengthening and regu-
larizing a more inclusive system of intergovernmental relations. As she
notes in Chapter 2 of this volume, the provincial premiers took a first
step (in late 2003) by initiating such a council. However, their creation
is still not yet much more than a vehicle for advancing provincial/ter-
ritorial interests as it includes neither national nor First Nations'
governments.

Two major reforms that would significantly alter electoral politics
are recommended by three separate Audit studies. The first, advocated
by Cross (2004), Gidengil et al. (2004), and White (2005), is for a major
change to the electoral system, with the adoption of some (unspecified)
form of proportional representation (PR). They are not so prescriptive
as to indicate the exact form such a system might take, but all are clear
that a move in that direction would enhance the democratic character
of the country's political life. However, the auditors are hardly unani-
mous here, for in his study of the electoral system, Courtney (2004)
reaches a quite different judgment. He points to the oft underrated
capacity of the current single-member plurality system to engender
broad coalition-building strategies by national political parties, which

is essential in a sprawling, diverse country such as Canada. This leads him to raise pointed questions about many of the assumed benefits of a shift to PR.

Enthusiasm for electoral reform is not new, and the issue once again found itself on the active agenda in much of the country during the early years of the twenty-first century. The Law Commission of Canada (since discontinued by the Harper government) recommended such a reform, and majority governments in British Columbia, Ontario, Quebec, New Brunswick, and Prince Edward Island all actively pursued it. Deliberative citizens' assemblies in BC and Ontario recommended different proportional systems; the Quebec government presented a draft bill for a regionalized PR system to the national assembly; and both New Brunswick's Commission on Legislative Democracy and Prince Edward Island's independent commissioner on electoral reform proposed mixed-member proportional systems for their provinces. No two of these proposals were identical, and not one of them has succeeded in being adopted. Public referendums to change their respective provincial electoral systems have now been held in British Columbia (twice), Ontario, and Prince Edward Island, but none managed to garner the required popular support. In the absence of a successful demonstration effect in one of the provinces, the present prospects for abandoning first past the post in favour of a proportional electoral system must appear very slim.

Nonetheless, the other reform endorsed by several auditors, the establishment of fixed electoral dates, has begun to take hold. British Columbia was the pioneer (in 2001) and has now held two provincial general elections on its fixed four-year calendar. Six other provinces – Ontario, Newfoundland and Labrador, New Brunswick, Prince Edward Island, Manitoba, and Saskatchewan – as well as the Northwest Territories have now followed suit. In 2007, parliament passed a law providing for a fixed election date for national elections, but when Prime Minister Harper (who had introduced the law) called the 2008 federal election, he indicated that it was not actually meant to apply to dysfunctional parliamentary situations. At a minimum, that was a major retreat from the spirit of the reform. It remains to be seen whether prime ministers and premiers will actually respect the principle of a fixed election date when political incentives tempt them otherwise and thus how effective such a reform will be.

Senate reform has long been one of the staples of democratic reformers in Canada; though two Audit studies (Smith 2004; Gidengil et al. 2004) recommend it, David Docherty's *Legislatures* (2005, 196) concluded that "no sane government would open up the constitutional can of worms that is Senate reform." In fact, the Harper Conservative government has taken the subject seriously and launched two significant initiatives. The first was to propose a fixed term for senators, the second to propose using elections to choose them. Neither of the government's proposals has yet been passed by parliament, and not surprisingly, both have been strongly resisted by a Liberal-dominated Senate. To demonstrate he was serious about the measure, Prime Minister Harper initially left all new Senate vacancies empty save for the symbolically significant appointment of Bert Brown following his victory in an Alberta Senate election. However, in the aftermath of the parliamentary "crisis" of November 2008, Harper reversed field and appointed eighteen new senators (pledged to support his reform agenda) during Christmas week. While contending that this was necessary to make parliament work effectively, he indicated that he had not abandoned the government's commitment to fundamental Senate change.

One final recommendation that emerges from the Audit analyses is Jennifer Smith's idea for a virtual region in Atlantic Canada (2004, 167, 155), which she describes as "not so much a proposal as the recognition of an integrative trend" that reflects "the slow process of unification from the bottom, or the ground up ... already under way." The notion that provincial governments might act together in ways that would increase their capacity for responsiveness is not applicable to just the (small, poorer) Atlantic provinces: regional meetings of Western premiers aim at much the same thing. The British Columbia-Alberta Trade, Investment and Labour Mobility Agreement is one recent important example of how provincial governments are moving to eliminate many of the internal barriers created by the country's federal structures. This sort of change may be as much a matter of political will as of constitutional engineering – but then, political reform almost always is.

Auditing Canadian Democracy

Auditing Canadian democracy was no easy task. Disagreements over just how to define or measure democracy meant that the project was inherently ambiguous, and most comparative measures suggest that Canada and Canadians have built one of the most successful societies and polities anywhere. The individuals who joined the Audit team agreed that, as the country entered a new century, issues of full and meaningful citizen *participation,* the capacity of the country to be genuinely *inclusive* of all its members, and the *responsiveness* of its institutions were the central democratic challenges to be faced. Each approached his or her particular audit in recognition that there was much to be celebrated but also identified opportunities for doing better within the constitutional framework that defines the country.

The Audit project deliberately eschewed the democratic audit methodology pioneered in the United Kingdom, which called for a small unified group to work to a carefully prepared checklist of characteristics. This approach had two important consequences that mark its final products. First, in the absence of a tightly defined set of criteria, the auditors worked with benchmark criteria – *participation, responsiveness, inclusivity* – that were themselves often in tension. This can be seen in Cross' recommendation for changed candidate selection procedures that would sacrifice some degree of local participation and responsiveness for increased inclusiveness. But, by its very nature, democracy necessitates a balance among competing values; that the Canadian Audit recognized this and forced its analyses to wrestle with the trade-offs required by contemporary Canada is one of its great strengths.

The second critical aspect of the project was the decision to engage a diverse group of scholars. All brought their own perspectives, expertise, and analytical approach to the subjects they addressed and, not surprisingly, did not always agree. Thus, as we have noted, there are conflicting interpretations about the merits and possibilities for strengthening Canadian democracy through electoral or Senate reform. But this is as it should be. The auditors' task was to lay out the competing evidence, not to sell their own personal agendas. It is for democratic citizens to consider their findings, engage the debates, and then make their own choices.

In this volume, we have summarized key findings of the auditors and pointed to a specific set of their recommendations that are aimed at strengthening the democratic life of Canadians. Individual Audit studies contain other proposals, but the list here provides a substantial program of reform. Each recommendation deserves careful consideration and healthy debate – some are items whose time appears to have come; others are now on the active political agenda and a matter of vigorous partisan difference; yet others still await their champions. But even if all were to be implemented, there would be no reason for easy complacency. As the Canadian population continues to grow and change, new challenges will arise to ensure that all are able to participate in a way that provides for responsive and accountable democratic government.

Works Cited

Amnesty International. 2006. *Amnesty International report.* London: Amnesty International.

–. 2009. *No more stolen sisters: The need for a comprehensive response to discrimination and violence against indigenous women in Canada.* London: Amnesty International.

Barney, Darin. 2005. *Communication technology.* Canadian Democratic Audit. Vancouver: UBC Press.

Carty, R. Kenneth. 2006. Regional responses to electoral reform. *Canadian Parliamentary Review* 29(1) (Spring): 22-26.

Courtney, John. 2004. *Elections.* Canadian Democratic Audit. Vancouver: UBC Press.

Cross, William. 2004. *Political parties.* Canadian Democratic Audit. Vancouver: UBC Press.

Cross, William, and Lisa Young. 2004. The contours of political party membership in Canada. *Party Politics* 10(4): 427-44.

Docherty, David. 2005. *Legislatures.* Canadian Democratic Audit. Vancouver: UBC Press.

Gidengil, Elisabeth, André Blais, Neil Nevitte, and Richard Nadeau. 2004. *Citizens.* Canadian Democratic Audit. Vancouver: UBC Press.

Howe, Paul, and David Northrup. 2000. Strengthening Canadian democracy: The views of Canadians. *Policy Matters* 1(5).

International Institute for Democracy and Electoral Assistance (IDEA). 2010. Voter turnout. http://www.idea.int/.

Martin, Paul. 2000. Empowering members of parliament, strengthening our democratic institutions. Public address, Assumption University, Windsor, 7 May.

–. 2002. Six-point plan for reforming the House of Commons. Public speech, Toronto, 21 October.

Monger, Joanne. 2004. International comparisons of labour disputes in 2002. *Labour Market Trends* 112(4): 145-52.

Russell, Peter. 2008. *Two cheers for minority government: The evolution of Canadian parliamentary democracy.* Toronto: Emond Montgomery.

Savoie, Donald. 1999. The rise of court government in Canada. *Canadian Journal of Political Science* 32(4): 635-64.

Smith, Jennifer. 2004. *Federalism.* Canadian Democratic Audit. Vancouver: UBC Press.

Stewart, D.K., and R.K. Carty. 2006. Many political worlds? Provincial parties and party systems. In *Provinces: Canadian provincial politics,* 2nd ed., ed. C. Dunn, 97-113. Peterborough, ON: Broadview Press.

White, Graham. 2005. *Cabinets and first ministers.* Canadian Democratic Audit. Vancouver: UBC Press.

World Bank Group. 2009. Worldwide governance indicators, 1996-2008. http://info.worldbank.org/.

Young, Lisa, and Joanna Everitt. 2004. *Advocacy groups.* Canadian Democratic Audit. Vancouver: UBC Press.

Contributors

Darin Barney is Canada Research Chair in Technology and Citizenship in the Department of Art History and Communication Studies at McGill University.

André Blais is Canada Research Chair in Electoral Studies in the Department of Political Science at the University of Montreal.

R. Kenneth Carty is Professor of Political Science at the University of British Columbia.

John Courtney is Professor Emeritus in the Department of Political Studies and Senior Policy Fellow of the Johnson-Shoyama Graduate School of Public Policy at the University of Saskatchewan.

William Cross is the Hon. Dick and Ruth Bell Chair for the Study of Canadian Parliamentary Democracy in the Department of Political Science at Carleton University.

David Docherty is Associate Professor of Political Science at Wilfrid Laurier University.

Joanna Everitt is Professor of Political Science and Dean of Arts at the University of New Brunswick, Saint John.

Elisabeth Gidengil is Hiram Mills Professor in the Department of Political Science at McGill University.

Richard Nadeau is Professor of Political Science at the University of Montreal.

Neil Nevitte is Professor of Political Science at the University of Toronto.

Jennifer Smith is Eric Dennis Memorial Professor of Government and Political Science at Dalhousie University.

Graham White is Professor of Political Science at the University of Toronto and is President of the Canadian Political Science Association.

Lisa Young is Professor of Political Science at the University of Calgary.

Index

Printed and bound in Canada by Friesens

Set in Meta and Eidetic Neo by Artegraphica Design Co. Ltd.

Copy editor: Deborah Kerr

Proofreader and indexer: Dianne Tiefensee